D0500056

Praise for
God's Story, Your Story

I love this man and have never been disappointed by anything Max Lucado has written. God's truth comes through poignantly and compassionately in *God's Story, Your Story*. It's a must-read. You won't be disappointed.

> STEPHEN ARTERBURN, founder and chairman
> of New Life Ministries; founder of Women of Faith
> conferences

One of the best storytellers alive today, Max Lucado demonstrates how the tapestry of our life intertwines with God's Word. *God's Story, Your Story* will inspire you to search for deeper meaning in your circumstances and cling to Scripture as your story unfolds.

> CRAIG GROESCHEL, senior pastor of LifeChurch.tv;
> author of *Weird*

Picking up a book by Max Lucado is like getting together with an old friend. You'll feel encouraged and enriched—and maybe even a little bit challenged if that friend is willing to be honest with you. *God's Story, Your Story* is like that.

> JIM DALY, president of Focus on the Family

All of us want to know that our life experiences matter and have transcendent meaning. We want to know our story so that we can make sense of our path and know the next step. With his engaging grace, Max illustrates for us how the Bible shows us our stories through those of its characters. A rare opportunity.

> Dr. John Townsend, psychologist,
> executive coach, and author of *Boundaries*

Do you ever feel a little lost in this world or wonder if your life really matters? With profound yet simple wisdom, Max opens wide God's story so that you can trace the Father's footprints. Tucked inside the pages of God's story you will find your own, and understand perhaps for the first time how greatly you are loved.

> Sheila Walsh, author of *The Shelter*
> *of God's Promises*

No one tells God's story better than Max Lucado. Now Max wants you to discover your story as well. This is more than a good read; it is a road map to an awesome life.

> Randy Frazee, senior minister of Oak Hills
> Church, San Antonio, Texas; author of
> *The Heart of the Story* and coauthor of *Real Simplicity*

GOD'S
STORY
your story

Other Titles by Max Lucado

INSPIRATIONAL

On the Anvil (1985)
No Wonder They Call Him the Savior (1986)
God Came Near (1987)
Six Hours One Friday (1989)
The Applause of Heaven (1990)
In the Eye of the Storm (1991)
And the Angels Were Silent (1992)
He Still Moves Stones (1993)
When God Whispers Your Name (1994)
A Gentle Thunder (1995)
In the Grip of Grace (1996)
The Great House of God (1997)
Just Like Jesus (1998)
When Christ Comes (1999)
He Chose the Nails (2000)
Traveling Light (2001)
A Love Worth Giving (2002)
Next Door Savior (2003)
Come Thirsty (2004)
It's Not About Me (2004)
Cure for the Common Life (2005)
Facing Your Giants (2006)
3:16 (2007)
Every Day Deserves a Chance (2007)
Cast of Characters (2008)
Fearless (2009)
Outlive Your Life (2010)
Max on Life (2011)
God's Story, Your Story (2011)

FICTION

An Angel's Story
The Christmas Candle
The Christmas Child

GIFT BOOKS

A Heart Like Jesus
Everyday Blessings
For These Tough Times
God's Mirror
God's Promises for You
God Thinks You're Wonderful
Grace for the Moment, Vols. I & II
Grace for the Moment Journal
In the Beginning
Just for You
Just Like Jesus Devotional
Let the Journey Begin
Max on Life series
Mocha with Max
One Incredible Moment
Safe in the Shepherd's Arms
The Cross
The Gift for All People
The Greatest Moments
Traveling Light for Mothers
Traveling Light Journal
Turn
Walking with the Savior
You: God's Brand-New Idea!

BIBLES (GENERAL EDITOR)

Grace for the Moment Daily Bible
He Did This Just for You (New Testament)
The Devotional Bible
The Lucado Life Lessons Study Bible

GOD'S STORY

your story

When His becomes yours

MAX LUCADO

New York Times BEST-SELLING AUTHOR

ZONDERVAN®

ZONDERVAN.com/
AUTHORTRACKER
follow your favorite authors

ZONDERVAN

God's Story, Your Story
Copyright © 2011 by Max Lucado

This title is also available as a Zondervan ebook. Visit www.zondervan.com/ebooks.

This title is also available in a Zondervan audio edition. Visit www.zondervan.fm.

Requests for information should be addressed to:

Zondervan, Grand Rapids, Michigan 49530

Library of Congress Cataloging-in-Publication Data

Lucado, Max.
    God's story, your story : when His becomes yours / Max Lucado.
       p. cm.
    Includes bibliographical references.
    ISBN 978-0-310-29403-0 (hardcover, jacketed)
    1. Christian life. I. Title.
BV4501.3.L826 2011
248.4—dc22   2011006758

11 12 13 14 15 16 17 18 /DCI/ 24 23 22 21 20 19 18 17 16 15 14 13 12 11 10 9 8 7 6 5 4 3 2 1

Denalyn and I happily dedicate this book
to my sister and brother-in-law
Joan and Fred Carrigan.
You've brought joy and laughter
to every page of our story,
and we love you!

GOD rewrote the text of my life
  when I opened the book of my heart to his eyes.

2 SAMUEL 22:25 MSG

CONTENTS

ACKNOWLEDGMENTS

Quite a cast made this production possible! Each one is worthy of a loud ovation:

Liz Heaney and Karen Hill monitored each sentence and helped me polish each paragraph. I deeply appreciate you both.

Carol Bartley applied her one-of-a-kind, sleuth-level copyediting. I am indebted to you.

Randy and Rozanne Frazee — I'm so grateful for the idea, even more grateful for the partnership.

Dudley Delffs oversaw every stage of creation and production. Great work, friend.

Byron Williamson and Steve and Cheryl Green managed to resuscitate this book more than once. Without you, who knows what would have happened?

Moe Girkins and the outstanding team at Zondervan elevated The Story initiative to a higher level. I am proud to work with you!

David Drury added his always-valuable theological insights.

Brad Tuggle offered valuable suggestions.

David Treat covered this book and the team in prayer.

My family: Brett and Jenna Bishop, Andrea and Sara Lucado. You teach me more about God's love than you will ever know.

My wife, Denalyn. God gave me you *and* heaven. Is it possible to be blessed too much? If so, I qualify. I love you!

INTRODUCTION

When God's Story Becomes Yours ...

RALLS, TEXAS, WAS A WEATHERED TUMBLEWEED OF A town in 1965. The city center consisted of a two-story courthouse framed by a weedy lawn and bricked roads. One drugstore had gone out of business; the second was not far behind. The shelves of the five-and-dime were dusty and empty, like the street upon which it sat. The closest facsimile of a traffic jam occurred every morning when the farmers left the diner parking lot after their sunrise coffee.

Someone had pressed the pause button and forgotten to release it.

Which was just fine with my grandparents, God bless 'em. Charles and Macey McDermott looked just like the farm couple in Grant Wood's painting, only not nearly as energetic. Grandpa, lanky and long faced; she, shorter and dark eyed. Neither one smiled much. They shuffled about in a two-bedroom frame house, chewing Brown's Mule tobacco, watching soap operas, and reading Zane Grey novels.

It was my mom's idea for me to spend a week with them. Let ten-year-old Max get to know his grandparents' and mom's hometown. So she gave me a chocolate bar and a kiss, loaded me on a Greyhound bus, and waved good-bye. The trip peaked with the candy bar. After one day I knew this was going to be the longest week of my life. My grandparents had no bicycles, baseballs, or basketball hoops. They knew no other ten-year-olds and lived too far out in the country for me to find any. Dullsville. I would have accepted an invitation to watch paint dry.

But then came the story.

Over lunch one day I asked my grandmother about the photo that hung in her bedroom: the sepia-toned picture that was professionally taken and handsomely set in an oval-shaped walnut frame. Who was this mystery man who occupied prime real estate above my grandmother's side of the bed? He stood next to a chair, one hand on its back and the other holding a fedora. His slender face came to a point at his nose. His forehead was whiter than the rest of his face, his hair slicked straight back, black and shiny, as if coated with engine grease. He was stiff and rigid, clearly uncomfortable in the three-piece suit and photography studio.

"That's Levi Thornton," Grandma told me, "your mother's first father. Your grandfather." I'd heard of this man. How he brought my mom to the farm country. How he died young. But where he came from? How he died? I didn't know.

So Grandma set out to tell me. Within a couple of sentences, I was lost in the story, bouncing in the cab of the 1929 Chevy pickup with Grandpa Levi, Grandma, and an eight-year-old version of my mom. They were migrating to the Texas Panhandle from Cherokee, Oklahoma, in search of an affordable farm and fertile soil. They found both. But then a drought took the crop, and tuberculosis took Levi's health. Macey drove the truck back to Cherokee, where Levi died in her arms. He was buried at the age of thirty-three.

Grandma's telling lasted more than a paragraph, of course, given that I was happy to listen and she was thrilled to talk. We shinnied up the family tree and spent the better part of the day exploring branches I had never known existed. As we did, my black-and-white week exploded into a Monet of colors.

Why do you suppose, now forty years removed, I

remember the day in such detail? I still see the kitchen in which we sat, its straight-backed chairs and Formica-topped table. I see Grandma spilling photos out of a box and details out of her heart as if neither had been taken off the shelf in quite some time. I recall an emotion akin to the one you felt when you learned about your great-grandfather's migration from Norway or a distant relation being one of the charter Royal Canadian Mounties. Perhaps you've traced your ancestry through the Apache's hunting grounds, African slave ships, or Polynesian sailors. We love to know where we came from.

We *need* to know where we came from. Knowing connects us, links us, bonds us to something greater than we are. Knowing reminds us that we aren't floating on isolated ponds but on a grand river.

That's why God wants you to know his story. Framed photos hang in his house. Lively talks await you at his table. A scrapbook sits in his living room, brimming with stories. Stories about Bethlehem beginnings and manger miracles. Enemy warfare in the wilderness and fishermen friends in Galilee. The stumbles of Peter, the stubbornness of Paul. All a part of the story.

But they are all subplots to the central message: "For God so loved the world that he gave his one and only Son, that whoever believes in him shall not perish but have eternal life" (John 3:16). This is the headline of the story: God saves his people! He casts his net over cities and individuals, princes and paupers, the Pontius Pilates of power and the Peters, Jameses, and Johns of the fishing villages. God takes on the whole mess of us and cleans us up.

This quest is God's story. And we are a part of it!

We can easily miss this. Life keeps pulling us down. The traffic, the troubles. The doctor visits and homework. Life is Ralls, Texas, and nothing more. No prelude or sequel. Just tumbleweeds and dust and birth and death. And the randomness of it all. One week you are having a baby; the next you are having to move out of your house. "Good news, a bonus!" "Bad news, a blizzard." Hectic. Haphazard. Playgrounds and cemeteries on the same block.

Is there a story line to this drama?

I asked the same question. About the same time I traveled to Ralls, I received another invitation. The local community theater group was staging the play *The Wizard of Oz*, and they needed some Munchkins. They recruited the children's choir (in which I sang second soprano, thank you very much) to play the parts. We learned the songs and practiced the dances, but our choir director overlooked one detail. He never told us the story. He assumed we'd seen the movie. I hadn't. As far as I knew, Toto was a chocolate candy, and the Yellow Brick Road was an avenue in Disneyland. I knew nothing of Kansas tornadoes or hot-air balloons. I didn't know how the story started or ended, but I found myself in the middle of it.

Dress rehearsal nearly did me in. A house crashed out of the sky. A queen floated in a bubble. A long-nosed witch waved her stick. "I'll get you, my pretty ..." I was wide-eyed and wondering what I'd gotten myself into. Life in Munchkinland can be a scary thing.

Unless you've read the screenplay. Unless you know the final act. When you enter the stage equipped with a script, everything changes. You know that in the end the witch melts. So let her cackle all she wants; her days are numbered. In the end, good wins.

Everything changes when you know the rest of your story.

As David discovered, "GOD rewrote the text of my life when I opened the book of my heart to his eyes" (2 Samuel 22:25 MSG). But what is the text of our lives?

The question is not a new one. Self-help gurus, talk-show hosts, and magazine headlines urge you to find your narrative. But they send you in the wrong direction. "Look inside yourself," they say. But the promise of self-discovery falls short. Can you find the plot of a book in one paragraph or hear the flow of a symphony in one measure? Can you uncover the plot of your life by examining your life? By no means. You are so much more than a few days between the womb and the tomb.

Your story indwells God's. This is the great promise of the Bible and the hope of this book. "It's in Christ that we find out who we are and what we are living for. Long before we first heard of Christ and got our hopes up, he had his eye on us, had designs on us for glorious living, part of the overall purpose he is working out in everything and everyone" (Ephesians 1:11 – 12 MSG).

Above and around us God directs a grander saga, written by his hand, orchestrated by his will, unveiled according to his calendar. And you are a part of it. Meaningless Munchkin? Not you. Stranded on the prairie in a creaky old farmhouse? No way. Your life emerges from the greatest mind and the kindest heart in the history of the universe: the mind and heart of God. "He makes everything work out according to his plan" (Ephesians 1:11 NLT).

Let's dive into his story, shall we? Our plan is simple: journey though the New Testament in search of God's narrative. We'll use the chronological Bible *The Story* as our guidebook, extracting a promise from each of its ten chapters.

Who knows? In his story we might find our own.

CHAPTER ONE

When God's Story Becomes Yours ...

ORDINARY MATTERS

THE PINT-SIZE JOSEPH SCURRIES ACROSS THE CHURCH stage, wearing sandals, a robe, and his best attempt at an anxious face. He raps on the door his dad built for the children's Christmas play, then shifts from one foot to the other, partly because he's supposed to act nervous. Mostly because he is exactly that.

The innkeeper answers. He too wears a tow sack of a robe and a towel turned turban. An elastic band secures a false beard to his face. He looks at Joseph and chokes back a giggle. Just a couple of hours ago the two boys were building a front-lawn snowman. Their moms had to tell them twice to get dressed for the Christmas Eve service.

Here they stand. The innkeeper crosses his arms; Joseph waves his. He describes a donkey ride from

Nazareth, five days on the open road, a census here in Bethlehem, and, most of all, a wife. He turns and points in the direction of a pillow-stuffed nine-year-old girl.

She waddles onto center stage with one hand on the small of her back and the other mopping her brow. She limps with her best portrayal of pregnant pain, though, if pressed, she would have no clue about the process of childbirth.

She plays up the part. Groan. Sigh. "Joseph, I need help!"

The crowd chuckles.

Joseph looks at the innkeeper.

The innkeeper looks at Mary.

And we all know what happens next. Joseph urges. The innkeeper shakes his head. His hotel is packed. Guests occupy every corner. There is no room at the inn.

I think some dramatic license could be taken here. Rather than hurry to the next scene, let Joseph plead his case. "Mr. Innkeeper, think twice about your decision. Do you know whom you are turning away? That's God inside that girl! You're closing the door on the King of the universe. Better reconsider. Do you really want to be memorialized as the person who turned out heaven's child into the cold?"

And let the innkeeper react. "I've heard some desperate appeals for a room, but *God inside a girl?* That girl? She has pimples and puffy ankles, for goodness' sake! Doesn't look like a God-mother to me. And you don't look too special yourself there … uh … What was your name? Oh yeah, Joe. Good ol' Joe. Covered head to toe with road dust. Take your tale somewhere else, buddy. I'm not falling for your story. Sleep in the barn for all I care!"

The innkeeper huffs and turns. Joseph and Mary exit. The choir sings "Away in a Manger" as stagehands wheel out a pile of hay, a feed trough, and some plastic sheep. The audience smiles and claps and sings along. They love the song, the kids, and they cherish the story. But most of all, they cling to the hope. The Christmas hope that God indwells the everydayness of our world.

The story drips with normalcy. This isn't *Queen* Mary or *King* Joseph. The couple doesn't caravan into Bethlehem with camels, servants, purple banners, and dancers. Mary and Joseph have no tax exemption or political connection. They have the clout of a migrant worker and the net worth of a minimum wage earner.

Not subjects for a PBS documentary.

Not candidates for welfare either. Their life is difficult but not destitute. Joseph has the means to pay taxes. They inhabit the populous world between royalty and rubes.

They are, well, normal. Normal has calluses like

Joseph, stretch marks like Mary. Normal stays up late with laundry and wakes up early for work. Normal drives the car pool wearing a bathrobe and slippers. Normal is Norm and Norma, not Prince and Princess.

Norm sings off-key. Norma works in a cubicle and struggles to find time to pray. Both have stood where Joseph stood and have heard what Mary heard. Not from the innkeeper in Bethlehem, but from the coach in middle school or the hunk in high school or the foreman at the plant. "We don't have room for you . . . time for you . . . a space for you . . . a job for you . . . interest in you. Besides, look at you. You are too slow . . . fat . . . inexperienced . . . late . . . young . . . old . . . pigeon-toed . . . cross-eyed . . . hackneyed. You are too . . . ordinary."

But then comes the Christmas story—Norm and Norma from Normal, Ohio, plodding into ho-hum Bethlehem in the middle of the night. No one notices them. No one looks twice in their direction. The innkeeper won't even clean out a corner in the attic. Trumpets don't blast; bells don't sound; angels don't toss confetti. Aren't we glad they didn't?

What if Joseph and Mary had shown up in furs with a chauffeur, bling-blinged and high-muckety-mucked? And what if God had decked out Bethlehem like Hollywood on Oscar night: red carpet, flashing lights, with angels interviewing the royal couple? "Mary, Mary, you look simply divine."

Had Jesus come with such whoop-de-do, we would have read the story and thought, *My, look how Jesus entered their world.*

But since he didn't, we can read the story and dream. *My, might Jesus be born in my world? My everyday world?*

Isn't that what you indwell? Not a holiday world. Or a red-letter-day world. No, you live an everyday life. You have bills to pay, beds to make, and grass to cut. Your face won't grace any magazine covers, and you aren't expecting a call from the White House. Congratulations. You qualify for a modern-day Christmas story. God enters the world through folks like you and comes on days like today.

The splendor of the first Christmas is the lack thereof.

Step into the stable, and cradle in your arms the infant Jesus, still moist from the womb, just wrapped in the rags. Run a finger across his chubby cheek, and listen as one who knew him well puts lyrics to the event:

"In the beginning was the Word" (John 1:1).

The words "In the beginning" take us to the beginning. "In the beginning God created the heavens and the earth" (Genesis 1:1). The baby Mary held was connected to the dawn of time. He saw the first ray of sunlight and heard the first crash of a wave. The baby was born, but the Word never was.

"All things were made through him" (1 Corinthians 8:6 NCV). Not *by* him, but *through* him. Jesus didn't fashion the world out of raw material he found. He created all things out of nothing.

Jesus: the Genesis Word, "the firstborn over all creation" (Colossians 1:15). He is the "one Lord, Jesus Christ, through whom God made everything and through whom we have been given life" (1 Corinthians 8:6 NLT).

And then, what no theologian conceived, what no rabbi dared to dream, God did. "The Word became flesh" (John 1:14). The Artist became oil on his own palette. The Potter melted into the mud on his own wheel. God became an embryo in the belly of a village girl. Christ in Mary. God in Christ.

Astounding, this thought of heaven's fetus floating within the womb. Joseph and Mary didn't have the advantage we have: ultrasound. When Denalyn was pregnant with each of our three daughters, we took full advantage of the technology. The black-and-white image on the screen looked more like Doppler radar than a child. But with the help of the doctor, we were able to see the arms and hands and the pierced nose and prom dress ... Wait, I'm confusing photos.

As the doctor moved the instrument around Denalyn's belly, he took inventory. "There's the head, the feet, the torso ... Well, everything looks normal."

Mary's doctor would have made the same announcement. Jesus was an ordinary baby. There is nothing in the story to imply that he levitated over the manger or walked out of the stable. Just the opposite. He "dwelt among us" (John 1:14 NKJV). John's word for *dwelt* traces its origin to *tabernacle* or *tent*. Jesus did not separate himself from his creation; he pitched his tent in the neighborhood.

The Word of God entered the world with the cry of a baby. His family had no cash or connections or strings to pull. Jesus, the Maker of the universe, the one who invented time and created breath, was born into a family too humble to swing a bed for a pregnant mom-to-be.

✠

God writes his story with people like Joseph and Mary ... and Sam Stone.

In the weeks before Christmas 1933, a curious offer appeared in the daily newspaper of Canton, Ohio. "Man Who Felt Depression's Sting to Help 75 Unfortunate

Families." A Mr. B. Virdot promised to send a check to the neediest in the community. All they had to do was describe their plight in a letter and mail it to General Delivery.

The plunging economy had left fathers with no jobs, houses with no heat, children with patched clothing, and an entire nation, it seemed, with no hope.

The appeals poured in.

"I hate to write this letter … it seems too much like begging … my husband doesn't know I'm writing … He is working but not making enough to hardly feed his family."

"Mr. Virdot, we are in desperate circumstances … No one knows, only those who go through it."

All of Canton knew of Mr. Virdot's offer. Oddly, no one knew Mr. Virdot. The city registry of 105,000 citizens contained no such name. People wondered if he really existed. Yet within a week checks began to arrive at homes all over the area. Most were modest, about five dollars. All were signed "B. Virdot."

Through the years, the story was told, but the identity of the man was never discovered. In 2008, long after his death, a grandson opened a tattered black suitcase that had collected dust in his parents' attic. That's where he found the letters, all dated in December 1933, as well as 150 canceled checks. Mr. B. Virdot was Samuel J. Stone.

His pseudonym was a hybrid of Barbara, Virginia, and Dorothy, the names of his three daughters.[1]

There was nothing privileged about Sam Stone. If anything, his upbringing was marred by challenge. He was fifteen when his family emigrated from Romania. They settled into a Pittsburgh ghetto, where his father hid Sam's shoes so he couldn't go to school and forced him and his six siblings to roll cigars in the attic.

Still, Stone persisted. He left home to work on a barge, then in a coal mine, and by the time the Depression hit, he owned a small chain of clothing stores and lived in relative comfort. He wasn't affluent, or impoverished, but he was willing to help.

Ordinary man. Ordinary place. But a conduit of extraordinary grace. And in God's story, ordinary matters.

CHAPTER TWO

When God's Story Becomes Yours ...

YOU KNOW SATAN'S NEXT MOVE

IF I WERE THE DEVIL, I'D BE TICKED OFF. TICKED OFF TO SEE you reading a Christian book, thinking godly thoughts, dreaming about heaven and other such blah-blah-blah.

How dare you ponder God's story! What about my story? I had my eyes on you . . . had plans for you. That's what I would think.

If I were the devil, I'd get busy. I'd assemble my minions and demons into a strategy session and give them your picture and address. I'd review your weaknesses one by one. *Don't think I don't know them. How you love to be liked and hate to be wrong. How cemeteries give you the creeps and darkness gives you the heebie-jeebies.*

I'd brief my staff on my past victories. *Haven't I had my share? Remember your bouts with doubt? I all but had you convinced that the Bible was a joke. You and your so-called faith in God's Word.*

I'd stealth my way into your mind. No frontal attacks for you. Witchcraft and warlocks won't work with your type. No. If I were the devil, I'd dismantle you with questions. *How do you know, I mean, truly know, that Jesus rose from the dead? Are you sure you really believe the gospel? Isn't absolute truth yesterday's news? You, a child of God? Come on.*

I might direct you to one of my churches. One of my "feel good, you're good, everything's good" churches. Half Hollywood, half pep talk. Glitz, lights, and love. But no talk of Jesus. No mention of sin, hell, or forgiveness. I'd asphyxiate you with promises of pay raises and new cars. Then again, you're a bit savvy for that strategy.

Distraction would work better. *I hate spiritual focus. When you or one like you gazes intently on God for any length of time, you begin to act like him. A nauseating sense of justice and virtue comes over you. You talk to God, not just once a week, but all the time. Intolerable.*

So I'd perch myself on every corner and stairwell of your world, clamoring for your attention. I'd flood you with e-mails and to-do lists. Entice you with shopping sprees and latest releases and newest styles. Burden you with deadlines and assignments.

If I were the devil, I'd so distract you with possessions and problems that you'd never have time to read the Bible. Especially the story of Jesus in the wilderness. *What a disaster that day was! Jesus brought me down. Coldcocked me. Slam-dunked one right over my head. He knocked my best pitch over the Green Monster. I never even landed a punch. Looking back, I now realize what he was doing. He was making a statement. He wanted the whole world to know who calls the shots in the universe.*

If I were the devil, I wouldn't want you to read about that encounter. So, for that reason alone, let's do.

> Then Jesus was led by the Spirit into the wilderness to be tempted by the devil. After fasting forty days and forty nights, he was hungry. The tempter came to him and said, "If you are the Son of God, tell these stones to become bread."
>
> Jesus answered, "It is written: 'Man shall not live on bread alone, but on every word that comes from the mouth of God.'"
>
> Then the devil took him to the holy city and had him stand on the highest point of the temple. "If you are the Son of God," he said, "throw yourself down. For it is written:
>
> "'He will command his angels concerning you,

and they will lift you up in their hands,

so that you will not strike your foot against

a stone.'"

Jesus answered him, "It is also written: 'Do not put the Lord your God to the test.'"

Again, the devil took him to a very high mountain and showed him all the kingdoms of the world and their splendor. "All this I will give you," he said, "if you will bow down and worship me."

Jesus said to him, "Away from me, Satan! For it is written: 'Worship the Lord your God, and serve him only.'"

Then the devil left him, and angels came and attended him.

MATTHEW 4:1–11

Jesus was fresh out of the Jordan River. He had just been baptized by John. At his baptism he had been affirmed by God with a dove and a voice: "You are my Son, whom I love; with you I am well pleased" (Luke 3:22). He stepped out of the waters buoyed by God's blessing. Yet he began his public ministry, not by healing the sick or preaching a sermon, but by exposing the scheme of Satan. A perfect place to begin.

How do we explain our badness? Our stubborn hearts

and hurtful hands and conniving ways? How do we explain Auschwitz, human trafficking, abuse? Trace malevolence upriver to its beginning, where will the river take us? What will we see?

If I were the devil, I'd blame evil on a broken political system. A crippled economy. The roll of the dice. The Wicked Witch of the West. I'd want you to feel attacked by an indefinable, nebulous force. After all, if you can't diagnose the source of your ills, how can you treat them? If I were the devil, I'd keep my name out of it.

But God doesn't let the devil get away with this and tells us his name. The Greek word for devil is *diabolos*, which shares a root with the verb *diaballein*, which means "to split." The devil is a splitter, a divider, a wedge driver. He divided Adam and Eve from God in the garden, and has every intent of doing the same to you. Blame all unrest on him. Don't fault the plunging economy or raging dictator for your anxiety. They are simply tools in Satan's tool kit. He is the

- serpent (Genesis 3:14; Revelation 12:9; 20:2)

- tempter (Matthew 4:3; 1 Thessalonians 3:5)

- enemy (Matthew 13:25, 39)

- evil one (Matthew 13:19; 1 John 2:13 – 14)

- prince of demons (Mark 3:22)

- father of lies (John 8:44)

- murderer (John 8:44)

- roaring lion (1 Peter 5:8)

- deceiver (Revelation 12:9 GWT)

- dragon (Revelation 12:7, 9; 20:2)

Satan is not absent from or peripheral to God's story. He is at its center. We can't understand God's narrative without understanding Satan's strategy. In fact, "the reason the Son of God appeared was to destroy the works of the devil" (1 John 3:8 ESV).

Nothing thrills Satan more than the current skepticism with which he is viewed. When people deny his existence or chalk up his works to the ills of society, he rubs his hands with glee. The more we doubt his very existence, the more he can work without hindrance.

Jesus didn't doubt the reality of the devil. The Savior strode into the badlands with one goal, to unmask Satan, and made him the first stop on his itinerary. "Then Jesus was led by the Spirit into the wilderness to be tempted by the devil" (Matthew 4:1).

Does God do the same with us? Might the Spirit of

God lead us into the wilderness? If I were the devil, I'd tell you no. I would want you to think that I, on occasion, snooker heaven. That I catch God napping. That I sneak in when he isn't looking and snatch his children out of his hand. I'd leave you sleeping with one eye open.

But Scripture reveals otherwise. The next time you hear the phrase "all hell broke loose," correct the speaker. Hell does not break loose. God uses Satan's temptation to strengthen us. (If I were the devil, that would aggravate me to no end.) Times of testing are actually times of training, purification, and strength building. You can even "consider it pure joy ... whenever you face trials of many kinds, because you know that the testing of your faith produces perseverance" (James 1:2 – 3).

God loves you too much to leave you undeveloped and immature. "God disciplines us for our good, that we may share in his holiness. No discipline seems pleasant at the time, but painful. Later on, however, it produces a harvest of righteousness and peace for those who have been trained by it" (Hebrews 12:10 – 11). Expect to be tested by the devil.

And watch for his tricks. You can know what to expect. "We are not ignorant of his schemes" (2 Corinthians 2:11 NASB).

When General George Patton counterattacked Field

Marshal Rommel in World War II, Patton is reported to have shouted in the thick of battle, "I read your book, Rommel! I read your book!" Patton had studied Rommel's *Infantry Attacks*. He knew the German leader's strategy and planned his moves accordingly.[2] We can know the same about the devil.

We know Satan will *attack weak spots first*. Forty days of fasting left Jesus famished, so Satan began with the topic of bread. Jesus' stomach was empty, so to the stomach Satan turned.

Where are you empty? Are you hungry for attention, craving success, longing for intimacy? Be aware of your weaknesses. Bring them to God before Satan brings them to you. Satan will tell you to turn stones into bread (Matthew 4:3). In other words, *meet your own needs*, take matters into your own hands, leave God out of the picture. Whereas Jesus teaches us to pray for bread (Matthew 6:11), Satan says to work for bread.

Besides, he said, "If you are the Son of God" (Matthew 4:3), you can do this. Ah, another ploy: *raise a question about identity*. Make Christians think they have to prove their position with rock-to-bread miracles. Clever. If Satan convinces us to trust our works over God's Word, he has us dangling from a broken limb. Our works will never hold us.

Jesus didn't even sniff the bait. Three times he repeated, "It is written ..."; "It is also written ..."; "it is written ..." (verses 4, 7, 10). In his book, God's book was enough. He overcame temptation, not with special voices or supernatural signs, but by remembering and quoting Scripture.

(If I were the devil, I wouldn't want you to underline that sentence.)

Satan regrouped and tried a different approach. This one may surprise you. He told Jesus to *show off in church*. "Then the devil took him to the holy city and had him stand on the highest point of the temple. 'If you are the Son of God,' he said, 'throw yourself down'" (verses 5–6).

Testing isn't limited to the desert; it also occurs in the sanctuary. The two stood on the southeastern wall of the temple, more than a hundred feet above the Kidron Valley, and Satan told Jesus to jump into the arms of God. Jesus refused, not because he couldn't, not because God wouldn't catch him. He refused because he didn't have to prove anything to anyone, much less the devil.

Neither do you. Satan is going to tell you otherwise. In church, of all places, he will urge you to do tricks: impress others with your service, make a show of your faith, call attention to your good deeds. He loves to turn church assemblies into Las Vegas presentations where people show off their abilities rather than boast in God's. Don't be suckered.

Satan's last shot began with a mountain climb. "The devil took him to a very high mountain" (verse 8). Another note out of Satan's playbook: *promise heights.* Promise the highest place, the first place, the peak, the pinnacle. The best, the most, the top. These are Satan's favorite words. The devil led Jesus higher and higher, hoping, I suppose, that the thin air would confuse his thinking. He "showed [Jesus] all the kingdoms of the world and their splendor. 'All this I will give you,' he said, 'if you will bow down and worship me'" (verses 8–9).

Oops. Satan just showed his cards. He wants worship. He wants you and me to tell him how great he is. He wants to write his own story in which he is the hero and God is an afterthought. He admitted as much:

> "I will ascend to the heavens;
>   I will raise my throne
>   above the stars of God;
>   I will sit enthroned on the mount of assembly,
>   on the utmost heights of Mount Zaphon.
>   I will ascend above the tops of the clouds;
>   I will make myself like the Most High."

ISAIAH 14:13–14

Satan wants to take God's place, but God isn't moving. Satan covets the throne of heaven, but God isn't leaving. Satan wants to win you to his side, but God will never let you go.

You have his word. Even more, you have God's help.

For our high priest [Jesus] is able to understand our weaknesses. When he lived on earth, he was tempted in every way that we are, but he did not sin. Let us, then, feel very sure that we can come before God's throne where there is grace. There we can receive mercy and grace to help us when we need it.

HEBREWS 4:15–16 NCV

The last two Greek words of that verse are *eukairon boētheian*. *Eukairos* means "timely" or "seasonable" or "opportune." *Boētheia* is a compound of *boē*, "to shout," and *theō*, "to run." Nice combination. We shout, and God runs at the right moment. God places himself prior to our need, and just before we encounter that need, he gives us what we need.

You don't have to face Satan alone. You know his schemes. He will attack your weak spots first. He will tell you to meet your own needs. When you question your identity as a child of God, that is Satan speaking. If you turn church into a talent show, now you know why.

Even more, now you know what to do.

Pray. We cannot do battle with Satan on our own. He is a roaring lion, a fallen angel, an experienced fighter, and an equipped soldier. He is angry—angry because he knows that his time is short (Revelation 12:12) and that God's victory is secure. He resents God's goodness toward us and our worship of God. He is a skillful, powerful, ruthless foe who seeks to "work us woe; His craft and power are great, and armed with cruel hate, on earth is not his equal."[3] But there is wonderful news for the Christian: Christ reigns as our protector and provider. We are more than conquerors through him (Romans 8:37).

Arm yourself with God's Word. Load your pistol with Scriptures and keep a finger on the trigger. And remember: "Our struggle is not against flesh and blood, but against the rulers, against the authorities, against the powers of this dark world and against the spiritual forces of evil in the heavenly realms" (Ephesians 6:12).

If I were the devil, I wouldn't want you to know that. But I'm not the devil, so good for you. And take that, Satan.

CHAPTER THREE

When God's Story Becomes Yours ...

YOU FIND
YOUR TRUE HOME

FOR ALL WE DON'T KNOW ABOUT MR. HOLDEN HOWIE, OF one thing we can be certain. He knew his birds would find their way home. Several times a day the square-bodied, gray-bearded New Zealander retrieved one of his pigeons from his Auckland aviary. Securing the feathered courier with one hand, he affixed the correspondence with the other. Some birds carried as many as five messages at a time, each one written on cigarette paper. Mr. Howie then released the bird into the South Pacific sky. It flew straight as a string to its nest on Great Barrier Island.[4]

Between 1898 and 1908, Mr. Howie delivered thousands of messages. His birds were speedy. They could travel in two hours the distance a boat would traverse in three days. Dependable. Storms rarely knocked the pigeons off course, and they never called in sick. And, most notably, they were accurate. They could find their nest. Why else would we call them homing pigeons?

Other birds fly faster. Other birds are stronger. Other birds boast larger plumes or stronger claws. But none have the navigational skill of the homing pigeon.

Some scientists believe pigeons have traces of magnetite in their beaks and brains that interplay with the magnetic field of the earth.[5] Others credit the birds' sense of hearing. Do they pick up a frequency other birds miss? Or do they sniff out their target with a keen sense of smell?

What we know is this: pigeons have an innate home detector.

So do you.

What God gave pigeons, he gave to you. No, not bird brains. A guidance system. You were born heaven equipped with a hunger for your heavenly home. Need proof?

Consider your questions. Questions about death and time, significance and relevance. Animals don't seem to ask the questions we do. Dogs howl at the moon, but we stare at it. How did we get here? What are we here for? Are we someone's idea or something's accident? Why on earth are we on this earth?

We ask questions about pain. The words *leukemia*

and *child* shouldn't appear in the same sentence. And war. Can't conflict go the way of phonograph records and telegrams? And the grave. Why is the dash between the dates on a tombstone so small? Something tells us this isn't right, good, fair. This isn't home.

From whence come these stirrings? Who put these thoughts in our heads? Why can't we, like rabbits, be happy with carrots and copulation? Because, according to Jesus, we aren't home yet.

Probably his best-known story follows the trail of a homeless runaway. Jesus doesn't give us a name, just a pedigree: rich. Rockefeller rich. Spoiled rich. A silver-spooned, yacht-owning, trust-funded, blue-blooded boy. Rather than learn his father's business, he disregarded his father's kindness, cashed in his stock, and drove his Mercedes to the big city.

As fast as you can say dead broke, he was exactly that. No friends, no funds, no clue what to do. He ended up in a pigpen of trouble. He fed hogs, slept in the mud, and grew so hungry he gave serious consideration to licking the slop. That's when he thought of home. He remembered lasagna and laughter at the dining room table. His warm bed, clean pajamas, and fuzzy slippers. He missed his father's face and longed for his father's voice. He looked around at the snorting pigs and buzzing flies and made a decision.

"I'll turn the pigpen into a home." He took out a loan from the piggy bank and remodeled the place. New throw rug over the mud. A La-Z-Boy recliner next to the trough. He hung a flat screen on the fence post, flipped the slop bucket upside down, and called it a lamp shade. He tied a ribbon on a sow's head and called her honey. He pierced the ear of a piglet and called him son. Within short order he'd made a home out of the pigsty and settled in for the good life.

OK, maybe he didn't. But don't we? Don't we do our best to make this mess a home? Do up and doll up. Revamp and redecorate. We face-lift this. Overhaul that. Salt on the slop and whitewash for the posts. Ribbons for her and tattoos for him. And, in time, the place ain't half bad.

We actually feel at home.

But then the flies come out. People die, earthquakes rumble, and nations rage. Families collapse, and children die of hunger. Dictators snort and treat people like, well, like pigs. And this world stinks.

And we have a choice. We can pretend this life is all God intended. Or . . .

We can come to our senses. We can follow the example of the prodigal son. "I will set out and go back to my father" (Luke 15:18).

Don't you love the image of the son setting out for the homestead: rising out of the mud, turning his back to the pigs, and turning his eyes toward the father? This is Jesus' invitation to us. Set your hearts on your home. "Seek first the kingdom of God" (Matthew 6:33 NKJV).

In his plan it's all about the King and his kingdom. He wrote the script, built the sets, directs the actors, and knows the final act—an everlasting kingdom. "And this is [God's] plan: At the right time he will bring everything together under the authority of Christ—everything in heaven and on earth" (Ephesians 1:10 NLT).

Reach for it!

The journey home is nice, but the journey is not the goal. I prepared part of this message on an airplane. As I looked around at fellow passengers, I saw content people. Thanks to books, pillows, and crossword puzzles, they passed the time quite nicely. But suppose this announcement were heard: "Ladies and gentlemen, this flight is your final destination. We will never land. Your home is this plane, so enjoy the journey."

Passengers would become mutineers. We'd take over the cockpit and seek a landing strip. We wouldn't settle for such an idea. The journey is not the destination. The vessel is not the goal. Those who are content with nothing more than joy in the journey are settling for too little satisfaction. Our hearts tell us there is more to this life than this life. We, like E.T., lift bent fingers to the sky. We may not know where to point, but we know not to call this airplane our home.

"God ... has planted eternity in the human heart" (Ecclesiastes 3:11 NLT). Mr. Howie released his pigeons from Auckland, and God released his children from the cage of time. Our privilege is to keep flapping until we spot the island. Those who do will discover a spiritual cache, a treasure hidden in a field, a pearl of great value (Matthew 13:44–46). Finding the kingdom is like finding a winning lottery ticket in the sock drawer or locating the cover to a jigsaw puzzle box. "Oh, this is how it's going to look."

In God's narrative, life on earth is but the beginning: the first letter of the first sentence in the first chapter of the great story God is writing with your life.

Do you feel as if your best years have passed you by? Hogwash. You will do your best work in heaven. Do you regret wasting seasons of life on foolish pursuits? So do I. But we can stop our laments. We have an eternity to make up for lost time. Are you puzzled by the challenges of your days? Then see yourself as an uncut jewel and God as a lapidary. He is polishing you for your place in his kingdom. Your biggest moments lie ahead, on the other side of the grave.

So "seek those things which are above, where Christ is, sitting at the right hand of God" (Colossians 3:1 NKJV). Scripture uses a starchy verb here. *Zēteite* ("to seek") is to "covet earnestly, strive after, to inquire for, desire, even require."

Seek heaven the way a sailor seeks the coast or a pilot seeks the landing strip or a missile seeks heat. Head for home the way a pigeon wings to the nest or the prodigal strode to his papa. "Think only about" it (3:2 NCV). "Keep your mind" on it (3:2 GWT). "Set your sights on the realities of heaven" (3:1 NLT). "Pursue the things over which Christ presides" (3:1 MSG). Obsess yourself with heaven!

And, for heaven's sake, don't settle for pigpens on earth.

I found myself saying something similar to my nephew and niece. I had taken them to the San Antonio Zoo, a perfect place for a three- and a five-year-old to spend a Saturday afternoon. A veteran kid-guide, I knew the path to take. Start small and end wild. We began with the lowly, glass-caged reptiles. Next we oohed and aahed at the parrots and pink flamingos. We fed the sheep in the petting zoo and tossed crumbs to the fish in the pond. But all along I kept telling Lawson and Callie, "We're getting closer to the big animals. Elephants and tigers are just around the corner."

Finally we reached the Africa section. For full effect I told them to enter with their heads down and their eyes on the sidewalk. I walked them right up to the elephant fence.

And just when I was about to tell them to lift their eyes, Lawson made a discovery. "Look, a doodlebug!"

"Where?" Callie asked.

"Here!" He squatted down and placed the pellet-sized insect in the palm of his hand and began to roll it around.

"Let me see it!" Callie said.

I couldn't lure them away. "Hey, guys, this is the jungle section."

No response.

"Don't you want to see the wild animals?"

No, they focused on the bug. There we stood, elephants to our left, lions to our right, only a stone's throw from hippos and leopards, and what were they doing? Playing with a doodlebug.

Don't we all? Myriads of mighty angels encircle us, the presence of our Maker engulfs us, the witness of a thousand galaxies and constellations calls to us, the flowing tide of God's history carries us, the crowning of Christ as King of the universe awaits us, but we can't get our eyes off the doodlebugs of life: paychecks, gadgets, vacations, and weekends.

Open your eyes, Christ invites. *Lift up your gaze.* "Seek first the kingdom of God" (Matthew 6:33 NKJV). Limit your world to the doodlebugs of this life, and, mark it down, you will be disappointed. Limit your story to the days between your birth and death, and brace yourself for a sad ending. You were made for more than this life.

Five hundred years ago, sailors feared the horizon. Sail too far and risk falling off the edge, they reasoned. Common wisdom of the ancients warned against the unseen. So did the monument at the Strait of Gibraltar. At its narrowest margin, Spaniards erected a huge marker that bore in its stone the three-word Latin slogan *Ne plus ultra* or "No more beyond."

But then came Christopher Columbus and the voyage of 1492. The discovery of the New World changed everything. Spain acknowledged this in its coins, which came to bear the slogan *plus ultra*—"more beyond."[6]

Why don't you chisel the *no* off your future? God has set your heart on home. Keep flying until you reach it.

CHAPTER FOUR

When God's Story Becomes Yours ...

YOU HEAR A VOICE
YOU CAN TRUST

You think it's hard to walk in the dark? Find it difficult to navigate a room with the lights off or your eyes closed? Try flying a small plane at fifteen thousand feet. Blind.

Jim O'Neill did. Not that he intended to do so. The sixty-five-year-old pilot was forty minutes into a four-hour solo flight from Glasgow, Scotland, to Colchester, England, when his vision failed. He initially thought he had been blinded by the sun but soon realized it was much worse. "Suddenly I couldn't see the dials in front of me. It was just a blur. I was helpless."

He gave new meaning to the phrase "flying blind."

Turns out, he'd suffered a stroke. O'Neill groped and found the radio of his Cessna and issued a Mayday alert.

Paul Gerrard, a Royal Air Force Wing Commander who had just completed a training sortie nearby, was contacted by air traffic controllers and took off in O'Neill's direction. He found the plane and began talking to the stricken pilot.

The commander told O'Neill what to do. His instructions were reassuring and simple: "A gentle right turn, please. Left a bit. Right a bit." He hovered within five hundred feet of O'Neill, shepherding him toward the nearest runway. Upon reaching it, the two began to descend. When asked if he could see the runway below, O'Neill apologized, "No sir, negative." O'Neill would have to land the plane by faith, not by sight. He hit the runway but bounced up again. The same thing happened on the second attempt. But on the eighth try, the blinded pilot managed to make a near-perfect landing.[7]

Can you empathize with O'Neill? Most can. We've been struck, perhaps not with a stroke, but with a divorce, a sick child, or a cancer-ridden body. Not midair, but mid-career, midsemester, midlife. We've lost sight of any safe landing strip and, in desperation, issued our share of Mayday prayers. We know the fear of flying blind.

Unlike O'Neill, however, we hear more than one voice. Many voices besiege our cockpit. The talk show host urges us to worry. The New Age guru says to relax.

The financial page forecasts a downturn. The pastor says pray; the professor says phooey. So many opinions! Lose weight. Eat low fat. Join our church. Try our crystals. It's enough to make you cover your ears and run.

And what if you follow the wrong voice? What if you make the same mistake as the followers of self-help guru James Arthur Ray? He promised to help people achieve spiritual and financial wealth, asserting to "double, triple, even multiply by ten the size of your business."

He gave more than financial counsel to the more than fifty clients who crowded into his 415-square-foot sweat lodge in Sedona, Arizona. They had paid him between nine thousand and ten thousand dollars apiece for a five-day spiritual warrior retreat. The participants had fasted for thirty-six hours as part of a personal spiritual quest, then ate a breakfast buffet before entering the saunalike hut that afternoon. People began passing out and vomiting, but were still urged to stay in the lodge. Two hours later, three of them were dead.[8]

Oh, the voices. How do we select the right one?

A more important question cannot be asked. In fact, a form of the question was asked by Jesus himself: "Who do you say I am?" (Mark 8:29).

He had led his disciples into Caesarea Philippi. The region was to religion what Wal-Mart is to shopping—

every variety in one place. A center of Baal worship. An impressive temple of white marble dedicated to the godhead of Caesar. Shrines to the Syrian gods. Here Jesus, within earshot of every spiritual voice of his era, asked his followers:

"Who do people say I am?"

They replied, "Some say John the Baptist; others say Elijah; and still others, one of the prophets."

"But what about you?" he asked. "Who do you say I am?"

Peter answered, "You are the Messiah."

MARK 8:27–29

When it came to expressing the opinions of others, the disciples were chatty. Everyone spoke. But when it came to this personal question, only Peter replied. We do well to wonder why. Why only one answer? Was Peter so confident and quick that the others had no time to speak? Did Peter drown out the replies of everyone else?

"YOU ARE THE MESSIAH!"

Maybe Peter's confession echoed off the walls of the temples. Or perhaps it didn't.

Perhaps no one else spoke because no one else knew what to say. Maybe John ducked his eyes. Philip looked away. Andrew cleared his throat. Nathanael kicked the dirt, then elbowed Peter. And Peter sighed. He looked at this lean-faced, homeless teacher from Nazareth and pondered the question, "Who do you say I am?"

It couldn't have been a new one for Peter. He must have asked it a thousand times: the night when Jesus walked off the beach into the bay without sinking, the day he turned a boy's basket into an "all you can eat" buffet, the time he wove a whip and drove the swindlers out of the temple. *Who is this man?*

Peter had asked the question. So have millions of other people. All serious students of Christ, indeed students of life, have stood in their personal version of Caesarea Philippi and contrasted Jesus with the great philosophers of the world and heard him inquire, "Who do you say I am?"

"You're a decent fellow," some have answered. After all, if you can't like Jesus, can you like anyone? In Jesus, the poor found a friend, and the forgotten found an advocate. Jesus was nothing if not good. True-blue. Solid. Dependable. Everyone's first choice for a best friend, right?

Sure, if you want a best friend who claims to be God on earth. For being such an affable sort, Jesus had a curious habit of declaring divinity.

His favorite self-designation was Son of Man. The title

appears eighty-two times in the four gospels, only twice by anyone other than Jesus.[9]

> "The Son of Man has nowhere to lay His head."
> (Matthew 8:20 NKJV)

> "The Son of Man must suffer many things."
> (Mark 8:31 NKJV)

> "They will see the Son of Man coming ..."
> (Mark 13:26 NKJV)

First-century listeners found the claim outrageous. They were acquainted with its origin in Daniel 7. In his visions the prophet Daniel saw "One like the Son of Man, coming with the clouds of heaven! ... Then to Him was given dominion and glory and a kingdom, that all peoples, nations, and languages should serve Him. His dominion is an everlasting dominion, which shall not pass away, and His kingdom the one which shall not be destroyed" (Daniel 7:13 – 14 NKJV).

"That's me," Jesus was saying. Every time he used the phrase "Son of Man," he crowned himself. Would a decent fellow walk around making such a claim? You want a guy like this in your neighborhood?

And what about his "I AM" statements? "I am the light

of the world." "I am the bread of life," "the resurrection and the life," and "the way, the truth, and the life." And most stunning, "Before Abraham was born, I am!"[10]

By claiming the "I AM" title, Jesus was equating himself with God.

Jesus claimed to be able to forgive sins — a privilege only God can exercise (Matthew 9:4 – 7). He claimed to be greater than Jonah, Solomon, Jacob, and even Abraham (Matthew 12:38 – 42; John 4:12 – 14; 8:53 – 56). Jesus said that John the Baptist was the greatest man who had ever lived but implied that he was greater (Matthew 11:11). Jesus commanded people to pray in his name (John 14:13 – 14). He claimed to be greater than the temple (Matthew 12:6), greater than the Sabbath (Matthew 12:8). He claimed his words would outlive heaven and earth (Mark 13:31) and that all authority in heaven and on earth had been given to him (Matthew 28:18 – 20).

Does a decent fellow say things like this? No, but a demented fool does.

Maybe Jesus was a megalomaniac on par with Alexander the Great or Adolf Hitler. But, honestly, could a madman do what Jesus did?

Look at the devotion he inspired. People didn't just respect Jesus. They liked him; they left their homes and businesses and followed him. Men and women alike tethered their hope to his life. Impulsive people like Peter. Visionaries like Philip. Passionate men like John, careful men like Thomas, methodical men like Matthew the tax collector. When the men had left Jesus in the grave, it was the women who came to honor him—women from all walks of life, homemaking to philanthropy.

And people were better because of him. Madmen sire madmen: Saddam Hussein created murderers, Joseph Stalin created power addicts, Charles Manson created wackos. But Jesus transformed common dockworkers and net casters into the authors of history's greatest book and founders of its greatest movement. "They stand like a row of noble pillars towering far across the flats of time. But the sunlight that shines on them, and makes them visible, comes entirely from Him. He gave them all their greatness; and theirs is one of the most striking evidences of His."[11]

And what about his teaching? What about the day when Jesus' enemies sent officers to arrest him? Because of the crowd, they couldn't reach him directly. As they were pushing through the people, the officers were so gripped by his words that they abandoned their assignment. Their hearts were arrested, and Jesus was not. They returned to their superiors without a prisoner. Their defense? "No man ever spoke like this Man!" (John 7:46 NKJV).

Christ stunned people with his authority and clarity. His was not the mind of a deranged wild man. Demented fool? No. Deceiving fraud? Some have said so.

Some believe that Jesus masterminded the greatest scheme in the history of humanity, that he out-Ponzied the swindlers and out-hustled the hucksters. If that were true, billions of humans have been fleeced into following a first-century pied piper over the edge of a cliff.

Should we crown Christ as the foremost fraud in the world?

Not too quickly. Look at the miracles Jesus performed. The four gospels detail approximately thirty-six miracles and reference many more. He multiplied bread and fish, changed water into wine, calmed more than one storm, restored sight to more one than blind man. He healed contagious skin diseases, gave steps to the lame, purged demons, stopped a hemorrhage, even replaced a severed ear.

Yet, in doing so, Jesus never grandstanded his miraculous powers. Never went for fame or profit. Jesus performed miracles for two reasons: to prove his identity and to help his people.

Around AD 120, a man named Quadratus wrote the emperor Hadrian, defending Christianity. His apologetic included this sentence: "The works of our Saviour were lasting, for they were genuine: those who were healed and those who were raised from the dead were seen ... not merely while the Saviour was on earth, but also after his death; they were alive for quite a while, so that some of them lived even to our day."[12]

Had Jesus been a fraud or trickster, the Jerusalem congregation would have died a stillborn death. People would have denounced the miracles of Christ. But they did just the opposite. Can you imagine the apostles inviting testimonies? "If you were a part of the crowd he fed, one of the dead he raised, or one of the sick he healed, speak up and tell your story."

And speak they did. The church exploded like a fire on a West Texas prairie. Why? Because Jesus performed public, memorable miracles. He healed people.

And he loved people. He paid no heed to class or nationality, past sins or present accomplishments. The neediest and loneliest found a friend in Jesus:

- a woman scarcely clothed because of last night's affair. Christ befriended and defended her. (John 8:3–11)

- an unscrupulous tax collector left friendless because of his misdealings. Christ became his mentor. (Luke 19:2–10)

• a multiple divorcée who drew from the well
  in the heat of the day to avoid the stares
  of the villagers. Jesus gave her his attention.
  (John 4:5–26)

Could a lying sham love this way? If his intent was to trick people out of their money or worship, he did a pitifully poor job, for he died utterly broke and virtually abandoned.

What if Peter was correct? "You are the Messiah" (Mark 8:29).

What if Jesus really was, and is, the Son of God? If so, then we can relish this wonderful truth: we never travel alone. True, we cannot see the runway. We do not know what the future holds. But, no, we are not alone.

We have what Jim O'Neill had: the commander's voice to guide us home. Let's heed it, shall we? Let's issue the necessary Mayday prayer and follow the guidance that God sends. If so, we will hear what O'Neill heard.

BBC News made the recording of the final four minutes of the flight available. Listen and you'll hear the patient voice of a confident commander. "You've missed the runway this time … Let's start another gentle right-hand turn … Keep the right turn coming … Roll out left … No need to worry … Roll out left. Left again, left again … Keep coming down … Turn left, turn left … Hey, no problem … Can you see the runway now?… So you cannot see the runway?… Keep coming down …"

And then finally, "You are safe to land."[13]

I'm looking forward to hearing that final sentence someday. Aren't you?

CHAPTER FIVE

When God's Story Becomes Yours …

YOU WON'T BE FORSAKEN

Tennessee gives drunk drivers a new wardrobe. The Volunteer State has a special gift for any person convicted of driving their streets under the influence of alcohol. A blaze orange vest. Offenders are required to wear it in public three different days for eight hours at a time while picking up litter from the side of the highway. Stenciled on the back in four-inch-tall letters are the words "I AM A DRUNK DRIVER."[14]

No doubt they deserve the punishment. In fact, given the threat they've imposed upon the highways, they deserve three days of public humiliation. I don't question the strategy of the state.

But I wonder why we do the same to ourselves. Why we dress ourselves in our mistakes, don the robe of poor choices. Don't we? We step into our closets and sort through our regrets and rebellion and, for some odd reason, vest up.

I DISAPPOINTED MY PARENTS.

I WASTED MY YOUTH.

I NEGLECTED MY KIDS.

Sometimes we cover the vest with a blouse or blazer of good behavior. Mrs. Adams did. She's not the only person who ever came to see me while wearing a vest, but she was the first. I was only days into my first full-time church position in Miami, Florida. I'd barely unpacked my books when the receptionist asked if I could receive a visitor.

The senior minister was occupied, and I was next in line. I stepped into the conference room, where she sat, stirring a cup of coffee. She was a slight woman, wearing a nice dress and carrying a designer purse. She looked at me for only a moment, then back at the cup. That I was several years her junior didn't seem to matter.

"I left my family," she blurted. No greeting, introduction, or small talk. Just a confession.

I took a seat and asked her to tell me about it. I didn't have to ask twice. Too much pressure, temptation, and stress. So she walked out on her kids—ten years before she came to see me! What struck me about her story was not what she had done but how long she'd been living with her guilt. A decade! And now, hungry for help, she had a request.

"Can you give me some work to do?"

"What? Do you need some money?"

She looked at me as though I were a doctor unacquainted with penicillin. "No, I need some work. Anything. Letters to file, floors to sweep. Give me some work to do. I'll feel better if I do some work for God."

Welcome to the vest system. Hard to hide it. Harder still to discard it. But we work at doing so. Emphasis on the word *work*. Overcome bad deeds with good ones. Offset bad choices with godly ones, stupid moves with righteous ones. But the vest-removal process is flawed. No one knows what work to do or how long to do it. Shouldn't the Bible, of all books, tell us? But it doesn't. Instead, the Bible tells us how God's story redeems our story.

Jesus' death on the cross is not a secondary theme in Scripture; it is the core. The English word *crucial* comes from the Latin for cross (*crux*). The crucial accomplishment of Christ occurred on the cross. Lest we miss the message, God encased the climax of his story in high drama.

The garden: Jesus crying out, the disciples running out, the soldiers bursting in.

The trials: early morning mockery and deceit. Jews scoffing. Pilate washing.

The soldiers: weaving thorns, slashing whips, pounding nails.

Jesus: bloodied, beaten. More crimson than clean. Every sinew afire with pain.

And God: He ebonized the sky and shook the earth. He cleaved the rocks and ripped the temple curtain. He untombed the entombed and unveiled the Holy of Holies.

But first he heard the cry of his Son.

"My God, my God, why have you forsaken me?" (Matthew 27:46)

Forsaken. Visceral, painful. The word has the connotations of abandonment, of desertion, of being helpless, alone, cast out, of being completely forgotten.

Jesus forsaken? Does Scripture not declare, "I have not seen the righteous forsaken" and assure that "the LORD . . . does not forsake His saints" (Psalm 37:25, 28 NKJV)?

Indeed it does. But in that hour Jesus was anything but righteous. This was the moment in which "God put the wrong on him who never did anything wrong" (2 Corinthians 5:21 MSG). "GOD . . . piled all our sins, everything we've done wrong, on him, on him. He was beaten, he was tortured, but he didn't say a word" (Isaiah 53:6 – 7 MSG).

He dressed Christ in vests. Our vests, each and every one.

I CHEATED MY FRIENDS.

I LIED TO MY WIFE.

I ABUSED MY CHILDREN.

I CURSED MY GOD.

As if Jesus deserved them, he wore them. Our sins, our vests, were put on Christ. "The LORD has laid on him the iniquity of us all" (Isaiah 53:6). "He bore the sin of many" (Isaiah 53:12). Paul proclaimed that God made Christ "to be sin" (2 Corinthians 5:21) and become "a curse for us" (Galatians 3:13). Peter agreed: " '[Jesus] himself bore our sins' in his body on the cross" (1 Peter 2:24).

This is the monumental offer of God. What does God say to the woman who wants to work and offset her guilt? Simple: the work has been done. My Son wore your sin on himself, and I punished it there.

"For Christ also suffered once for sins, the just for the unjust, that He might bring us to God" (1 Peter 3:18 NKJV).

On August 16, 1987, Northwest Airlines flight 255 crashed after taking off from the Detroit airport, killing 155 people. The lone survivor was four-year-old Cecelia from Tempe, Arizona. Rescuers found her in such good condition that they wondered if she'd actually been on the flight. Perhaps she was riding in one of the cars into which the airplane crashed. But, no, her name was on the manifest.

While the exact nature of events may never be known, Cecelia's survival may have been due to her mother's quick response. Initial reports from the scene indicate that, as the plane was falling, her mother, Paula Cichan, unbuckled her own seat belt, got down on her knees in front of her daughter, and wrapped her arms and body around the girl. She separated her from the force of the fall ... and the daughter survived.[15]

God did the same for us. He wrapped himself around us and felt the full force of the fall. He took the unrelaxed punishment of the guilty. He died, not like a sinner, but as a sinner—in our place. "By a wonderful exchange our sins are now not ours but Christ's, and Christ's righteousness is not Christ's but ours."[16] His sacrifice is a sufficient one. Our merits don't enhance it. Our stumbles don't diminish it. The sacrifice of Christ is a total and unceasing and accomplished work.

"It is finished," Jesus announced (John 19:30). His

prayer of abandonment is followed by a cry of accomplishment. Not "It is begun" or "It is initiated" or "It is a work in progress." No, "It is finished."

You can remove your vest. Toss the thing in a trash barrel, and set it on fire. You need never wear it again. Does better news exist? Actually, yes. There is more. We not only remove our vest; we don his! He is "our righteousness" (1 Corinthians 1:30)

God does not simply remove our failures; he dresses us in the goodness of Christ! "For all of you who were baptized into Christ have clothed yourselves with Christ" (Galatians 3:27).

Think about this for a moment. When you make God's story yours, he covers you in Christ. You wear him like a vest. Old labels no longer apply—only labels that would be appropriately worn by Jesus Christ. Can you think of a few phrases for your new vest? How about

- royal priest (1 Peter 2:9)

- complete (Colossians 2:10 NKJV)

- free from condemnation (Romans 8:1)

- secure (John 10:28)

- established and anointed one
  (2 Corinthians 1:21 NKJV)

- God's coworker (2 Corinthians 6:1)

- God's temple (1 Corinthians 3:16–17)

- God's workmanship (Ephesians 2:10 NKJV)

How do you like that outfit?

"Now you're dressed in a new wardrobe. Every item of your new way of life is custom-made by the Creator, with his label on it. All the old fashions are now obsolete" (Colossians 3:10 MSG). Don't mess with the old clothes any longer. "As far as the east is from the west, so far has he removed our transgressions from us" (Psalm 103:12). How far is the east from the west? Further and further by the moment. Travel west and you can make laps around the globe and never go east. Journey east and, if you desire, maintain an easterly course indefinitely. Not so with the other two directions. If you go north or south, you'll eventually reach the North or South Pole and change directions. But east and west have no turning points.

Neither does God. When he sends your sins to the east and you to the west, you can be sure of this: he doesn't see you in your sins. His forgiveness is irreversible. "He does not treat us as our sins deserve or repay us according to our iniquities" (Psalm 103:10).

Headline this truth: when God sees you, he sees his

Son, not your sin. God "blots out your transgressions" and "remembers your sins no more" (Isaiah 43:25). No probation. No exception. No reversals.

He did his due diligence. He saw your secret deeds and heard your unsaid thoughts. The lies, the lusts, the longings — he knows them all. God assessed your life from first day to last, from worst moment to best, and made his decision.

"I want that child in my kingdom."

You cannot convince him otherwise.

Look on his city gates for proof. In the last pages of the Bible, John describes the entrance to the New Jerusalem:

> She had a great and high wall with twelve gates . . . and names written on them, which are the names of the twelve tribes of the children of Israel. . . .
>
> Now the wall of the city had twelve foundations, and on them were the names of the twelve apostles of the Lamb.
>
> REVELATION 21:12, 14 NKJV

God engraved the names of the sons of Jacob on his gateposts. More ragamuffins than reverends. Their rap sheets include stories of mass murder (Genesis 34), incest (38:13 – 18), and brotherly betrayal (37:17 – 28). They behaved more like the 3:00 a.m. nightclub crowd than a Valhalla of faith. Yet God carved their names on the New Jerusalem gates.

And dare we mention the names on the foundations? Peter, the apostle who saved his own skin instead of his Savior's. James and John, who jockeyed for VIP seats in heaven. Thomas, the dubious, who insisted on a personal audience with the resurrected Jesus. These were the disciples who told the children to leave Jesus alone (Luke 18:15), who told Jesus to leave the hungry on their own (Matthew 14:15), and chose to leave Jesus alone to face his crucifixion (Matthew 26:36–45). Yet all their names appear on the foundations. Matthew's does. Peter's does. Bartholomew's does.

And yours? It's not engraved in the gate, but it is written in the Book of the Lamb. Not in pencil marks that can be erased, but with blood that will not be removed. No need to keep God happy; he is satisfied. No need to pay the price; Jesus paid it.

All.

Lose your old vest. You look better wearing his.

CHAPTER SIX

When God's Story Becomes Yours ...

YOUR FINAL CHAPTER BECOMES A PREFACE

CARL MCCUNN, AN AFFABLE TEXAN WITH A LOVE OF THE outdoors, moved to Alaska in the late 1970s. He took a trucking job on the Trans-Alaska Pipeline, where he made good money, fast friends, and concocted an adventure that still stirs bewilderment in the forty-ninth state.

At the age of thirty-five, he embarked on a five-month photography expedition in the wild. Friends describe how seriously he prepared for the quest, devoting a year to plan making and detail checking. He solicited advice and purchased supplies. And then, in March 1981, he hired a bush pilot to drop him at a remote lake near the Coleen River, some seventy miles northeast of Fort Yukon. He took two rifles, a shotgun, fourteen hundred pounds of provisions, and five hundred rolls of film.

He set up his tent and set about his season of isolation, blissfully unaware of an overlooked detail that would cost him his life.

He had made no arrangement to be picked up.

His unbelievable blunder didn't dawn on him until August. We know this because of a hundred-page loose-leaf diary the Alaska state troopers found near his body the following February. In an understatement the size of Mount McKinley, McCunn wrote: "I think I should have used more foresight about arranging my departure."

As the days shortened and air chilled, he began searching the ground for food and the skies for rescue. He was running low on ammunition. Hiking out was impossible. He had no solution but to hope someone in the city would notice his absence.

By the end of September, the snow was piling, the lake was frozen, and supplies were nearly gone. His body fat began to metabolize, making it more difficult to stay warm. Temperatures hovered around zero, and frostbite began to attack his fingers and toes.

By late November, McCunn was out of food, strength, and optimism. One of his final diary entries reads, "This is sure a slow and agonizing way to die."[17]

Isolated with no rescue. Trapped with no exit. Nothing to do but wait for the end. Chilling.

And puzzling. Why no exit strategy? Didn't he know that every trip comes to an end? It's not like his excursion would last forever.

Ours won't.

This heart will feel a final pulse. These lungs will empty a final breath. The hand that directs this pen across the page will fall limp and still. Barring the return of Christ, I will die. So will you. "Death is the most democratic institution on earth. . . . It allows no discrimination, tolerates no exceptions. The mortality rate of mankind is the same the world over: one death per person."[18]

Or, as the psalmist asked, "Who can live and not see death, or who can escape the power of the grave?" (Psalm 89:48). Young and old, good and bad, rich and poor. Neither gender is spared; no class is exempt. "No one has power over the time of their death" (Ecclesiastes 8:8).

The geniuses, the rich, the poor — no one outruns it or outsmarts it. Julius Caesar died. Elvis died. John Kennedy died. Princess Diana died. We all die. Nearly 2 people a second, more than 6,000 an hour, more than 155,000 every day, about 57 million a year.[19] We don't escape death.

The finest surgeon might enhance your life but can't eliminate your death. The Hebrew writer was blunt: "People are destined to die once" (Hebrews 9:27). Exercise all you want. Eat nothing but health food, and pop fistfuls of vitamins. Stay out of the sun, away from alcohol, and off drugs. Do your best to stay alive, and, still, you die.

Death seems like such a dead end.

Until we read Jesus' resurrection story.

"He is not here. He has risen from the dead as he said he would" (Matthew 28:6 NCV).

It was Sunday morning after the Friday execution. Jesus' final breath had sucked the air out of the universe. As his body seemed to be a-moldering in the grave, no one was placing bets on a resurrection.

His enemies were satisfied with their work. The spear to his side guaranteed his demise. His tongue was silenced. His last deed done. They raised a toast to a dead Jesus. Their only concern was those pesky disciples. The religious leaders made this request of Pilate: "So give the order for the tomb to be made secure until the third day. Otherwise, his disciples may come and steal the body and tell the people that he has been raised from the dead" (Matthew 27:64).

No concern was necessary. The disciples were at melt-down. When Jesus was arrested, "all the disciples forsook Him and fled" (Matthew 26:56 NKJV). Peter followed from a distance but caved in and cursed Christ. John watched Jesus die, but we have no record that John gave any thought to ever seeing him again. The other followers didn't even linger; they cowered in Jerusalem's cupboards and corners for fear of the cross that bore their names.

No one dreamed of a Sunday morning miracle. Peter didn't ask John, "What will you say when you see Jesus?" Mary didn't ponder, *How will he appear?* They didn't encourage each other with quotes of his promised return. They could have. At least four times Jesus had said words like these: "The Son of Man is being betrayed into the hands of men, and they will kill Him. And after He is killed, He will rise the third day."[20] You'd think someone would mention this prophecy and do the math. "Hmm, he died yesterday. Today is the second day. He promised to rise on the third day. Tomorrow is the third day ... Friends, I think we'd better wake up early tomorrow."

But Saturday saw no such plans. On Saturday the Enemy had won, courage was gone, and hope caught the last train to the coast. They planned to embalm Jesus, not talk to him.

> When the Sabbath was over, Mary Magdalene, Mary the mother of James, and Salome bought spices so that they might go to anoint Jesus' body. Very early on the first day of the week, just after sunrise, they were on their way to the tomb and they asked

each other, "Who will roll the stone away from the entrance of the tomb?"

MARK 16:1–3

Easter parade? Victory march? Hardly. More like a funeral procession. It may have been Sunday morning, but their world was stuck on Saturday.

It was left to the angel to lead them into Sunday.

There was a violent earthquake, for an angel of the Lord came down from heaven and, going to the tomb, rolled back the stone and sat on it. His appearance was like lightning, and his clothes were white as snow. The guards were so afraid of him that they shook and became like dead men.

The angel said to the women, "Do not be afraid, for I know that you are looking for Jesus, who was crucified. He is not here; he has risen, just as he said. Come and see the place where he lay."

MATTHEW 28:2–6

God shook up the cemetery. Trees swayed, and the ground trembled. Pebbles bounced, and the women struggled to maintain their balance. They looked in the direction of the tomb only to see the guards — scared stiff, paralyzed, and sprawled on the ground. Hard to miss the irony: the guards of the dead appear dead, while the dead one appears to be living. Take that, Devil. Remember the famous play on Nietzsche's statement?[21]

"GOD is DEAD!"

Nietzsche.

"NIETZSCHE is DEAD!"

God."

The angel sat on the dislodged tombstone. He did not stand in defiance or crouch in alertness. He sat. Legs crossed and whistling? In my imagination at least. The angel sat upon the *stone*. Again, the irony. The very rock intended to mark the resting place of a dead Christ became the resting place of his living angel. And then the announcement.

"He has risen."

Three words in English. Just one in Greek. *Ēgerthē*. So much rests on the validity of this one word. If it is false, then the whole of Christianity collapses like a poorly told joke. Yet, if it is true, then God's story has turned your final chapter into a preface. If the angel was correct, then you can believe this: Jesus descended into the coldest cell of death's prison and allowed the warden to lock the door and smelt the keys in a furnace. And just when the demons began to dance and prance, Jesus pressed pierced hands against the inner walls of the cavern. From deep within he shook the cemetery. The ground rumbled, and the tombstones tumbled.

And out he marched, the cadaver turned king, with the mask of death in one hand and the keys of heaven in the other. *Ēgerthē!* He has risen!

Not risen from sleep. Not risen from confusion. Not risen from stupor or slumber. Not spiritually raised from the dead; *physically* raised. The women and disciples didn't see a phantom or experience a sentiment. They saw Jesus in the flesh. "It is I myself!" he assured them (Luke 24:39).

The Emmaus-bound disciples thought Jesus was a fellow pilgrim. His feet touched the ground. His hands touched the bread. Mary mistook him for a gardener. Thomas studied his wounds. The disciples ate fish that he cooked. The resurrected Christ did physical deeds in a physical body. "I am not a ghost," he explained (Luke 24:39 NLT). "Handle Me and see, for a spirit does not have flesh and bones as you see I have" (verse 39 NKJV).

The bodily resurrection means everything. If Jesus lives on only in spirit and deeds, he is but one of a thousand dead heroes. But if he lives on in flesh and bone, he is the King who pressed his heel against the head of death. What he did with his own grave he promises to do with yours: empty it.

A curious thing happened as I was rewriting this chapter. While reading the above paragraph, I heard my computer signal an e-mail arrival. I stopped to read it. A friend had just returned from the funeral of his ninety-six-year-old aunt, and he wanted to tell me about it.

Max,

Until about a year ago, you couldn't keep up with my Aunt Wanda. Seriously—she had such energy you just couldn't believe it. Her eyesight was failing so completely that her energy almost made it dangerous to go to unfamiliar places with her. Her eyes couldn't see the crack in the sidewalk that she was about to trot over at ninety miles an hour!!!

About a year ago she started having difficulty breathing. The doctor found a mass in her chest that was almost certainly cancer. But at ninety-five there was little reason to do surgery—even exploratory. The better plan was to keep her comfortable.

It was only in the last three days of her life that the mass became painful to the point she needed medication to fight the pain. It became so severe so quickly that she was given enough morphine to sedate her and basically keep her in an unconscious state.

But as she began to pass from this world into the

next, her sight became clear, she was released of the pain, and even in her unconscious state, she began to have conversations with those who had gone before her. She saw her mother (who was her best friend) and talked to her. And, my favorite part, she saw my dad and their brother.

My dad and their brother (Uncle Marvin) were constantly playing practical jokes on their sister (Aunt Wanda). She always referred to them as "the boys" or "those boys." I have no idea what they did or how they greeted her at heaven's door, but whatever it was made her laugh so hard that she literally pulled her legs up to her chest and doubled over laughing. "I can't believe you boys! Oh, my goodness . . . you boys!" She literally took her last breaths laughing. I can't wait to find out what she saw. But she saw something grand!"[22]

You will too.

Will you die laughing? I don't know. But die in peace, for certain. Death is not the final chapter in your story. In death you will step into the arms of the One who declared, "I am the resurrection and the life. The one who believes in me will live, even though they die; and whoever lives by believing in me will never die" (John 11:25–26).

Winston Churchill believed this. The prime minister

planned his own funeral. According to his instructions, two buglers were positioned high in the dome of St. Paul's Cathedral. At the conclusion of the service, the first one played taps, the signal of a day completed. Immediately thereafter, with the sounds of the first song still ringing in the air, the second bugler played reveille, the song of a day begun.[23]

Appropriate song. Death is no pit but a passageway, not a crisis but a corner turn. Dominion of the grim reaper? No. Territory of the Soul Keeper, who will some-day announce, "Your dead will live, your corpses will get to their feet. All you dead and buried, wake up! Sing! Your dew is morning dew catching the first rays of sun, the earth bursting with life, giving birth to the dead" (Isaiah 26:19 MSG).

Play on, bugler. Play on.

CHAPTER SEVEN

When God's Story Becomes Yours ...

POWER MOVES IN

WHAT GOT INTO PETER? SEVEN WEEKS AGO HE WAS HIDING because of Jesus; today he is proclaiming the death of Jesus. Before the crucifixion, he denied Christ; now he announces Christ. On the eve of Good Friday, you couldn't get him to speak up. Today, you can't get him to shut up! "My fellow Jews, and all of you who are in Jerusalem, listen to me. Pay attention to what I have to say" (Acts 2:14 NCV).

What got into Peter?

He was a coward at the crucifixion. A kind coward but a coward nonetheless. A comment from a servant girl undid him. A soldier didn't bludgeon him. The Sanhedrin didn't browbeat him. Rome didn't threaten to export him to Siberia. No, a waitress from the downtown diner heard his accent and said he knew Jesus. Peter panicked. He not only denied his Lord; he bleeped the very idea. "Then Peter began to place a curse on himself and swear, 'I don't know the man!'" (Matthew 26:74 NCV).

But look at him on the day of Pentecost, declaring to a throng of thousands, "God has made Jesus—the man you nailed to the cross—both Lord and Christ" (Acts 2:36 NCV). Gutsy language. Lynch mobs feed on these accusations. The same crowd that shouted, "Crucify him!" could crucify him.

From wimp to warrior in fifty days. What happened?

Oh, how we need to know. We admire the Pentecost Peter yet identify with the Passover one. We battle addictions we can't shake, pasts we can't escape, bills we can't pay, sorrow that won't fade.

Our convictions wrinkle, and resolve melts. And we wonder why. We look at other believers and ask, Why is her life so fruitful and mine so barren? Why is his life so powerful and mine so weak? Aren't we saved by the same Christ? Don't we read the same Scripture and rally around the same cross? Why do some look like the early Peter and others like the latter? Or, better question, why do I vacillate between the two in any given week?

Jesus embedded an answer in his final earthly message. He told Peter and the other followers, "Wait here to receive the promise from the Father which I told you about. John baptized people with water, but in a few days you will be baptized with the Holy Spirit" (Acts 1:4–5 NCV).

What got into Peter?

God's Spirit did. Ten days after Jesus' ascension into heaven, "all of them were filled with the Holy Spirit" (Acts 2:4). The followers experienced a gushing forth, a tremendous profusion. They were drenched in power. They all were "sons and daughters … young men … old men … servants, both men and women" (Acts 2:17–18). The Holy Spirit, in his own time and according to his own way, filled the followers with supernatural strength.

Didn't Jesus promise this event? As his days on earth came to an end, he said, "But very truly I tell you, it is for your good that I am going away. Unless I go away, the Advocate will not come to you; but if I go, I will send him to you" (John 16:7).

The bad news: Jesus was going away. The wonderful news: Jesus was sending them the Spirit. During his earthly ministry Jesus lived near the disciples. The Holy Spirit, however, would live *in* the disciples. What Jesus did with the followers, the Spirit would do through them and us. Jesus healed; the Spirit heals through us. Jesus taught; the Spirit teaches through us. Jesus comforted; the Spirit comforts through us. The Spirit continues the work of Christ.

The Holy Spirit is not enthusiasm, compassion, or bravado. He might stimulate such emotions, but he himself is a person. He determines itineraries (Acts 16:6), distributes spiritual gifts (1 Corinthians 12:7–11), and selects church leaders (Acts 13:2). He teaches (John 14:26), guides (John 16:13), and comforts (John 16:7 KJV).

"He dwells with you and will be in you" (John 14:17 NKJV). Occasional guest? No sir. The Holy Spirit is a year-round resident in the hearts of his children. As God's story becomes our story, his power becomes our power. Then why do we suffer from power failures?

I believe we make the mistake the Welsh woman made. She lived many years ago in a remote valley but determined that it would be worth the cost and trouble to have electricity in her home. Several weeks after the installation, the power company noticed that she had barely used any. So they sent a meter reader to see what was wrong.

"Is there a problem?" he asked.

"No," she answered, "we're quite satisfied. Every night we turn on the electric lights to see how to light our lamps."[24]

We're prone to do likewise: depend on God's Spirit

to save us but not sustain us. We are like the Galatians whom Paul asked, "After beginning by means of the Spirit, are you now trying to finish by means of the flesh?" (Galatians 3:3). We turn to him to get us started, and then continue in our own strength.

The Christians in Ephesus did this. The apostle Paul assured them that they had received the Spirit. God "put his special mark of ownership on you by giving you the Holy Spirit that he had promised" (Ephesians 1:13 NCV). Even so, he had to urge them to be "filled with the Spirit" (Ephesians 5:18). Interesting. Can a person be saved and not full of the Holy Spirit? They were in Ephesus.

And in Jerusalem. When the apostles instructed the church to select deacons, they said, "So, brothers and sisters, choose seven of your own men who are good, full of the Spirit and full of wisdom" (Acts 6:3 NCV). The fact that men "full of the Spirit" were to be chosen suggests that men lacking in the Spirit were present. We can have the Spirit but not let the Spirit of God have us.

When God's Spirit directs us, we actually "keep in step with the Spirit" (Galatians 5:25). He is the drum major; we are the marching band. He is the sergeant; we are the platoon. He directs and leads; we obey and follow. Not always that easy, is it? We tend to go our own way.

Some time ago I purchased a new cartridge for my

computer printer. But when I used it, no letters appeared on the page. It was half an hour before I noticed the thin strip of tape covering the outlet of the cartridge. There was plenty of ink, but until the tape was removed, no impression could be made.

Is there anything in your life that needs to be removed? Any impediment to the impression of God's Spirit? We can grieve the Spirit with our angry words (Ephesians 4:29 – 30; Isaiah 63:10) and resist the Spirit in our disobedience (Acts 7:51). We can test or conspire against the Spirit in our plottings (Acts 5:9). We can even quench the Spirit by having no regard for God's teachings. "Never damp the fire of the Spirit, and never despise what is spoken in the name of the Lord" (1 Thessalonians 5:19 – 20 Phillips).

Here is something that helps me stay in step with the Spirit. We know that the "fruit of the Spirit is love, joy, peace, patience, kindness, goodness, faithfulness, gentleness, self-control" (Galatians 5:22 – 23 NASB). God's Spirit creates and distributes these characteristics. They are indicators on my spiritual dashboard. So whenever I sense them, I know I am walking in the Spirit. Whenever I lack them, I know I am out of step with the Spirit.

I sensed his corrective pull just yesterday at a Sunday service. A dear woman stopped me as I was entering the building. She didn't agree with a comment I had made in a sermon the week before and wanted to express her opinion ... in the foyer ... in a loud voice ... ten minutes prior to the service.

What's more, she pressed the nerve of my pet peeve. "Other people feel the same way." Grrr. Who are these "other people"? How many "other people" are there? And why, for crying out loud, don't "other people" come and talk to me?

By now it was time for the service to begin. I was more in a mood to hunt bear than to preach. I couldn't get my mind off the woman and the "other people." I drove home from the morning assembly beneath a cloud. Rather than love, joy, peace, and patience, I felt anger, frustration, and impatience. I was completely out of step with the Spirit. And I had a choice. I could march to my own beat, or I could get back in rhythm. I knew what to do.

I made the phone call. "I didn't feel like we quite finished the conversation we began in the foyer," I told her. So we did. And over the next fifteen minutes, we discovered that our differences were based on a misunderstanding, and I learned that the "other people" consisted of her and her husband, and he was really OK.

To walk in the Spirit, respond to the promptings God gives you.

Don't sense any nudging? Just be patient and wait. Jesus told the disciples to "*wait* for the gift my Father promised ... the Holy Spirit" (Acts 1:4–5, emphasis mine). Abraham waited for the promised son. Moses waited forty years in the wilderness. Jesus waited thirty years before he began his ministry. God instills seasons of silence in his plan. Winter is needed for the soil to bear fruit. Time is needed for the development of a crop. And disciples wait for the move of God. Wait for him to move, nudge, and direct you. Somewhat as I'm learning to wait on my dance teacher.

Yes, Denalyn and I are taking dance lessons. This was her announcement to me on our twenty-eighth wedding anniversary. She's been making such comments for years. "We need to learn to dance, honey." "What's there to learn?" was my stock reply, and I would remind her of the night we waltzed our way across the dance floor at my niece's wedding reception in 1985. She would mumble something about tractor-trailers having more finesse and drop the subject.

Of late she's been picking it back up. Now that our third little bird has winged her way out of our nest, it's time for the Mr. and Mrs. to slide their heels. So for my anniversary gift, she loaded me in the car, drove me to a shopping center, and parked in front of the Fred Astaire Dance Studio. (I know where they got the name. I just sat there and … uh … stared.)

Our instructor is young enough to be our son. He wears a moustache-less beard and an innocent smile, and I wonder if he'd more quickly teach an elephant to pirouette than me to waltz. He spent the better part of the first class reminding me to "gently lead" my wife. "Place your hand beneath her shoulder blade and guide her."

He said I shoved and dragged her. Denalyn agreed. And to convey his point, he danced with me. He matched one hand on mine, placed the other beneath my left shoulder blade, and off we went, *forward, forward, slide, slide,* following the beat of Barry Manilow across the room. I know, it's not a pretty sight. But it was a good lesson. I learned to follow his lead. He nudged me this way, led me that way, and at the end I even did a nice twirl.

(Just kidding about the twirl. It was more of a tumble.)

It's nice to be led by a master. Won't you let your Master lead you?

> He guides the humble in what is right
> and teaches them his way.
>
> PSALM 25:9

Whether you turn to the right or to the left, your ears will hear a voice behind you, saying, "This is the way; walk in it."

ISAIAH 30:21

Wait on the Spirit. If Peter and the apostles needed his help, don't we? They walked with Jesus for three years, heard his preaching, and saw his miracles. They saw the body of Christ buried in the grave and raised from the dead. They witnessed his upper room appearance and heard his instruction. Had they not received the best possible training? Weren't they ready?

Yet Jesus told them to wait on the Spirit. "Do not leave Jerusalem, but wait for the gift my Father promised … the Holy Spirit" (Acts 1:4–5).

Learn to wait, to be silent, to listen for his voice. Cherish stillness; sensitize yourself to his touch. "Just think — you don't need a thing, you've got it all! All God's gifts are right in front of you as you *wait expectantly* for our Master Jesus to arrive on the scene" (1 Corinthians 1:7–8 MSG, emphasis mine). You needn't hurry or scurry. The Spirit-led life does not panic; it trusts.

God's power is very great for us who believe. That power is the same as the great strength God used to raise Christ from the dead and put him at his right side in the heavenly world.

EPHESIANS 1:19–20 NCV

The same hand that pushed the rock from the tomb can shove away your doubt. The same power that stirred the still heart of Christ can stir your flagging faith. The same strength that put Satan on his heels can, and will, defeat Satan in your life. Just keep the power supply open. Who knows, you may soon hear people asking, "What's gotten into you?"

CHAPTER EIGHT

When God's Story Becomes Yours . . .

THE RIGHT
DOORS OPEN

I CAME HOME THE OTHER DAY TO A HOUSE OF BLOCKED doors. Not just shut doors, closed doors, or locked doors. Blocked doors.

Blame them on Molly, our nine-year-old, ninety-pound golden retriever, who, on most fronts, is a great dog. When it comes to kids and company, Molly sets a tail-wagging standard. But when it comes to doors, Molly just doesn't get it. Other dogs bark when they want out of the house; Molly scratches the door. She is the canine version of Freddy Krueger. Thanks to her, each of our doors has Molly marks.

We tried to teach her to bark, whine, or whistle; no luck. Molly thinks doors are meant to be clawed. So Denalyn came up with a solution: doggy doors. She installed

Molly-sized openings on two of our doors, and to teach Molly to use them, Denalyn blocked every other exit. She stacked furniture five feet deep and twice as wide. Molly got the message. She wasn't going out those doors.

And her feelings were hurt. I came home to find her with drooping ears and limp tail. She looked at the blocked door, then at us. "How could you do this to me?" her eyes pleaded. She walked from stack to stack. She didn't understand what was going on.

Maybe you don't either. You try one door after another, yet no one responds to your résumé. No university accepts your application. No doctor has a solution for your illness. No buyers look at your house.

Obstacles pack your path. Road, barricaded. Doorway, padlocked. You, like Molly, walk from one blocked door to another. Do you know the frustration of a blocked door? If so, you have a friend in the apostle Paul.

He, Silas, and Timothy were on their second missionary journey. On his first one Paul enjoyed success at every stop. "They began to report all things that God had done with them and how He had opened a door of faith to the Gentiles" (Acts 14:27 NASB). God opened doors into Cyprus, Antioch, and Iconium. He opened the door of grace at the Jerusalem council and spurred spiritual growth in every city. "The churches were being strengthened in the faith, and were increasing in number daily" (Acts 16:5 NASB).

The missionaries felt the gusts at their backs, and then, all of a sudden, headwinds.

> Paul and his companions traveled throughout the region of Phrygia and Galatia, having been kept by the Holy Spirit from preaching the word in the province of Asia. When they came to the border of Mysia, they tried to enter Bithynia, but the Spirit of Jesus would not allow them to.
>
> ACTS 16:6–7

Paul set his sights on Asia. Yet no doors opened. So the three turned north into Bithynia but encountered more blocked doors. They jiggled the knobs and pressed against the entrances but no access. We aren't told how or why God blocked the door. Just that he did.

He still does.

God owns the key to every door. He is "opening doors no one can lock, locking doors no one can open" (Revelation 3:7 MSG). Once God closes a door, no one can open it. Once God shut the door of Noah's ark, only he could open it. Once he directed the soldiers to seal the tomb of Jesus, only he could open it. Once he blocks a door, we cannot open it. During a season of blocked doors, we, like Molly, can grow frustrated.

A few years ago, many of us at Oak Hills were convinced that our church needed a new sanctuary. We were bursting at the seams. Wouldn't God want us to build a larger auditorium? We thought so. We prayed for forty days and sought counsel from other churches. We weighed our options and designed a new facility. Sensing no divine reservation, we began the campaign.

All of a sudden the wind turned. In less than six months, construction costs increased 70 percent! Gulp. Still, we continued. We reduced the scope of the project and challenged the congregation to ante up more money. Even with their astounding generosity, we didn't raise enough money to build the sanctuary. I will never forget the weight I felt when I announced our decision not to build.

Didn't we pray? Didn't we seek God's will? Why would God close the door? Might it have something to do with this — the worst recession since the Great Depression looming less than a year away? God was protecting us. Moreover, within three months I would be diagnosed with a heart condition. God was protecting us.

It was a classic God's story/our story contrast. From our perspective we saw setbacks. God, however, saw an opportunity, an opportunity to keep us out of dangerous debt and bolster our leadership team with a new senior minister, Randy Frazee. A plan to protect us from a budget-busting mortgage and to grant us fresh leadership. God closed the wrong doors so he could lead us through the right one.

As God's story becomes yours, closed doors take on a new meaning. You no longer see them as interruptions of your plan but as indications of God's plan.

This is what Paul learned. God blocked his missionary team from going north, south, or east. Only west remained, so they ended up at Asia's westernmost point. They stood with their toes in the sand and looked out over the sea. As they slept, "Paul had a vision of a man of Macedonia standing and begging him, 'Come over to Macedonia and help us'" (Acts 16:9).

The closed doors in Asia led to an open-armed invitation to Europe. "Therefore, sailing from Troas, we ran a straight course to Samothrace, and the next day came to Neapolis, and from there to Philippi" (Acts 16:11 – 12 NKJV). They ran a "straight course." The wind was at their back. Blocked passages became full sails.

After several days Paul and his team went out of the city of Philippi to the riverside to attend a Jewish prayer service. While there, they met Lydia. "One of those listening was a woman from the city of Thyatira named Lydia, a dealer in purple cloth. She was a worshiper of God. The Lord opened her heart to respond to Paul's message" (Acts 16:14).

Read that verse too quickly, and you'll miss this account of the first convert in the West. Christianity was born in the East, and here the seeds of grace rode the winds of sovereignty over the Aegean Sea, fell on Grecian soil, and bore fruit in Philippi. Christ had his first European disciple ... and she was a she!

Is Lydia the reason the Holy Spirit blocked Paul's path? Was God ready to highlight the value of his daughters? Perhaps. In a culture that enslaved and degraded women, God elevated them to salvation co-heirs with men. Proof? The first person in the Western world to receive the Christian promise or host a Christian missionary was a female.

With her support Paul and his team got to work. Their efforts in Philippi were so effective that the pagan religious leaders were angered. They saw the people turning away from the temples and feared the loss of income. So they conjured up a story against Paul and Silas.

Then the multitude rose up together against them; and the magistrates tore off their clothes and commanded them to be beaten with rods. And when they had laid many stripes on them, they threw them into prison, commanding the jailer to keep them securely. Having received such a charge, he put them into the inner prison and fastened their feet in the stocks.

ACTS 16:22–24 NKJV

Listen closely. Do you hear it? The old, familiar sound of keys turning and locks clicking. This time the doors swung closed on the hinges of a prison. Paul and Silas could have groaned, "Oh no, not again. Not another locked door."

But they didn't complain. From the bowels of the prison emerged the most unexpected of sounds: praise and prayer. "About midnight Paul and Silas were praying and singing hymns to God, and the other prisoners were listening to them" (Acts 16:25).

Their feet were in stocks, yet their minds were in heaven. How could they sing at a time like this? The doors were slammed shut. Their feet were clamped. Backs ribboned with wounds. From whence came their song? There is only one answer: they trusted God and aligned their story to his.

The ways of the LORD are right;
the righteous walk in them.

HOSEA 14:9

"God will always give what is right to his people who cry to him night and day, and he will not be slow to answer them."

LUKE 18:7 NCV

When God locks a door, it needs to be locked. When he blocks a path, it needs to be blocked. When he stuck Paul and Silas in prison, God had a plan for the prison jailer. As Paul and Silas sang, God shook the prison. "At once all the prison doors flew open, and everyone's chains came loose" (Acts 16:26).

There God goes again, blasting open the most secure doors in town. When the jailer realized what had happened, he assumed all the prisoners had escaped. He drew his sword to take his life.

When Paul told him otherwise, the jailer brought the two missionaries out and asked, "What must I do to be saved?" (Acts 16:30). Paul told him to believe. He did, and he and all his family were baptized. The jailer washed their wounds, and Jesus washed his sins. God shut the door of the jail cell so that he could open the heart of the jailer.

God uses closed doors to advance his cause.

He closed the womb of a young Sarah so he could display his power to the elderly one.

He shut the palace door on Moses the prince so he could open shackles through Moses the liberator.

He marched Daniel out of Jerusalem so he could use Daniel in Babylon.

And Jesus. Yes, even Jesus knew the challenge of a blocked door. When he requested a path that bypassed the cross, God said no. He said no to Jesus in the garden of Gethsemane so he could say yes to us at the gates of heaven.

God's goal is people. He'll stir up a storm to display his power. He'll keep you out of Asia so you'll speak to Lydia. He'll place you in prison so you'll talk to the jailer. He might even sideline a quarterback in the biggest game of the season. This happened in the 2010 BCS National Championship Game. Colt McCoy, the University of Texas quarterback, had enjoyed four years of open doors. He was the winningest signal caller in the history of collegiate football. But in the National Championship Game, the most important contest of his university career, a shoulder injury put him out of the game in the first quarter. "Slam" went the door. Colt spent most of the game in the locker room.

I don't know if he, like Paul and Silas, was singing, but we know he was trusting. For after the game, he said these words:

> I love this game.... I've done everything I can to contribute to my team.... It's unfortunate I didn't get to play. I would have given everything I had to be out there with my team. But ... I always give God the glory. I never question why things happen the way they do. God is in control of my life. And I know that, if nothing else, I'm standing on the rock.[25]

Even on a bad night, Colt gave testimony to a good God. Did God close the door on the game so he could open the door of a heart?

Colt's father would say so. A young football player approached Brad McCoy after he returned from the game and asked, "I heard what your son said after the game, but I have one question. What is the rock?" McCoy responded, "Well, son, we sing about him at church," and began singing the hymn:

> *My hope is built on nothing less*
> *Than Jesus' blood and righteousness.*
> *I dare not trust the sweetest frame,*

But wholly lean on Jesus' Name.
On Christ, the solid Rock, I stand,
All other ground is sinking sand;
All other ground is sinking sand.[26]

It's not that our plans are bad but that God's plans are better.

"My thoughts are nothing like your thoughts,"
    says the LORD.
"And my ways are far beyond anything you
        could imagine.
For just as the heavens are higher than
        the earth,
    so my ways are higher than your ways
    and my thoughts higher than your thoughts."

ISAIAH 55:8–9 NLT

This is what I'm trying to teach Molly. Our family blocks doors so she can have better doors.

And this is what God is trying to teach us. Your blocked door doesn't mean God doesn't love you. Quite the opposite. It's proof that he does.

CHAPTER NINE

When God's Story Becomes Yours ...

ALL THINGS WORK FOR GOOD

Robben Island consists of three square miles of windswept land off the southern tip of Africa. Over the centuries it has served as the home for a prison, leper colony, mental asylum, and naval base. Most significantly, it was the home of one of the most famous political prisoners in history, Nelson Mandela.

He opposed the South African apartheid, a system designed to extend the rule and privileges of the white minority and diminish those of the blacks. It ensured that the 14 percent minority would control the rest of the population. Under apartheid, blacks were excluded from the "whites only" buses, "whites only" beaches, and "whites only" hospitals. Blacks could not run for office or live in a white neighborhood.

Apartheid legalized racism.

Mandela was the perfect man to challenge it. As a descendant of royalty, he was educated in the finest schools. As the son of a Christian mother, he embraced her love for God and people. Under the tutelage of a tribal chief, he learned the art of compromise and consensus. And as a young black lawyer in Cape Town, he experienced "a thousand slights, a thousand indignities, a thousand unremembered moments,"[27] which produced an inward fire to fight the system that imprisoned his people.

By the mid-1950s, Mandela was a force to be reckoned with. Passionate. Bitter. Given to retaliation. With his enviable pedigree and impressive stature (six feet two inches, 245 pounds), he was, for many, the hope of the black culture. But then came the events of August 5, 1962. Government officials arrested Mandela, convicted him of treason, and sent him to prison. For the next twenty-seven years, he stared through wired windows. And he wondered, surely he wondered, how a season in prison could play a part in God's plan.

You've asked such questions yourself. Perhaps not about time in prison but about your time in a dead-end job, struggling church, puny town, or enfeebled body. Certain elements of life make sense. But what about autism, Alzheimer's, or Mandela's prison sentence on Robben

Island? Was Paul including these conditions when he wrote Romans 8:28?

> And we know that in all things God works for the good of those who love him, who have been called according to his purpose.

We know ... There are so many things we do not know. We do not know if the economy will dip or if our team will win. We do not know what our spouse is thinking or how our kids will turn out. We don't even know "what we ought to pray for" (Romans 8:26). But according to Paul, we can be absolutely certain about four things. We know ...

1. *God works.* He is busy behind the scenes, above the fray, within the fury. He hasn't checked out or moved on. He is ceaseless and tireless. He never stops working.

2. *God works for the good.* Not for our comfort or pleasure or entertainment, but for our ultimate good. Since he is the ultimate good, would we expect anything less?

3. *God works for the good of those who love him.*

Behold the benefit of loving God! Make his story your story, and your story takes on a happy ending. Guaranteed. Being the author of our salvation, he writes a salvation theme into our biography.

4. *God works in all things. Panta*, in Greek. Like "*panoramic*" or "*panacea*" or "*pandemic*." All-inclusive. God works, not through a few things or through the good things, best things, or easy things. But in "all things" God works.

Puppet in the hands of fortune or fate? Not you. You are in the hands of a living, loving God. Random collection of disconnected short stories? Far from it. Your life is a crafted narrative written by a good God, who is working toward your supreme good.

God is not slipshod or haphazard. He planned creation according to a calendar. He determined the details of salvation "before the foundation of the world" (1 Peter 1:20 NKJV). The death of Jesus was not an afterthought, nor was it Plan B or an emergency operation. Jesus died "when the set time had fully come" (Galatians 4:4), according to God's "deliberate plan and foreknowledge" (Acts 2:23).

God, in other words, isn't making up a plan as he goes along. Nor did he wind up the clock and walk away. "The

Most High God rules the kingdom of mankind and sets over it whom he will" (Daniel 5:21 ESV). He "executes judgment, putting down one and lifting up another" (Psalm 75:7 ESV). "The LORD will not turn back until he has executed and accomplished the intentions of his mind" (Jeremiah 30:24 ESV). Look at those verbs: God *rules, sets, executes, accomplished.* These terms confirm the existence of heavenly blueprints and plans. Those plans include you. "In him we were also chosen, . . . according to the plan of him who works out everything in conformity with the purpose of his will" (Ephesians 1:11).

This discovery changes everything! It changed the outlook of the mom Denalyn and I visited in the maternity ward two days ago. She had miscarried a child. Her face awash with tears and heart heavy with questions, she reached through the fog and held on to God's hand. "This will work out for good, won't it, Max?" I assured her it would, and reminded her of God's promise: "'For I know the plans I have for you,' declares the LORD, 'plans to prosper you and not to harm you, plans to give you hope and a future'" (Jeremiah 29:11).

The apostle Paul's life is proof. We know just enough of his story to see God's hand in each phase of it. Here is how Paul began his testimony: "I am indeed a Jew, born in Tarsus of Cilicia, but brought up in this city at the feet of

Gamaliel, taught according to the strictness of our fathers' law, and was zealous toward God as you all are today" (Acts 22:3 NKJV).

Paul grew up in Tarsus. He called it "an important city" (Acts 21:39 NLT). He wasn't exaggerating. Tarsus sat only a few miles from the coast and served as a hub for sailors, pirates, and merchants from all sections of Europe and Asia. Any child raised in Tarsus would have heard a dozen languages and witnessed a tapestry of cultures.

Tarsus was also a depot city on the Roman highway system. The empire boasted a network of roads that connected business centers of the ancient world. Ephesus. Iconium. Derbe. Syrian Antioch and Caesarea. While young Paul likely didn't visit these cities, he grew up hearing about them. Tarsus instilled a Mediterranean map in his heart and a keen intellect in his mind. Tarsus rivaled the academic seats of Alexandria and Athens. Paul conversed with students in the streets and, at the right age, became one himself. He learned the lingua franca of his day: Greek. He mastered it. He spoke it. He wrote it. He thought it.

Paul not only spoke the international language of the world; he carried its passport. He was born a Jew and a Roman citizen. Whenever he traveled through the empire, he was entitled to all the rights and privileges of a Roman citizen. He could enter any port and demand a judicial hearing. He could even appeal to Caesar. He was treated, not as a slave or foreigner, but as a freeman. How did his father acquire such a status? Perhaps in exchange for tents. Paul, himself a tentmaker, likely learned his craft from his father, who probably created durable gear for the ever-mobile Roman soldiers.

Young Paul left Tarsus with everything an itinerant missionary would need: cultural familiarity, linguistic skills, documents for travel, and a trade for earning a living. That was only the beginning.

Paul's parents sent him to Jerusalem for rabbinical studies. He memorized large sections of the Torah and digested massive amounts of rabbinical law. He was a valedictorian-level student, a Hebrew of Hebrews. Paul later wrote: "I was advancing in Judaism beyond many of my own age among my people, so extremely zealous was I for the traditions of my fathers" (Galatians 1:14 ESV).

An interesting side note. Paul and Jesus may have passed each other on the streets of Jerusalem. If Paul was a member of the Sanhedrin court when he persecuted the church, he would have been at least thirty years old, the minimum-age requirement for being a member of the court. That would make him roughly the same age as Jesus, who was crucified in his early thirties. Which raises this fanciful question: Did young Paul and young Jesus find themselves in Jerusalem at the same time? A twelve-year-old Messiah and his father. A young Saul and his studies. If so, did the Christ at some point cast a glance at his future apostle-to-be?

We know God did. Before Paul was following God, God was leading Paul. He gave him an education, a vocation, the necessary documentation. He schooled Paul in the law of Moses and the language of Greece. Who better to present Jesus as the fulfillment of the law than a scholar of the law?

But what about Paul's violence? He confessed: "I persecuted this Way to the death, binding and delivering into prisons both men and women" (Acts 22:4 NKJV). He tore husbands from their homes and moms from their children. He declared jihad against the church and spilled the blood of disciples. Could God use this ugly chapter to advance his cause?

More than a hypothetical question. We all have seasons that are hard to explain. Before we knew God's story, we made a mess of our own. Even afterward, we're prone to demand our own way, cut our own path, and hurt people in the process. Can God make good out of our bad?

He did with Paul.

"Now it happened, as I journeyed and came near Damascus at about noon, suddenly a great light from heaven shone around me. And I fell to the ground and heard a voice saying to me ..."

ACTS 22:6–7 NKJV

"I'm going to give you a taste of your own medicine."
"Back to the dust with you, you Christian-killer."
"Prepare to meet your Maker!"

❖

Did Paul expect to hear words like these? Regardless, he didn't. Even before he requested mercy, he was offered mercy. Jesus told him:

"I have a job for you. I've handpicked you to be a servant and witness to what's happened today, and to what I am going to show you.

"I'm sending you off to open the eyes of the outsiders so they can see.... I'm sending you off to present my offer of sins forgiven, and a place in the family."

ACTS 26:16–18 MSG

Jesus transformed Paul, the card-carrying legalist, into a champion for mercy. Who would have thought? Yet who would be better qualified? Paul could write epistles of grace by dipping his pen into the inkwell of his own heart. He'd learned Greek in the schools of Tarsus, tentmaking in the home of his father, the Torah at the feet of Gamaliel. And he learned about love when Jesus paid him a personal visit on Damascus Highway.

"All things" worked together.

I saw an example of this process in our kitchen. My intent was to chat with Denalyn about some questions. She was stirring up a delicacy for someone's birthday. She assured me she could talk and bake at the same time. So I talked. She baked. But as she baked, I stopped talking.

Had I never witnessed the creation of cuisine? *Au contraire!* I've applauded the society of Julia Child since I was a child. We who do not cook stand in awe of those who do. And I did.

Denalyn buzzed about the kitchen like the queen of the hive. She snatched boxes off the shelves, pulled bowls out of the pantry. I've been known to stare at an open refrigerator for days in search of mayonnaise or ketchup. Not Denalyn. She grabbed the carton of eggs with one hand and butter with the other, never pausing to look.

She positioned the ingredients and utensils on the

table as a surgeon would her tools. Once everything was in place, off she went. Eggs cracking, yolks dropping. Shake this, stir that. Pour out the milk. Measure the sugar. Sift, mix, and beat. She was a blur of hands and elbows, a conductor of the kitchen, the Cleopatra of cuisine, the da Vinci of da kitchen, the lord of the lard, the boss of the bakery.

She popped the pan into the oven, turned the knob to 350 degrees, wiped her hands with a towel, turned to me, and said the words I longed to hear: "Want to lick the bowl?" I fell at her feet and called her blessed. Well, maybe not. But I did lick the bowl, spatula, and beaters. And I did wonder if Denalyn's work in the kitchen is a picture of God's work in us.

All the transfers, layoffs, breakdowns, breakups, and breakouts. Difficulties. Opportunities. Sifted and stirred and popped into the oven. Heaven knows, we've felt the heat. We've wondered if God's choice of ingredients will result in anything worth serving.

If Nelson Mandela did, no one could blame him. His prison life was harsh. He was confined to a six-by-six-foot concrete room. It had one small window that overlooked the courtyard. He had a desk, a mattress, a chair, three blankets, and a rusted-iron sanitary bucket for washing and shaving. Meals came from corn: breakfast was a porridge of corn scraped from the cob; lunch and supper consisted of corn on the cob; coffee was roasted corn mixed with water.

Mandela and the other prisoners were awakened at 5:30 a.m. They crushed rocks into gravel until noon, ate lunch, then worked until 4:00 p.m. Back in the cell at 5:00, asleep by 8:00. Discrimination continued even into the prison. Africans, like Mandela, were required to wear short pants and were denied bread.

Yet God used it all to shape Mandela. The prisoner read widely: Leo Tolstoy, John Steinbeck, Daphne du Maurier. He exercised daily: a hundred fingertip push-ups, two hundred sit-ups, fifty deep knee bends. Most of all he honed the capacity to compromise and forgive. He developed courtesy in all situations, disarming even the guards who had been placed to trouble him. He became particularly close to one jailer who, over two decades, read the Bible and discussed Scripture with Mandela. "'All men,' Mandela reflected later, 'have a core of decency, and … if their heart is touched, they are capable of changing.'"[28]

After twenty-seven years of confinement, at the age of seventy-two, Mandela was released. Those who knew him well described the pre-prison Mandela as "cocky and pugnacious." But the refined Mandela? "I came out mature," he said. He was devoted to "rationality, logic, and compromise." Journalists noted his lack of bitterness. Others observed that he was "unmarred by rancor."[29] Within four years Mandela was elected president and set out to lead South Africa out of apartheid and into a new era of equality.

God needed an educated, sophisticated leader who'd mastered the art of patience and compromise, so he tempered Mandela in prison.

He needed a culture-crossing, Greek-speaking, border-passing, Torah-quoting, self-supporting missionary, so he gave grace to Paul, and Paul shared grace with the world.

And you? In a moment before moments, your Maker looked into the future and foresaw the needs and demands of your generation. He instilled, and is instilling, within you everything you need to fulfill his plan in this era. "God made us to do good works, which God planned in advance for us to live our lives doing" (Ephesians 2:10 NCV).

If that doesn't take the cake, I don't know what does.

CHAPTER TEN

When God's Story Becomes Yours ...

GOD WILL
COME FOR YOU

WITH HOPES OF EARNING EXTRA CASH, MY DAD ONCE TOOK a three-month job assignment in New England. I was ten years old, midway between training wheels and girlfriends. I thought much about baseball and bubble gum. Can't say I ever thought once about Bangor, Maine. Until Dad went there.

When he did, I found the town on the map. I calculated the distance between the Texas plains and the lobster coast. My teacher let me write a report on Henry Wadsworth Longfellow, and Dad sent us a jug of maple syrup. Our family lived in two worlds, ours and his.

We talked much about my father's pending return. "When Dad comes back, we will ... fix the basketball net ... take a trip to Grandma's ... stay up later." Mom used his coming to comfort and caution. She could do both with the same phrase. With soft assurance, "Your dad will be home soon." Or clenched teeth, "Your dad will be home soon." She circled his arrival date on the calendar and crossed out each day as it passed. She made it clear: Dad's coming would be a big deal.

It was. Four decades have weathered the memories, but these remain: the sudden smell of Old Spice in the house; his deep, bellowing voice; gifts all around; and a happy sense of settledness. Dad's return changed everything.

The return of Christ will do likewise.

Jude has a name for this event: "the great Day" (Jude 6).

The great Day will be a normal day. People will drink coffee, endure traffic snarls, laugh at jokes, and take note of the weather. Thousands of people will be born; thousands will die.

> The Arrival of the Son of Man will take place in times like Noah's. Before the great flood everyone was carrying on as usual, having a good time right up to the day Noah boarded the ark. They knew nothing—until the flood hit and swept everything away.
>
> MATTHEW 24:37–39 MSG

The tourists on Thailand's coast come to mind. They spent the morning of December 26, 2004, applying suntan lotion and throwing beach balls, unaware that a tsunami-stirred wave was moving toward them at the speed of a jetliner. Christ's coming will be equally unexpected. Most people will be oblivious, playing on the beach.

His shout will get our attention. "For the Lord Himself will descend from heaven with a shout" (1 Thessalonians 4:16 NKJV). Before we see angels, hear trumpets, or embrace our grandparents, we will be engulfed by Jesus' voice. John heard the voice of God and compared it to "the sound of many waters" (Revelation 1:15 NKJV). Perhaps you've stood at the base of a cataract so loud and full of fury that you had to shout to be heard. Or maybe you've heard the roar of a lion. When the king of beasts opens his mouth, every head in the jungle lifts. The King of kings will prompt the same response: "The Lord will roar from on high" (Jeremiah 25:30).

Lazarus heard such a roar. His body was entombed and his soul in paradise when Jesus shouted into both places: "[Jesus] cried with a loud voice, 'Lazarus, come forth!' And he who had died came out" (John 11:43–44 NKJV). Expect the same shout and shaking of the corpses on the great Day. "The dead will hear the voice of the Son of God.... All who are ... in their graves will hear his voice. Then they will come out" (John 5:25, 28–29 NCV).

The shout of God will trigger the "voice of an archangel ... with the trumpet of God" (1 Thessalonians 4:16 NKJV). The archangel is the commanding officer. He will dispatch armies of angels to their greatest mission: to gather the children of God into one great assemblage. Envision these silvered messengers spilling out of the heavens into the atmosphere. You'll more quickly count the winter snowflakes than you will number these hosts. Jude announced that "the Lord is coming with thousands and thousands of holy angels to judge everyone" (verses 14–15 CEV). The population of God's armies was too high for John to count. He saw "ten thousand times ten thousand, and thousands of thousands" (Revelation 5:11 NKJV).

They minister to the saved and battle the devil. They keep you safe and clear your path. "He has put his angels in charge of you to watch over you wherever you go" (Psalm 91:11 NCV). And on the great Day, they will escort you into the skies, where you will meet God. "He'll dispatch the angels; they will pull in the chosen from the four winds, from pole to pole" (Mark 13:27 MSG).

Whether you are in Peoria or paradise, if you're a follower of Jesus, you can count on an angelic chaperone into the greatest gathering in history. We assume the demons will gather the rebellious. We aren't told. We are told, however, that the saved and lost alike will witness the assembly. "All the nations will be gathered before him" (Matthew 25:32).

The Population Reference Bureau estimates that 106 billion people have been born since the dawn of the human race.[30] Every single one of them will stand in the great assembly of souls. He who made us will convene us. "The LORD, who scattered his people, will gather them" (Jeremiah 31:10 NLT). "All the ends of the earth shall see the salvation of our God" (Isaiah 52:10 ESV).

At some point in this grand collection, our spirits will be reunited with our bodies:

> It will happen in a moment, in the blink of an eye, when the last trumpet is blown. For when the trumpet sounds, those who have died will be raised to live forever. And we who are living will also be transformed. For our dying bodies must be transformed into bodies that will never die; our mortal bodies must be transformed into immortal bodies.
>
> 1 CORINTHIANS 15:52–53 NLT

Paradise will give up her souls.

The earth will give up her dead, and the sky will stage a reunion of spirit and flesh. As our souls reenter our bodies, a massive sound will erupt around us: "On that day heaven will pass away with a roaring sound. Everything that makes up the universe will burn and be destroyed. The earth and everything that people have done on it will be exposed" (2 Peter 3:10 GWT).

Jesus called this "the re-creation of the world" (Matthew 19:28 MSG). God will purge every square inch that sin has contaminated, polluted, degraded, or defiled. But we may not even notice the reconstruction, for an even greater sight will appear before us: "the Son of Man coming on the clouds in the sky with power and great glory" (Matthew 24:30 GWT).

God has often used clouds to indicate his presence. He led the Israelites with a cloudy pillar. He spoke to Moses through the mist on Sinai, and to Jesus through the cloud at the transfiguration. Clouds symbolize his hiddenness, but on the great Day they will declare his visible presence. Note the preposition. "the Son of Man coming *on* the clouds" (emphasis mine). Subtle distinction. Great declaration. Every person, prince, pauper, saint, sinner — every eye will see Jesus. "All the nations will be gathered before him" (Matthew 25:32).

By this point we will have seen much: the flurry of

angels, the ascension of the bodies, the great gathering of the nations. We will have heard much: the shout of God and the angel, the trumpet blast, and the purging explosion. But every sight and sound will seem a remote memory compared to what will happen next: "He will be King and sit on his great throne" (Matthew 25:31 NCV).

This is the direction in which all of history is focused. This is the moment toward which God's plot is moving. The details, characters, antagonists, heroes, and subplots all arc in this direction. God's story carries us toward a coronation for which all creation groans:

> For everything, absolutely everything, above and below, visible and invisible, rank after rank after rank of angels—*everything* got started in him and finds its purpose in him.... He was supreme in the beginning and—leading the resurrection parade— he is supreme in the end.
>
> COLOSSIANS 1:16, 18 MSG

God's creation will return to its beginning: a one-king kingdom. Our earth is plagued by multiple competing monarchs, each one of us climbing ladders and claiming thrones. But we will gladly remove our crowns when Christ comes back for us.

During one of the crusades, Philippe Auguste, king of France, gathered his noble knights and men to call them to be strong in battle. He placed his crown on a table with the inscription "To the most worthy." He pledged the crown as the prize to be given to the bravest fighter.

They went to battle and returned victorious and encircled the table on which the crown had been placed. One of the nobles stepped forward, took the crown, and put it on the head of the king, saying, "Thou, O King, art the most worthy."[31]

On the great Day you'll hear billions of voices make the identical claim about Jesus Christ. "Every knee will bow to the name of Jesus—everyone in heaven, on earth, and under the earth. And everyone will confess that Jesus Christ is Lord" (Philippians 2:10–11 NCV).

Multitudes of people will bow low like a field of wind-blown wheat, each one saying, "Thou, O King, art the most worthy."

There will be one monumental difference. Some people will continue the confession they began on earth. They will crown Christ again, gladly. Others will crown him for the first time. They will do so sadly. They denied Christ on earth, so he will deny them in heaven.

But those who accepted him on earth will live with God forever. "I heard a voice thunder from the Throne:

'Look! Look! God has moved into the neighborhood, making his home with men and women! They're his people, he's their God'" (Revelation 21:3 MSG). The narrator makes the same point four times in four consecutive phrases:

"God has moved into the neighborhood"

"making his home with men and women"

"They're his people"

"he's their God"

The announcement comes with the energy of a six-year-old declaring the arrival of his father from a long trip. "Daddy's home! He's here! Mom, he's back!" One statement won't suffice. This is big news worthy of repetition. We shall finally see God face-to-face. "They will see his face" (Revelation 22:4).

Let this sink in. You will see the face of God. You will look into the eyes of the One who has always seen; you will behold the mouth that commands history. And if there is anything more amazing than the moment you see his face, it's the moment he touches yours. "He will wipe every tear from their eyes" (Revelation 21:4).

God will touch your tears. Not flex his muscles or

show off his power. Lesser kings would strut their stallions or give a victory speech. Not God. He prefers to rub a thumb across your cheek as if to say, "There, there ... no more tears."

Isn't that what a father does?

There was much I didn't understand about my father's time in Maine. The responsibilities of his job, his daily activities, the reason he needed to go. I was too young to comprehend all the details. But I knew this much: he would come home.

By the same token, who can understand what God is doing? These days on earth can seem so difficult: marred by conflict, saddened by separation. We fight, pollute, discriminate, and kill. Societies suffer from innumerable fiefdoms, small would-be dynasties. *What is this world coming to?* we wonder. God's answer: A great Day. On the great Day all of history will be consummated in Christ. He will assume his position "far above all rule and authority and power and dominion ... not only in this age but also in the one to come" (Ephesians 1:21 NASB). And he, the Author of it all, will close the book on this life and open the book to the next and begin to read to us from his unending story.

When God's Story Becomes Yours ...

YOU WILL FINALLY GRADUATE

MAY 19, 2007, WAS A SPLENDID NIGHT FOR AN OUTDOOR graduation. The South Texas sky was as blue as a robin's egg. A just-passed rain shower perfumed the air. Thirty-four members of the Lucado clan occupied a sizable section of the amphitheater seats in honor of high-school-graduating Sara, my youngest daughter.

Never accused of timidity, we Lucados attempted to do the wave as Sara walked across the platform. We more closely resembled popping popcorn ... but Sara heard our support. Graduation warrants such displays. There's nothing small about the transfer of tassels. Cut the cake and call the newspaper. Applaud the closing, not of a chapter, but of a tome. Graduation is no small matter.

What we didn't know, however, is that two Lucado

women were graduating the same evening. About the same time Sara stepped across the platform, my mom stepped into paradise. Sara and Thelma, separated in age by seventy-six years, yet joined by the same graduation date.

Applause for the first. Tears for the second. *Hooray* for Sara. *Oh, my* about Mom. Gladness. Sadness. The sorrow is understandable. Reactions to graduation and death shouldn't be identical.

Yet should they be so different?

Both celebrate completion and transition. And both gift the graduate with recognition: a diploma to one and a brand-new life to the other.

> It will take only a second — as quickly as an eye blinks — when the last trumpet sounds. The trumpet will sound, and those who have died will be raised to live forever, and we will all be changed. This body that can be destroyed must clothe itself with something that can never be destroyed. And this body that dies must clothe itself with something that can never die.
>
> 1 CORINTHIANS 15:52 – 53 NCV

As God's story becomes your story, you make this

wonderful discovery: you will graduate from this life into heaven. Jesus' plan is to "gather together in one all things in Christ" (Ephesians 1:10 NKJV). "All things" includes your body. Your eyes that read this book. Your hands that hold it. Your blood-pumping heart, arm-hinging elbow, weight-supporting torso. God will reunite your body with your soul and create something unlike anything you have seen: an eternal body.

You will finally be healthy. You never have been. Even on the days you felt fine, you weren't. You were a sitting duck for disease, infections, airborne bacteria, and microbes. And what about you on your worst days?

Last Sunday as I sat in front of our church, my eyes seemed to radar toward the physically challenged. A recent retiree with a rush of white hair just found out about a brain tumor. So did a thirtyish mother of three. "I thought it was a migraine," she had told me earlier in the week.

Philip is in law school and a wheelchair. I haven't seen Adam in several weeks. He's a Juilliard grad. Multiple sclerosis has silenced his keyboard. Doctors are giving another member two months to live.

I hate disease. I'm sick of it.

So is Christ. Consider his response to the suffering of a deaf mute. "He took him aside from the multitude, and put His fingers in his ears, and He spat and touched his tongue. Then, looking up to heaven, He sighed, and said to him, 'Ephphatha,' that is, 'Be opened'" (Mark 7:33–34 NKJV).

Everything about this healing stands out. The way Jesus separates the man from the crowd. The tongue and ear touching. The presence of Aramaic in the Greek account. But it's the sigh that we notice. Jesus looked up to heaven and sighed. This is a sigh of sadness, a deep breath, and a heavenly glance that resolves, "It won't be this way for long."

Jesus will heal all who seek healing in him. There are no exceptions to this promise — no nuances, fine-print conditions, or caveats. To say some will be healed beyond the grave by no means diminishes the promise. The truth is this: "When Christ appears, *we shall be like him*, for we shall see him as he is" (1 John 3:2, emphasis mine).

"We shall be like him." Let every parent of a Down syndrome or wheelchair-bound child write these words on the bedroom wall. Let the disabled, infected, bedridden, and anemic put themselves to sleep with the promise "We shall be like him." Let amputees and the atrophied take this promise to heart: "We shall be like him." We shall graduate from this version of life into his likeness.

You'll have a spiritual body. In your current state,

your flesh battles your spirit. Your eyes look where they shouldn't. Your taste buds desire the wrong drinks. Your heart knows you shouldn't be anxious, but your mind still worries. Can't we relate to Paul's confession? "I truly delight in God's commands, but it's pretty obvious that not all of me joins in that delight. Parts of me covertly rebel, and just when I least expect it, they take charge" (Romans 7:22–23 MSG).

Your "parts" will no longer rebel in heaven. Your new body will be a spiritual body, with all members cooperating toward one end. Joni Eareckson Tada's words are powerful on this point. She has been confined to a wheelchair since the age of seventeen. Yet the greatest heavenly attraction for her is not new legs but a new soul.

I can't wait to be clothed in righteousness. Without a trace of sin. True, it will be wonderful to stand, stretch, and reach to the sky, but it will be more wonderful to offer praise that is pure. I won't be crippled by distractions. Disabled by insincerity. I won't be handicapped by a ho-hum halfheartedness. My heart will join with yours and bubble over with effervescent adoration. We will finally be able to fellowship fully with the Father and the Son.

For me, this will be the best part of heaven.[32]

In heaven "there shall be no more curse" (Revelation 22:3 NKJV). As much as we hate carcinomas and cardiac arrests, don't we hate sin even more? Cystic fibrosis steals breath, but selfishness and stinginess steal joy. Diabetes can ruin the system of a body, but deceit, denial, and distrust are ruining society.

Heaven, however, has scheduled a graduation. Sin will no longer be at war with our flesh. Eyes won't lust, thoughts won't wander, hands won't steal, our minds won't judge, appetites won't rage, and our tongues won't lie. We will be brand-new.

Some of you live in such road-weary bodies: knees ache, eyes dim, skin sags. Others exited the womb on an uphill ride. While I have no easy answers for your struggle, I implore you to see your challenge in the scope of God's story. View these days on earth as but the opening lines of his sweeping saga. Let's stand with Paul on the promise of eternity.

So we're not giving up. How could we! Even though on the outside it often looks like things are falling apart on us, on the inside, where God is making new life, not a day goes by without his unfolding grace. These hard times are small potatoes compared to the coming good times, the lavish celebration prepared for us. There's far more here than meets the eye. The things we see now are here today, gone tomorrow. But the things we can't see now will last forever.

2 CORINTHIANS 4:16–18 MSG

I write these words during the final hours of a two-week vacation. I've passed the last dozen days with my favorite people, my wife and daughters. We've watched the sun set, fish jump, and waves crash. We've laughed at old stories and made new memories. A trip for the ages.

At its inception, however, I got searched at airport security. I removed my shoes and handed my boarding pass to the official. He instructed me to step over to the side. I groaned as he waved his wand over my body. Why single me out? Isn't it enough that we have to plod barefoot through a scanner? Do they think I am a terrorist? You can tell that I don't like the moments at airport security. But as I remember this vacation, I won't reflect on its irritating inauguration. It was necessary but quickly lost in the splendor of the vacation.

You suppose we'll someday say the same words about this life? "Necessary but quickly lost in the splendor of heaven." I have a hunch we will. We'll see death differently too. We'll remember the day we died with the same fondness we remember graduation day.

By the way, if I graduate before you do, you'll see me waiting for you. I'll be the one in the stands starting the wave.

DISCUSSION
AND
ACTION GUIDE

PREPARED BY DAVID DRURY

You've just read Max's carefully detailed study of the great news: Your life story plays a role in the larger story of God. Can any news be more thrilling? God's story—truth, not fiction or myth or fantasy—is a great story. And your story is a part of the larger story written by God.

This guide is designed to help you reflect on *God's Story, Your Story* and take action on the ideas contained in the book, to see how your own story fits into the grand plot of God's story. Each chapter guide has questions to consider on your own or with a group devoted to discussing the book. Have your Bible handy in order to dig into the Scripture verses noted. The action steps reinforce the chapter through practical activities.

In the end, the greatness of the Bible is that *the* story, God's story, can become *your* story. It's not just a tale to be told or a yarn to be spun; it's a life to be lived, a hope to be grasped, a truth to be told.

CHAPTER 1: *When God's Story Becomes Yours . . .*
ORDINARY MATTERS

Questions for Discussion

1. Where do you see the idea of God's word in the creation story? Build a list of all the moments in Genesis 1 when God speaks.

2. Read aloud Genesis 1:1 and John 1:1. What might it mean that Jesus was "with God" and "was God" in the beginning?

3. In what ways was Jesus like you? And how is Jesus different from you?

4. Discuss how it might be reassuring that Jesus was "normal" and like you in many ways? How might it be reassuring to know he is unlike you in other ways?

5. Think about an ordinary person you know who has been a giver of extraordinary grace. What motivated that person?

6. Read Matthew 6:1–4 together. Gain a new perspective by considering why it might mean more to receive a blessing without knowing the identity of the giver.

7. In what ways do you need God to "dwell" with you this week? (See John 1:14.)

Ideas for Action

1. In the next week, pool some financial resources together as a group in order to be a blessing to someone in need. Like Sam Stone in the chapter, go to great lengths to conceal your identity. Select one person in the group to be the treasurer so each gift is anonymous.

2. Take time this week to memorize portions of John 1:1 – 18. Some of the most memorable verses to tuck away in your heart in this section are verses 5, 12, 14, and 17. Choose at least one verse to begin.

3. On your own this week, consider whom you could bless in secrecy. Don't share with family members or friends that you took an action to meet someone's need — keep it between you and God (see Matthew 6:1 – 4).

CHAPTER 2: *When God's Story Becomes Yours ...*
YOU KNOW
SATAN'S NEXT MOVE

Questions for Discussion

1. This chapter talks about the distractions of "possessions and problems." Share with the group the distractions you seem to encounter most—distractions that keep you from engaging the story of God in Scripture.

2. What kind of personal attacks does the Enemy plot? How does he attempt to divide people? Have you seen the Devil at work? Do you tend to underestimate or overestimate the Devil's activity?

3. Together study 1 John 3:1–10, asking the following questions:

   • How does being a child of God help us in our battle against the Enemy?

   • Do you think the Enemy considers it a victory for him when we "keep sinning"? (See 1 John 3:6, 8–9.)

   • In 1 John 3:10, righteousness is equated with obeying God's commands and loving each other. Where else in Scripture do you see a reinforcement of these claims?

   • Is there a victory over sin that you would feel

comfortable sharing with the group? Praise the Lord for these wins over the Enemy. Give God the glory.

4. Have you experienced a "wilderness" period in your life? When have you been most tempted and needed God's power over darkness?

5. Share the strategies you suspect the Enemy is using these days (this chapter mentions a few strategies Satan used on Jesus: trying to exploit weak spots, bringing to the surface identity issues, showing off, and promising heights). Pray for one another. Ask for God's strength to overcome Satan's strategies.

Ideas for Action

1. This week, consider any division residing in your own soul. Journal the two opposing ideas that seem to be pulling at you, one from God and one from Satan. Pray for strength to choose the path of God.

2. Take time to pray over these Scriptures daily this week: Revelation 12:12 and Romans 8:37. Become more urgent in your private prayers, praying against the Enemy and asking for God's protection.

3. Memorize at least one Scripture as a reminder that your story is God's story, not the Enemy's tall tale of division and lies. As you repeat this Scripture, thank God for equipping you for every spiritual battle (Ephesians 6:12).

CHAPTER 3: *When God's Story Becomes Yours . . .*
YOU FIND YOUR
TRUE HOME

Questions for Discussion

1. In what ways do you long for the kingdom of God and heaven to come? Instead of talking about what you imagine will happen, talk about *why* you want it to happen. Share reasons you have for anticipating the day when all will change for eternity.

2. As a group, compile a list of what is wrong with the world today. What makes us discontent in a righteous way?

3. How does the story of Scripture show that God will mend these problems in the world? What part of the change will happen by God's hand in the future? What part of the change is the responsibility of God's children in the meantime?

4. Are we too content to "live in the pigsty" rather than long for home, as the prodigal son did? Why?

5. Why is it important that we not only enjoy the journey but also long for the destination of eternity with God? How does this adjust the way we talk about "journey" and "destination" as Christians?

6. Describe how it might affect one's life to believe there is "no more beyond" this world. How should it change us to believe there is "more beyond"?

Ideas for Action

1. Find a spot to place Scripture in front of you this week—the bathroom mirror, the family calendar, your bedside table, your computer monitor. Where else might you post Scripture? In your wallet, next to your television, on the fridge? Some good Scriptures to post are Matthew 6:33 and Colossians 3:1, which were cited in this week's chapter.

2. What "distracting doodlebugs" do you focus on with your head down? What minor things take up too much of your focus? What big things might you miss with your head down and a narrow focus?

3. Make a list of the things that worried you or got you down a year ago. Note how the "plan came together" with God's guidance. If you are still struggling, write a prayer of appeal specifically addressing that worrisome matter. Pray it daily. Then write about how God responds (see Ephesians 1:10).

CHAPTER 4: *When God's Story Becomes Yours . . .*
YOU HEAR A VOICE
YOU CAN TRUST

Questions for Discussion

1. Create a list of the voices that compete for our attention today. Discuss how we respond to these voices.

2. Read Mark 8:27 – 30 as a group. Share how people today describe who Jesus is.

3. C. S. Lewis echoed many others when he claimed in *Mere Christianity* that it was a foolish thing to say, "I'm ready to accept Jesus as a great moral teacher, but I don't accept His claim to be God." He pointed out that if Jesus was "merely a man and said the sort of things Jesus said," he would be either a "lunatic" or something much worse: a fraudulent liar who set us up. Discuss this quote in your group, and answer the following questions:

   • If Jesus was a lunatic, what would be the implications?

   • What if Jesus was a liar?

   • What are the implications if Jesus is Lord?

4. Some scholars say that Jesus never claimed to be God. Look up Scriptures that relate to the identity of Jesus (such as Mark 2:27 – 28; Luke 5:20; John 1:1, 14; 11:43 – 44; Philippians 2:5 – 11; Colossians 1:15; 1 Timothy 3:16; Hebrews 1:2 – 3, 8; 2 Peter 1:16 – 17.)

How do such passages influence your view of who
Jesus is?

5. What is the best way to have constructive conversations
with someone who thinks Jesus was just a good moral
teacher?

6. In what ways do you need to hear the clear guiding
voice of God in this season of your life? Pray for these
concerns as a group before your meeting ends.

Ideas for Action

1. This week, study through the first book of the Gospel
accounts of Jesus (see Matthew 2:2, 11; 8:2; 9:18; 14:33;
15:25; 20:20; 28:9, 17). Take note of the moments when
Jesus was worshiped, and consider how out of place
this was in the religious culture of the day. As you pray
this week, use these Scriptures as your guide to worship
and prayer, making the story of Matthew your story of
worship.

2. For the next five days, spend an increasing amount of
time alone with Jesus Christ merely listening for his
voice. Start with just 3 minutes sitting with no music
and without reading or writing your own thoughts. On
day two, go for 6 minutes. Then 9, 12, 15, and 18, so
that by next week you'll be in the habit of listening for
more than 20 minutes a day.

3. Set up a one-on-one meeting with someone else in the group this week. Instead of giving each other advice, ask each other what you believe God is saying in your time alone, and help each other discern the voice of your commander and Lord, Jesus Christ.

CHAPTER 5: *When God's Story Becomes Yours . . .*
YOU WON'T BE FORSAKEN

Questions for Discussion

1. What does "forsaken" mean to you? Share a time in your life when you felt forsaken. How did someone encourage you?

2. Think about someone you know who feels forsaken. Discuss how you could encourage that person individually or as a group.

3. Read John 19 aloud, taking turns to read sections from one version. After reading the crucifixion story spend time in prayer, thanking Jesus for his redemptive work.

4. How *crucial* is the cross to your personal story? In what ways has the fact that Jesus died on the cross (*crux*) changed your life? How would your life be different today if Jesus hadn't died on the cross?

5. What "vests" of yours — symbols of your sin — have been removed? What about your past does the cross of Christ cover?

Ideas for Action

1. Cut a poster board so it looks like a vest and put it on the wall. Write words on this symbolic vest thanking God for covering you with his forgiveness. Write sins, then cross them out, or list words of redemption.

2. In private this week, write down on one side of a sheet of paper what you used to be like without Christ; on the other side, write down your new identity in him. If you can, share about the experience next time you meet. Here are some examples:

OLD	NEW
I was alone because of sinful choices.	I am complete in Christ.
I was accused and ashamed.	I am free from condemnation.
I was fearfully running from God's purpose for my life.	I am established and anointed.
I was lazy and unmotivated.	I am God's coworker.
I was harming my body with my actions.	I am God's workmanship.
I was living without care or responsibility.	I am a royal priest in God's eyes.
I was unethical.	I am honest and hard-working.
I was a bad parent.	I am a good, intentional parent.
I was feeling forsaken.	I am forgiven.
I was prone to wander.	I am a faithful spouse.
I was addicted.	I am dependent only on God.

CHAPTER 6: *When God's Story Becomes Yours . . .*
YOUR FINAL CHAPTER
BECOMES A PREFACE

Questions for Discussion

1. In what season of your life did you begin to have assurance that you had been saved and would spend eternity with God? Do you have that same assurance now?

2. What experiences have most influenced your view of your own mortality? When have you grappled with your own death or the deaths of those you know and love?

3. What would you say to someone who claims to be spiritual but doesn't believe in the resurrection? How would you describe the role the resurrection plays in your own life? What difference does it make?

4. Do Christians today act more like the disciples behaved before or after the resurrection? What could we do to be "resurrection people" in the way we worship, serve, and relate to one another?

5. Read John 20:10–31 as a group. How are you like Thomas in this story? Do you know someone who plays a Thomas role? Notice that even though he doubted, Thomas remained with the other disciples. Why

might it be important to do our doubting in Christian community?

Ideas for Action

1. Build a list of the things you may not be able to accomplish in this life but hope to do in the next life. Now build a list of things that can only be accomplished in this life. Reorder your priorities around these lists.

2. Intentionally set up a time to speak with someone who questions his or her eternity with God. As much as possible, give that person hope. Witness to them by sharing your faith in Jesus Christ. If they are ready, help them take the step of putting their faith in Jesus and receiving the assurance of eternal life.

3. If you do not have a close relationship with a person far from God, take time this week to begin to build such relationships. If all your days are spent with other Christians, adapt your schedule to spend more time with the kind of people Jesus gave priority to in his brief ministry.

CHAPTER 7: *When God's Story Becomes Yours ...*
POWER MOVES IN

Questions for Discussion

1. Consider times in your life when you may have disowned Christ in perhaps less overt ways than Peter did. Describe those attitudes and actions of people that become other ways of disowning Christ.

2. The chapter asks, "What got into Peter?" How would you answer this question? (See Acts 2:4, 17–18.)

3. These days, do you feel more like the early Peter or the later one? Or do you vacillate between the two in any given week?

4. What was the difference between Jesus living *near* the disciples and the Spirit living *in* them? What were the results? Do you long for such results in your life? What difference might that make in your life right now?

5. What is your greatest need for the Holy Spirit in your life? (See Galatians 3:3.)

6. List the things that limit God's Spirit from moving. (See Isaiah 63:10; Acts 5:9; 7:51; Ephesians 4:29–30; 1 Thessalonians 5:19–20.)

Ideas for Action

1. Let this be the week of waiting. Wait for the Spirit. Wait expectantly for the Holy Spirit to guide and empower you. Carve out time to just sit, wait, and listen for the Spirit's words of reassurance. (See Acts 1:4–5 and 1 Corinthians 1:7–8.)

2. On a small card, write the fruit of the Spirit as a list: love, joy, peace, patience, kindness, goodness, faithfulness, gentleness, self-control. Carry the card around with you, and check yourself often as to whether you are walking in the Spirit or walking your own way.

3. Think about a Christian who exhibits the fruit of the Spirit. Ask him to meet for coffee or lunch. Discover his path of faith. Ask how the Spirit came into his life. What changes resulted? Pray together for strength from the Spirit.

CHAPTER 8: *When God's Story Becomes Yours . . .*
THE RIGHT
DOORS OPEN

Questions for Discussion

1. What blocked doors have you encountered in your life? As you look back on them, how might God have been protecting you by blocking your path?

2. On the other hand, has God opened a door in your life? Explain what happened and how you could see his hand at work.

3. If this group were locked away in prison for your faith, what are the songs you would remember and sing to praise God and pass the time? Make a list, and then sing some of these songs together.

4. Sarah, Moses, and Daniel were Old Testament characters who encountered blocked doors so that another door could be opened. Who are some of your favorite Bible characters who have similar stories of God closing paths and then opening others?

5. What blocked doors are you facing right now? Pray for one another that God would blast them open in his perfect timing.

Ideas for Action

1. On your own this week, start a journal about the open and closed doors in front of you. Over time, note those open and closed doors in relation to decisions that needed to be made. Praise God for each open and closed door.

2. Seek out a trusted Christian mentor and speak to him or her about the closed doors that most frustrate you in your life. Ask for their perspective on these situations. Listen to their wisdom on why God may be closing those options to you.

CHAPTER 9: *When God's Story Becomes Yours . . .*
ALL THINGS WORK
FOR GOOD

Questions for Discussion

1. In what kind of circumstances is it difficult for people to see "all things" as working together for the good of those who love him? (See Romans 8:28).

2. Break into groups of two or three and share more of your stories with each other. Notice how God may have been working all things together for good in each person's story.

3. Which of your life experiences or privileges is God using, as he did with Paul, to his advantage? How are you uniquely able to do what others may not be able to do?

4. How would you like God to sift and stir the difficult situations you see around you into a well-prepared ending to the story? Describe the preferred future you would like to see in these situations.

5. Consider how you might be included in someone else's story of redemption. What role might you have to play in seeing that preferred future become reality?

Ideas for Action

1. Write a note to someone in a difficult situation and include Scriptures that encourage him or her. (See some of the Scriptures used in this chapter: Psalm 75:7; Jeremiah 29:11; 30:24; Daniel 5:21; Acts 2:23; Ephesians 1:11; 2:10; Galatians 4:4; 1 Peter 1:20.)

2. Visit an elderly person in a nursing home or someone who is in the hospital. Pray for them and encourage them in their difficult season.

3. Make a "life map" on a big sheet of paper or by using sticky notes on a desk. Start by listing all the difficult experiences of your life, and then key milestones of change and opportunity. Note high points of joy. Go back when you've mapped out your life and praise the Lord for how God used all of it together for some good in you and through you.

CHAPTER 10: *When God's Story Becomes Yours . . .*
GOD WILL COME
FOR YOU

Questions for Discussion

1. Many people are tempted to speculate on and even predict when Christ will return. How does Matthew 24:37–39 instruct us about that temptation?

2. Who would you most like to see in the resurrected life? (See John 5:25–29.) Think about someone close to you or someone who was a major influence on your life. Is there someone from Scripture or history you would like to meet after the resurrection?

3. What aspects of the final judgment do you anticipate with joy and what parts might you be fearful about? What about those who will "rise to be condemned" (see John 5:29)?

4. Why would you like a "transformed body?" (See 1 Corinthians 15:52–53.) Describe a disabled person you know who longs to see this day.

5. What evil things in the world will be corrected in the final judgment? What can we do to prepare the world for this change by changing some of those evils now?

Ideas for Action

1. In your devotional time this week, study the following Scriptures that pertain to the final judgment: Psalm 50:6; 94:1–3; Matthew 25:31–32; John 5:22, 27; Acts 10:39–43.

2. Intentionally spend time this week changing what you can to prepare the world for the return of Christ. Share your faith with unbelieving friends, challenge systems of oppression, treat God's creation better, and be clear about your own longing expectations of eternity.

3. Journal your own story this week if you've yet to do so. Capture the high and low points, and tell the story of how God has saved you and is using you for his purposes. Use one page to note the kinds of things he's doing in you right now; then use another page for the hopes you have as your story continues to align with God's story.

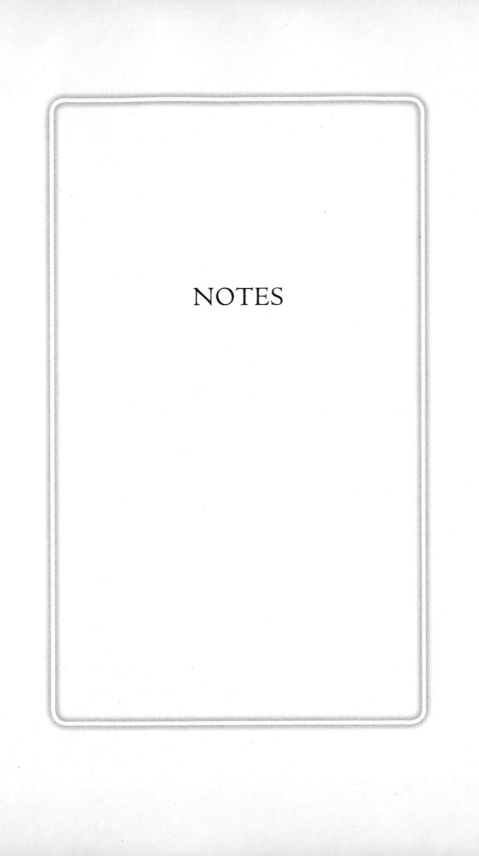

NOTES

1. Ted Gup, "Hard Times, a Helping Hand," *New York Times*, December 22, 2008, www.nytimes.com/2008/12/22/opinion/22gup.html (September 27, 2010).

2. Cited in Richard Mayhue, *Unmasking Satan: Understanding Satan's Battle Plan and Biblical Strategies for Fighting Back* (Grand Rapids: Kregel, 2001), 22.

3. Martin Luther, "A Mighty Fortress Is Our God" (1529), *Lyrics Era*: www.lyricsera.com/433137-lyric-Religious+Music-A+Mighty+Fortress+Is+Our+God.html (October 1, 2010).

4. See A. E. Le Roy, "The Great Barrier Island," in *Journal of the Auckland-Waikato Historical Societies* (April 1978), *Great Barrier Island Tourist Directory*: www.thebarrier.co.nz/History/AELeRoy.htm (October 1, 2010).

5. See Charles Walcott, "Magnetic Orientation in Homing Pigeons," in *IEEE Transactions on Magnetics* 16 (September 1980): 1008–13, *IEEEXplore*: ieeexplore.ieee.org/xpl/freeabs_all.jsp?arnumber=1060868 (October 1, 2010).

6. Cited in John Gilmore, *Probing Heaven* (Grand Rapids: Baker, 1989), 65.

7. Paul Stokes, "Blinded Pilot Guided to Safe Landing by RAF" (© Telegraph Media Group Limited 2008; used by permission), *Telegraph.co.uk* (November 7, 2008), www.telegraph.co.uk/news/newstopics/howaboutthat /3400429/Blinded-pilot-guided-to-safe-landing-by-RAF .html (October 1, 2010).

8. "Sweat Lodge Death Investigation Turns to Self-Help Guru James Arthur Ray" (October 12, 2009), *CBS News*: www.cbsnews.com/8301-504083_162-5378668 -504083.html (September 14, 2010); Mike Fleeman, "James Arthur Ray arrested in Sweat Lodge Deaths" (February 3, 2010), *People*: www.people.com/article/ 0,,20341429,00.html (September 14, 2010).

9. In the NIV, "Son of Man" appears eighty-two times in the Gospels. In Luke 24:7 the angels use the term to refer to Jesus, and in John 12:34 the crowd quotes Jesus describing himself as the Son of Man and asks what the name means. Twice in Mark's narrative (8:31; 9:9), Mark uses the term in paraphrasing Jesus' words.

10. John 8:12; 6:35; 11:25; 14:6 (NKJV); 8:58.

11. James Stalker, *The Life of Christ* (1880; repr., Arlington Heights, Ill.: Christian Liberty, 2002), 82.

12. Quoted in J. John and Chris Walley, *The Life: A Portrait of Jesus* (Milton Keynes, UK: Authentic Media, 2003), 126.

13. "Blind pilot guided to land by RAF" (November 7, 2010), *BBC News*: news.bbc.co.uk/2/hi/uk_news/england /north_yorkshire/7715345.stm; the audio account is embedded in the article (September 14, 2010).

14. "Tennessee Drunk Driving Laws," *Edgar Snyder & Associates*, www.edgarsnyder.com/drunk-driving/statute -limitations/tennessee-drunk-driving-laws.html (September 14, 2010).

15. Cited in Bryan Chapell, *The Promises of Grace: Living in the Grip of God's Love* (1992; repr., Grand Rapids: Baker, 2001), 142. Note: This report was disputed by some authorities.

16. Martin Luther, quoted in Donald G. Bloesch, *Essentials of Evangelical Theology* (San Francisco: HarperSanFrancisco, 1978), 1:148.

17. The story is told in Jon Krakauer, *Into the Wild* (New York: Anchor, 1996), 80–84.

18. Fred Carl Kuehner, "Heaven or Hell," in *Fundamentals of the Faith*, ed. Carl F. H. Henry (Grand Rapids: Zondervan, 1969), 233.

19. Based on mortality rates from "The World Factbook," last updated September 29, 2010, *Central Intelligence Agency*: www.cia.gov/library/publications/the-world -factbook/geos/xx.html (October 1, 2010). The figures are based on estimates of 8.37 deaths per 1,000 population (2009 estimate) and a world population of 6,768,181,146 (July 2010 estimate).

20. Mark 9:31 NKJV; see also 8:31; 10:33 – 34; 14:28

21. "Theology: The God Is Dead Movement" (October 25, 1965), *Time*: www.time.com/time/magazine/article /0,9171,941410 – 3,00.html (September 14, 2010).

22. Chaz Corzine, e-mail message to author, August 3, 2010. Used by permission.

23. Billy Graham, "Remarks by Dr. Billy Graham at Richard Nixon's Funeral" (April 27, 1994), *Watergate.info*: www .watergate.info/nixon/94-04-27_funeral-graham.shtml (September 14, 2010).

24. Cited in Jeff Strite, "The Power of Persistent Prayer," *SermonCentral.com*: www.sermoncentral.com/sermons/ the-power-of-persistent-prayer-jeff-strite-sermon-on -prayer-how-to-49222.asp (September 14, 2010).

25. Mark Schlabach, "Injury Swipes McCoy's One Goal" (January 7, 2010), *ESPN*: sports.espn.go.com/ncf/bowls09/ columns/story?columnist=schlabach_mark&id=4807219 (September 15, 2010); "Colt McCoy Postgame Interview

Video: 'I Would Have Given Everything to Be Out There'" (March 18, 2010), *The Huffington Post*: www .huffingtonpost.com/2010/01/08/colt-mccoy-postgame -inter_n_415841.html (October 1, 2010).

26. Edward Mote, "My Hope Is Built on Nothing Less" (1834), *Hymns*: www.hymns.me.uk/my-hope-is-built-on -nothing-less-favorite-hymn.htm (October 28, 2010); put to music in 1863 by composer William Bradbury.

27. David Aikman, *Great Souls: Six Who Changed the Century* (Nashville: Word, 1998), 78. Many of the details of Mandela's life described in this chapter are taken from pages 61 – 123 of *Great Souls*.

28. Aikman, *Great Souls*, 108.

29. Aikman, *Great Souls*, 116, 64.

30. Figures vary widely. The figure 106 billion is cited by Carl Haub, "How Many People Have Ever Lived on Earth" (November/December 2002), *Population Reference Bureau*: www.prb.org/Articles/2002/HowMany PeopleHaveEverLivedonEarth.aspx (October 1, 2010).

31. Cited in Paul Lee Tan, *Encyclopedia of 7700 Illustrations: Signs of the Times* (Rockville, Md.: Assurance, 1988), #5470.

32. Joni Eareckson Tada, *Heaven: Your Real Home* (Grand Rapids: Zondervan, 1995), 41.

GOD'S STORY

your story

OTHER PRODUCTS AVAILABLE!

The experience doesn't have to end with this book. Here's a brief look at some of the other *God's Story, Your Story* products that will allow you and others to explore God's plan of eternal redemption that is being told through our very own lives right now.

❖ **Church Campaign**
ISBN: 978-0310683-025

Includes:
• 1 six-session DVD
• 1 Small Group
  Participants Guide
• 1 Hardcover book
• 1 Getting Started Guide

❖ **Youth Edition**
ISBN: 978-0310725-466

❖ **Small Group Curriculum**
ISBN: 978-0310684-336

Includes:
• 1 six-session DVD
• 1 Participants Guide

❖ **Spanish Edition**
ISBN: 978-0829759-099

❖ **Audio CD**
ISBN: 978-0310318-866

inspired by THE STORY
POWERED BY ZONDERVAN

BOOKS AND CURRICULUM FOR ALL AGES
PERFECT FOR SUNDAY SCHOOL AND SMALL GROUPS

ADULT CURRICULUM

Adult curriculum helps small groups of any form or size learn, discuss, and apply the themes in *The Heart of the Story*. Designed to be used independently or as part of *The Story* 31-week campaign.

TEEN CURRICULUM

Experiential learning and fun; creative; best-in-class HD video and lesson plans help teens clearly understand *The Story*.

CHILDREN'S BOOKS AND CURRICULUM

Three new children's books, including *The Story for Children* by Max Lucado, help bring the Bible to life for readers of any age. Reproducible lesson plans make for easy implementation in children's programs.

To order visit www.TheStory.com

THE STORY
POWERED BY ZONDERVAN

Share Your Thoughts

With the Author: Your comments will be forwarded to the author when you send them to *zauthor@zondervan.com*.

With Zondervan: Submit your review of this book by writing to *zreview@zondervan.com*.

Free Online Resources at
www.zondervan.com

Zondervan AuthorTracker: Be notified whenever your favorite authors publish new books, go on tour, or post an update about what's happening in their lives at www.zondervan.com/authortracker.

Daily Bible Verses and Devotions: Enrich your life with daily Bible verses or devotions that help you start every morning focused on God. Visit www.zondervan.com/newsletters.

Free Email Publications: Sign up for newsletters on Christian living, academic resources, church ministry, fiction, children's resources, and more. Visit www.zondervan.com/newsletters.

Zondervan Bible Search: Find and compare Bible passages in a variety of translations at www.zondervanbiblesearch.com.

Other Benefits: Register to receive online benefits like coupons and special offers, or to participate in research.

ZONDERVAN

ZONDERVAN.com/
AUTHORTRACKER
follow your favorite authors

Also by Ernest K. Gann

ISLAND IN THE SKY

BLAZE OF NOON

BENJAMIN LAWLESS

FIDDLERS GREEN

THE HIGH AND THE MIGHTY

SOLDIER OF FORTUNE

TWILIGHT FOR THE GODS

THE TROUBLE WITH LAZY ETHEL

FATE IS THE HUNTER

OF GOOD AND EVIL

IN THE COMPANY OF EAGLES

SONG OF THE SIRENS

THE ANTAGONISTS

BAND OF BROTHERS

FLYING CIRCUS

BRAIN 2000

THE AVIATOR

THE MAGISTRATE

GENTLEMEN OF ADVENTURE

THE TRIUMPH

THE BAD ANGEL

THE BLACK WATCH

THE
BLACK
WATCH

The Men
Who Fly America's
Secret Spy Planes

ERNEST K. GANN

Random House New York

Gann, Ernest Kellogg.
The black watch : The men who fly America's secret spy planes / by Ernest
K. Gann.
p.   cm.
ISBN 0-394-57507-5
1. Aerial reconnaissance.   2. United States. Air Force. Squadron, 99th.
3. U-2 (Reconnaissance aircraft)   4. SR-71 (Jet reconnaissance plane)
I. Title.
UG763.G36   1989
358.4'5—dc20   89-3919

Manufactured in the United States of America
24689753
First Edition

To my comrades without arms—the members of the 99th Strategic Reconnaissance Squadron and the 5th Strategic Training Squadron, United States Air Force

Author's Note

History often mocks us and has a malevolent habit of turning upon itself and upon those who make it. Contemporary history is extremely fickle and sometimes conceals the logic that inspires action—or lack of it. If I tell you a secret and you do not believe it, it becomes a nonevent even though it actually happened.

The events herein are based on fact. For obvious purposes I have changed certain locales and sometimes interchanged names, and have felt obliged to avoid pinpointing events and men exactly—even in time span. It would contribute nothing to the purpose of this work if I burdened the reader with dates, hours, places, and the precise identification of the many individuals who act upon this high stage. The author is also guilty of certain instances of historical neglect; for example, Lieutenant Colonel Steven Brown, who does exist, is hardly mentioned in this book, yet one of the major sequences happened to him and he received an extremely rare award for his skill and courage—a peacetime Distinguished Flying Cross. And many of the men who walk or fly through these pages are no longer on the job, or have been transferred elsewhere. That is the military way.

I have never received any "official" permission to write this book, although the prolonged research included a few hours flying the U-2 at low altitudes and two "high flights." While I tried repeatedly to seek some kind of paper giving me formal permission, I am now persuaded it will never come, nor was there any intention that official sanction would be on file. Bureaucrats and national intelligence are a poor mix, so if you want to accomplish anything that is at all sensitive you must run around end. That also is the military way.

I am honored to salute those special men who at some risk to their careers helped me to do so.

ERNEST K. GANN
Friday Harbor, Washington

Contents

THE BLACK WATCH

Prologue

The Article squats like a stricken toad in the pre-dawn darkness. It is painted a flat black, and so its outlines are vague and its bulk mysteriously uncertain. It might be something a giant lepidopterist would pin in his prize display case, an object to meditate upon, a rare specimen worth continually reviewing when countless others have been garbaged.

When the CIA owned the first of the breed, it was known as "Article 341," a handy way of saying that it was nothing of interest or perhaps did not actually exist.

In the world of intelligence many things do not exist.

No one enjoys the game of "I've got a secret" more than the CIA—except the military. There are some things so secret they are declared forever invisible by invisible spokesmen. The official term is "classified."

Tonight there are more than a score of dark figures moving about the Article. It is bitter cold and when they pass a light, their breathing creates the spew of dragons and intermixes in strangely embroidered patterns. When they are not prodding or twisting or manipulating a part of the Article, they huddle in small groups while all around them lights flash and blink with the relentless repetition of a disco. There are red flashing lights atop the "mobile" cars, a red flasher on the small tractor that is waiting to pull the Article, and on the van that has brought the technical representatives, and on a truck for those who will unlock the pogo sticks that support the Article's wings. In the distance a green light beacon flashes on top of the control tower.

Before dawn another van arrives, also festooned with flashing lights. It resembles an ambulance. The doors open and something approximating a human figure emerges. He wears a bulky clown suit and a goldfish-bowl helmet. He is connected to his life-support system by wires and hoses extending from a small metal case. It will be ten hours before he eats, except for what nourishment he can take via a straw that he will insert through a special valve in his helmet.

He walks toward the Article awkwardly, confined by the garment that will serve as his armor against the extremely hostile high environment for which he is bound. It is as if he has been mummified by the slick yellow material of his clown suit, and thus able to continue the aging process within his very private world.

The man-figure climbs a metal set of stairs known as a "howdah" that has been placed alongside the body of the Article and can be compared to trying to mount an elephant that refuses to kneel. At the top two men await him; they perform like *novicios* dressing a matador. He disappears between them, and somewhere near the black belly of the Article a generator driven by a turbine engine tears apart the early morning tranquillity. Moments later the Article displays a red and green light blossom on each wingtip. Then both vanish. They are not to be seen again, because espionage is mostly illusion and the game must be played by absurd rules.

People who are not privy to the activities of the Article are not supposed to discover they really take place.

The actual number of humans who guide the mysterious Articles varies with time, yet seldom numbers more than twenty. The fewer the number, the fewer the possibility of mistakes. The lack of total reliability in human beings is always a problem in intelligence work, and here the risk is complicated by the necessity to operate in such high country.

The darkness cloaks details within the goldfish-bowl helmet, but once a flash of light strikes the faceplate and a pair of eyes blink in annoyance. The soft red of the instrument-panel lights is soothing, bright flashes are hard on concentration. And the mission rules. Nothing else matters.

To smile. No foreign government knows the whereabouts of all the U-2s except the Russians.

One:

The World

Wars have come and gone for Americans: Against
Nazi Germany, against the Japanese, against the Koreans, the
Chinese, the Vietnamese, the Libyans and—with a sword in ill-
fitting disguise—against the Egyptians, the Nicaraguans, the Cu-
bans, and the Iranians. Our principle adversary is also in disguise,
maneuvering as if the rest of the world were blind, as if it were
unthinkable to acknowledge that their henchmen are utterly dependent on and responsible to the only other major power in the
world. And so, despite some humiliating defeats, our hapless
warriors are still stationed everywhere.

We must know about these events that have changed and keep
changing. We must somehow contrive to see if there is any
buildup of military hardware in Ethiopia while reassuring ourselves that the Ethiopians have not suddenly taken to home-style
manufacture. We must know these details about the Ethiopians
because, like it or not, the world is now one unit, the nations
ill-kept and scraggly, yet tangled in various ways with each other.
Likewise, we must be aware of military movements in the deserts
of Algeria, any undue acquisition of military ordnance in Guate-
mala, the state of agricultural crops in war-bashed Iran and Iraq,

and a significant increase in ship movements in the hitherto stagnant port of Lagos.

Samsamme Mango, Muckle Flugga, Unst, Yell, Rangoon, and Mindanao—it is our obligation to know the situation there better than we once knew our own frontiers. We are busybodys because we *have* to be. If the Libyans suddenly start the construction of an odd plant in a remote desert location, we must know if it is a factory for canning dates, or something less palatable.

The reality of a benign world community is still far down the line, and while Pearl Harbor–type surprises are extremely unlikely, there must never be another such event. We must watch—or we may perish.

The French can tell us about lack of intelligence. They folded in pathetic retreat before the German panzers of World War II, dying in battles that were lost before they began. Ignorance, not lack of courage or even numbers, initially brought the French to their knees.

And yet we persist in wearing the cloak of harmony, a heartwarming tendency that carries a certain rustic charm until the blood of innocence drains from our eyes.

Observing our behavior in wonder are Department 8, Directorate S of the KGB's First Directorate, and the "Special Branch" and "Special Center" of the Soviet GRU. Despite Gorbachev's air of sweetness and light, those not-so-clandestine organizations have men directly responsible for the functioning, financing, and training of terrorist groups throughout the world. "Glasnost" is a hopeful label, but it looks strangely askew against the amount of military hardware being shipped overseas through the port of Nikolayev on the Black Sea. The Soviets invariably suggest that they are responding to "dangerous situations" as far away as Cuba, Nicaragua, various new African nations, Peru, and, of course, Southeast Asia. In Cuba, at their main communications site, the Soviets are careful to monitor our space and military signals and even domestic telephone calls. Such busybodying on their part may at least keep their two-thousand-man combat brigade from more serious mischief. *Their* satellites are maintaining their own watch—on us. Soviet knowledge of our industrial as well as our military situation leaves us enacting what appears to be a secret force.

The Western world does have its troubles, but the Soviets are cursed with boundless internal ailments—the basic reason for *glasnost*. Actually the Russian word is not an exact equivalent of our word "openness." It means rather that things are "more open than they have been," which is very thin encouragement. The new policy is an attempt by Gorbachev, a very clever man, to assuage the wild divergencies in Soviet society and thus increase the strength of the nation as a whole. The language problem alone is extremely sticky, and while the study of Russian is demanded of all students, their mother tongue can be Ukranian, Latvian, Lithuanian, Estonian, Georgian, Armenian, Tartar, or Pashto. Gorbachev recognizes that because of the language puzzle, any large-scale military action involving Soviet troops would be greatly handicapped and might lead to disaster. Even in peacetime the language barrier creates resentment among some units. They know they will not be chosen to fly jets unless they are fluent in the official language of the land.

Only in space have the Soviets stuck to their original program, and they have succeeded considerably beyond our own admirable, if floundering, efforts. The Soviets have never been concerned with landing men on the moon or any other planetary body. Their space performance so far has been quite obvious—the establishment of a space station (or several) to be permanently occupied by specialist teams who might be equipped with nuclear cannons. Command of space to the Soviets is more than a vague ambition. They accept it as a vital part of their future, and we must concede that it is also ours if we are to survive.

All people want peace, and perhaps now is the greatest opportunity for it since the beginning of mankind. But the era of international trust has not yet arrived, and while it is expensive to keep informed, espionage is still a necessity.

Our spy business is divided among four kinds of operatives. We have our satellites, which are, inconveniently, not always in the right place at the right time, and whose greatest disadvantage is predictability and vulnerability in a time of war. And we have our spy planes. These elements are supplemented by an assortment of ground spooks in the CIA, the defense agency, and the various military intelligence arms.

The Soviets have a separate arm of their air force charged with the immediate defense of their frontiers. It is known as VPVO (Voiska Protvovzdushmoi), and includes every activity from radar stations to interception aircraft. In some sense VPVO is similar to "Looking Glass," our flying command post, which is aloft twenty-four hours of every day. The general on board is heavily dependent on information gathered by the four sources.

For reasons they keep to themselves, the Soviets seem to have little faith in aerial reconnaissance. They did try to build their own version of a spy plane, but its performance was disappointing. They rely instead on their multitudes of ground operatives, who do succeed in digging out a certain amount of "classified" material. They can usually buy whatever else they yearn to know at the newsstand.

The rationale for our airborne spies is that they anticipate trouble rather than waiting for it. While no overt action on the part of our planetary neighbors has been stopped by intelligence since the Cuban missile affair, we at least know our adversaries' strengths and weaknesses. And many of their projects have been frustrated before reaching the danger point.

Sorties flown in spy planes are only a part of the intelligence effort, and not even the chiefs of staff know exactly how every element of a mission is interwoven. Spy pilots who are sitting right on top of the mission have only a very sketchy knowledge of what is going on in that long snout projecting ahead of their eyes.

Our intelligence system is based firmly on "need to know," and is deliberately compartmentalized to prevent scraps of information from being put together and forming a whole. This security policy has its own acronym, SCI—for Sensitive Compartmented Information.

The SCI throws a black cloak over a host of agencies, committees, and political busybodies, each of which may be entitled to receive certain intelligence gleanings relative to a specified situation. But no more. SCI hopes to keep the details of intelligence collection immune from discovery, and has so far been reasonably successful.

Despite glasnost, the undeniable charm of Gorbachev, and the daisy chain of amiabilities currently encircling most affairs between the two major powers, we must remind ourselves that in one way or another *the Soviets have violated every treaty we have made with them.* Geneva, a city dripping with money wasted on "conferences," many of which are doomed to failure before the first limousine arrives at the entrance to the meeting hall, would be devastated if supposedly well-meaning diplomats canceled their almost-continuous rendezvous.

The Soviets, who luxuriate in the bourgeois amenities of Geneva, continue to violate SALT I and SALT II, the ABM treaty and the Helsinki Final Act, while busily buying trinkets to take back to Mother Russia when the conference is at last admitted to have accomplished little or nothing. The Soviets do their violating when it is convenient for them, almost as if they were small boys practicing a grisly laugh for the school play at Halloween. They know we cannot catch them in the act 99 percent of the time, so the urge to cheat just a little becomes irresistible.

As far as we know (or are confessing to know), one example is immediate. The installation of a massed phased-array radar at Krasnoyarsk is an undeniable violation of the ABM treaty. The same goes for the relatively new complex near Abalakova.

So far we have demurely ignored the fact that we have made similar violations with our complex at Shemya. And Greenland. And elsewhere.

We do have a reasonable assessment of the Russian ICBM sites at Kostroma, Derashnya, Yedrovo, and a number of other strategically located installations. But what of it? If the Soviets really want to take on the expense and trouble of concealing the majority of their missile sites, it probably could be done and we would never know about them. Yet the trade-off is not worth it because, we may suppose from past performance, in spite of glasnost they have other things to hide, and a few missile and radar decoys are intended to keep us amused and guessing. Cynics have been quick to label glasnost part of the same con.

It is all very well and even heartening to hear Gorbachev say he is going to reduce various categories in the Soviet armed forces. It is also somewhat like hearing a multimillionaire announcing that he is going to give a hundred dollars to charity—he will hardly miss it. Gorbachev's most welcome gesture will not put a serious dent in the incredible and terrible host of tanks the Soviets have at hand. And their armies are so formidable, a few hundred thousand troops will hardly be missed except at mealtimes.

The Soviets have not taken our accusation of treaty violations in exactly the way we might have wished. They play the game according to long-established rules and accuse us of the same conduct. They also quote a report of our Joint Chiefs of Staff, which blandly states that the Soviets are "almost" innocent—a claim that leaves our accusatory administrations gasping for air.

The current melting of U.S.–Soviet relations, suddenly warmed even more by a great natural catastrophe (the earthquake in Armenia), unquestionably eases tension between the two nations, and Gorbachev may even become the darling of international statesmanship.

Suspicion is the concubine of international politicians, and we are inclined to forget that the Soviet Union is the only nation in the world that is entirely surrounded by hostile neighbors. So at least the Russians have a sound reason for their paranoid worries.

Perhaps we would suffer the same complexes if the geographical situation were reversed. Meanwhile, we had best keep our pistol in its holster—and just in case, keep our spies in the air.

Even now, with the occasional fragrance of true peace touching the atmosphere, we remain stunned by the quantities of weapons of the Soviet military establishment and the inferences that must be drawn from them. What do you do with fifty-two thousand main battle tanks all poised at NATO Europe?

The presumption is that the tanks will work, along with the rest of their military hardware, but there are reports that insist the opposite. Ever since the famous Yak fighter plane of World War II, the Soviets have displayed a talent for producing "field fixable" weapons and systems. It was often said that to repair a Yak, a mechanic needed a screwdriver, a pair of pliers, and a wrench. And a minimum of knowledge.

If we slide into one of those rare moments of military honesty, we realize that the technical demands of modern warfare are so complex a considerable percentage of our material is bound to malfunction even before it is deployed against a foe. We no longer waste manpower by carrying the flag into battle. Instead, we need battalions of electronic engineers to keep the terrible machinery grinding.

So do the Soviets.

Perhaps it is not unreasonable that we should occasionally take a peek at their activities. Our best spies are a flock of high-flying birds.

Two:

The Birds

Vaulting over the ravaged face of the most beautiful planet we know, sailing high upon the searing hot winds of their engines, is a small group of men who perhaps better than any others, except astronauts, understand their insignificance. If they were lacking it before, they have a way of developing religion when their voyages are done. They have been privileged to view our radiantly blue home from a locale hardly imagined a few centuries ago, and they are the more thoughtful because of their experience. Some of their original ebullience becomes lost in the high altitudes, and their habitat takes on a new seriousness. They look down on millions of acres for which various peoples claim ownership, and some nights they are treated to the spectacle of thunderstorms exploding like a magician's carpet in the far below.

After a time on the job, these men change subtly at first, until finally they are a little different from other men. A part of the change is natural maturation, but an airman with the most high-tech, computerized mind will admit that when he views the "terminator" from the cockpit of his puny little machine, something happens deep within him. Some spiritual energy removes him permanently from his flying peers. At the very high reconnaissance altitudes he has never been so alone, so utterly dependent on his machine and self, so isolated from all that is normal. He is aware that there is a certain amount of danger in every sortie, yet if he is to survive he must manage to spit in its eye. Aloft he finds himself the sole proprietor of an enormous and glorious hall—his to accept and his to conquer. Alone. Here, in a sort of pre-heaven, he knows that there can be occasional forays into a treacherous and unforgiving hell.

Danger is an irresolute foe and only a very few men seek it deliberately. A convenient escape relay in our brain closes only when danger is actually present; meanwhile, it is easy to pretend it is not even there. Courage comes of carrying on more or less efficiently when the relay is closed, and the percentage of that opportunity varies greatly. There is no danger in going to sea, driving a car, or robbing a bank, unless something goes differently than planned. The same goes for flying. All professional airmen are aware of it, and so foolishness around airplanes is not tolerated.

At Beale Air Force Base in northern California there is a stable of three aircraft types that can do considerable damage to the human carcass if they are allowed to have their own way. They are safe enough, because they are exceedingly well managed. Not one of them carries any kind of armament.

There is the U-2. Sometimes it is called the TR-1 in a rather quaint attempt to modify its sinister image as a spy plane. It is still a spy plane no matter what the label. It could not fight its way out of a flock of balloons.

The U-2 is not a large aircraft, but does have an enormous 103-foot wingspan, which helps it operate at altitudes long thought impossible. It is extraordinarily lightweight, essentially an overgrown glider with a jet engine. The regular U-2s at Beale are assigned to the 99th Squadron of the United States Air Force and are single-seaters. The trainers are two-place airplanes, painted white, and belong to the 5th Strategic Reconnaissance

Training Squadron. Both types have fantastic climb rates (as much as 6,000 feet per minute), and cruise at normal airliner 420-knot speed, although at altitudes airliners could never achieve. They also have a talent for metamorphosis: Taxiing toward the runway, a U-2 looks like an airplane that has had too much to drink, but once in the sky it becomes a most graceful bird.

Then there is the exotic, even erotic SR-71, which in the hangar looks like a gigantic science-fiction beetle crouched for attack. It is an ugly beast of an airplane; there is something frightening about it even though it is innocent of armament. Owned by the 1st Aero Squadron, an outfit that came into being under General Pershing during the Mexican War, the SR-71 operates at altitudes even above the U-2, considerably above eighty thousand feet, and is the fastest plane in the world. It too is a spy plane, and its flights require so many people that they are often referred to as "launchings." The enormous expense of operating it has compelled the air force to use it less; the U-2s can do the routine missions, while satellites have become ever more sophisticated and useful. So much of the time the SRs stand glowering ominously in their special hangars, lamp black and somewhat intimidating even when at rest.

The commander of the 1st Aero Squadron at Beale is Kinego, a sepia-eyed handsome man whose eyebrows signal his restless nature and boundless energy.

Rivalry between U-2 airmen and those still tending the SR-71s is constant and often imaginative. "Yes," the U-2 people smirk, "the SR does fly faster than a bullet. It also has about the same range."

There are two tanker squadrons at Beale, the 349th and the 350th, and both range the world. They also refuel the ravenous SRs. Tankermen are mostly resigned to the fact that their demanding job is far from glamorous. For if they are not in the proper place in the sky at just the perfect time and ready to give a transfusion, their customers may very well die. When an SR slides into view looking like a determined barracuda just below the tanker's tail, there is no time to ask for a charge card. The SR burns twenty gallons of very special fuel every minute it is in full flight, which is one of the many reasons the air force has severely restricted its use.

Although the U-2s have been refueled in midair, their built-in range of ten hours plus is about all a solo human being can tolerate at such high altitudes.

Now, Kinego is inclined to smile wistfully and says he spends most of his time addressing fifth-graders on the wonders of the SR-71s. He is not jesting. Beside the enormous operational costs, the fastest, highest-flying airplane in the world is a victim of "vanishing vendors," which is one way of saying that the original manufacturers of the SR-71's highly specialized parts have gone out of business long ago. The resulting lack of reserve parts supply includes the powerful thirty-four thousand-pound thrust (J-58) engines, and when Kinego or any other SR-71 man is asked about its future, no one has an answer.

Like any outstanding accomplishment, flying the fastest and most mysterious aircraft in the world inevitably persuades a man that he matches his equipment: He is a unique, extraordinarily gifted aviator and an all-around wonderful guy. The utter secrecy inherent in the job combines with an aura of pure class and inspires a not-always-restrained swagger. Hence there is often a certain condescension in the manner of SR-71 pilots and the "backseaters" who keep their fancy flying machine exactly on target. They are inclined to regard the U-2 as a work mule, with a speed to match that animal.

The reaction of the U-2 people is hardly surprising. Their roost at Beale is down the hall from Kinego's territory and, as the 99th Squadron, represents the sole unit in the air force devoted to operational flights in the U-2. They are commanded by Lieutenant Colonel Driskill, a handsome, ultrarelaxed officer who makes no attempt to ease the sense of rivalry between the two organizations. He sometimes joins in the continuous exchange of good-natured barbs that mark the difference between two types of aircraft flown by men who have somehow assimilated their characters.

The SR-71 "backseaters," or RSOs (Reconnaissance Systems Operators), are only vicariously interested in the manipulation of the SR-71s. They lack even a hint of a flight control in their separate cockpits. Instead, the cockpit is crammed with navigational devices, most important among them the astro-nav, which constantly displays the precise position of the SR using pre-programmed fixes on the stars. Away with the old sextant and chronometer; the same stars that once guided the ancients now tell the RSO to put the rock in his other hand. North is that way.

SR pilot and "backseater" are married to each other, after due process of consent. It is a marriage of more than convenience, and divorce or even separation while the two airmen are flying together rarely occurs. The pair must work as a perfectly coordinated team, a situation possible only if they are inexorably linked to each other. An SR driver knows what his partner is talking about just by the tone of his voice. He must. The extraordinary aircraft enables them to see far beyond what most men will ever see; the charging black bull of a vehicle that becomes their uttermost world is in a hurry. It transits a mile every two seconds. The very lives of the two men depend on an absence of disagreement.

This mano-a-mano approach creates its own problems. If a "backseater" decides to go skiing with his family, his pilot is likely to display at least a frown of disapproval.

"Suppose you break your leg? What do I do?" The concern is

genuine, because if one member of a team is grounded, the other falls automatically into the same dreary state.

Even a sneeze brings an anxious "Are you feeling all right?" So mixing SR crews is almost never done.

The continuous badinage between two such vigorous neighbors is the joy of U-2 pilots, who find it a rich opportunity to minimize the undeniable glamour of the SR-71. They refer to it as the "sled," and since the sled drivers seem to make a more romantic impression on the public, they are said to deliberately fly toward thunderstorms because they mistake them for camera flashbulbs. They also say the difference between a porcupine and the SR-71 is that the porcupine has the pricks on the outside.

The SR crews claim they are the wine-and-cheese set of the aviators and fly a "cerebral" aircraft.

The U-2 men say the difference between finding a dead skunk and a dead sled driver on the freeway is that there are always skid marks just before the skunk.

The sled drivers insist the U-2 boys are merely jealous, but lose a few points when they are referred to as Nats Ass (National Asset) drivers, and are easily distinguished by their Gucci patent-leather boots, pressed flight suits, manicured fingernails, white turtleneck shirts, and hairstyling by Christopher J's.

If a sled driver seeks to defend his flying machine with some reference to its operating expense and consequent gift of employment to countless citizens, the U-2 drivers agree. They suggest that the Chrysler Corporation was saved from bankruptcy just by the number of ground-bound vehicles required to launch an SR-71. They say that, indeed, if the actual cost of flying the SR-71 is "classified," isn't that because it is the most expensive project ever conceived by man, other than the Alaska Pipeline? Which, of course, was built specifically to support the SR-71.

As for the SR's vaunted ability to survey more than one hundred thousand square miles of the earth's surface in an hour's time, the U-2 pilots concede that may be so if there is a tanker squadron on both ends.

The Nats Ass drivers do not have an easy time. While both Kinego and Driskill are genial friends, their squadron mates rarely mix when day is done. Along the flight line both types look the other way when passing the other's aircraft. It is not appropriate to cheat on one's love, even via a lascivious glance.

The unit emblem of the SR-71 squadron features the word HABU, the name of a deadly Okinawan snake. The relationship is obscure to all but Okinawans, who occasionally see one of the big black birds launching out of the American base at Kadena and claim they look alike.

The difference in the lives of the two squadron members is as vast as the difference of their flying machines, yet there is one common denominator. They are all obsessed with their work and their flying machines, and they understand each other for their dedication. Those very few who feel differently do not last long.

Deep down beneath the harmless rivalry at Beale lurks a disturbing vision. Stand at one of the exit gates of the Lockheed Corporation in Burbank, California, which once built the SR-71s and still builds a limited number of U-2s. Watch the thousands of employees depart at four-thirty in the afternoon. Observe them, with empty lunch buckets in hand, climb into well-polished cars and drive God-only-knows how far to their homes. It is almost impossible not to ask what happens if the military-industrial complex stumbles and falls down in an era of true and blessed peace. Will the thousands of ex–Lockheed workers find employment building roads and bridges, and if so, where? Their skills are aeronautical, ill-matched to driving bulldozers, laying asphalt, or forging steel. In no other American enterprise is the ultimate employment destiny of a nation so unpredictable.

Not far from the flight line at Beale, and isolated from the rest of the base, stands a ten-story building containing something called "Pave Paws." It comprises two enormous radar systems so arranged that they can pick up and identify any major addition to the five thousand odd items already floating in space. There are similar installations in Alaska, Greenland, and a few other remote locations, and presumably they would identify any long-range missiles aimed at targets within the United States.

The trouble is that Pave Paws is a tardy spy. Once it locks on and identifies an approaching threat, there remain only five to ten minutes before arrival time—hardly enough time to mix a good martini and say hello to eternity. Thus we could go lurching innocently toward Armageddon, unless somehow we can anticipate and so have time to cancel any dangerous activities of our possible adversaries.

Unfortunately there is now no place to hide except beneath the surface of the oceans, and even that refuge is becoming vulnerable.

The military-industrial complex plays a heavy hand in all this high-altitude hocus-pocus, and not only in the photographic and electronic systems. The variety of equipment is changing constantly, but certain items are now relatively standard on U-2s. There is usually a modified X-band radar, and a forward-looking infrared system; there is side-looking radar, with a slant range of better than one hundred miles, and probably also a PLSS (Precision Emitter Location Strike System). Despite progress in solid-state microelectronics, all these ultrafancy gizmos do weigh down the aircraft. It is a common pilot complaint that the newer Articles, being some five thousand pounds heavier, will not reach the altitudes possible in the older models.

Cameras are primary equipment in all spy planes, although the type varies from one aircraft to the next. There is the old "B" camera, a brainchild of Dr. Edwin Land, father of the Polaroid. Any camera carried high aloft is vastly more complex than even the finest camera used in earthly environments. The whole object of the mission is lost if the resolution is not almost perfect, but the factors working against that goal are formidable: Compensation must be made for the aircraft's movement, and the focus must be adjusted whenever the altitude varies even slightly, and exposure must be automatically controlled when various cloud surfaces are reflecting light and what is of interest lies in shadow.

The lenses of the various U-2 cameras are marvels of oracular acuity, and their working environment must be protected from temperature changes, pressure changes, and even on rare occasions high-altitude humidity. There is a type "H" camera, which can cover oblique shots either left or right, and a KA-102-A camera that can also be aimed to seven positions.

It is no longer necessary to "overfly" a country and possibly cause a Francis Gray Powers rumpus. Now, we can stand on tiptoe and peek over the windowsill.

But in the intelligence business seeing is not always believing; illusions abound, and the talent of specialists is often required to differentiate fact from fiction. These are the photo interpreters, a unique, almost mystic profession whose members are apt to display a passion for the eye-rolling airs of secrecy. It is said they can spot a sardine at twenty miles and turn it into a red herring.

Many of the photo interpreters are women, who seem to have a special aptitude for detail. Interpreters of both sexes prefer to work from negatives, which give them higher resolution than prints, and they all live in a world as seen through a microscope. They often make solid deductions from the apparently insignificant. Is that covered truck transporting food or ammunition? Its tracks in the mud, coupled with other information, may reveal the answer.

❖

There has always been an abundance of credit-takers for any successful enterprise, but in the case of the U-2 the inspiration belonged to a relatively obscure air force major, John Seaberg, the onetime chief of new developments at Wright Field in Dayton, Ohio. He was an unusual man, an engineer with an extra quotient of imagination. As long ago as 1953, Seaberg was convinced the air force needed a reconnaissance aircraft that could fly high enough to avoid interception by missiles or other aircraft. He took his ideas to his superior, William Lamar, who invited a few relatively small aircraft manufacturers in for discussion. Martin, Bell, and Fairchild confessed they were perplexed by the high-altitude-flight demands. The best available engine, they believed, would deliver only 7 percent normal horsepower at the altitudes Seaberg and Lamar envisioned. Was that enough to keep any practical flying machine airborne? The higher the altitude, the less the density of atmosphere—there is a lot of space between molecules. Since any engine requires a generous ration of air to function at all, how in that high semidesert of consumable particles could an aircraft maintain flying speed on such a starvation diet?

The key, everyone realized, was not so much in the horrendous business of designing a completely new engine, but in the airframe itself. Radical thinking was demanded to carry out a radical concept.

It takes a host of skilled people to launch any new aircraft, and staggering amounts of money. Pratt and Whitney, a company whose superb engines had created a sect of idolatry among those whose lives had depended on them, came through with an axial flow "J-57," and the unthinkable at least looked feasible.

Next was the money.

Seaberg and company appeared before the Killian Committee,* which was charged with discovering if the Soviet Union

---

*James R. Killian, president of the Massachusetts Institute of Technology, was chairman.

was contemplating another Pearl Harbor. President Eisenhower had taken to caressing his bald head more often than usual, and waggling his eyebrows uneasily; for he had been listening to the diatribes delivered by the Soviet leaders and was wondering if their threats were just bluster reflecting too much vodka, or were they a prelude to something serious? It was even more frustrating than dealing with that prime British ass Montgomery before the invasion of France. At least there was excellent intelligence then. Now, the secretary of defense did not know what the Russians were up to, and Allen Dulles, chief of the CIA, did not know. Something had to be done, Eisenhower realized, as he longed for the simplicity of giving a military order. This sneaky business was not for a true soldier. There were too many unpredictables.

There was now the vexing problem of energetic drive and secrecy—unnatural companions.

Who could handle this project without too many people knowing about it? There was that fellow at Lockheed . . . whatever his name was. Kelly, or something? Which goes first, the memory or the bladder? "What's his real name?"

"Clarence Johnson, Mr. President."

When he reported to the White House, Clarence "Kelly" Johnson was already a star in the aeronautical world. His international renown had been achieved by the production of important aircraft such as the P-38, the F-80 fighters, the Constellation airliner, and the supersonic F-104.

When Johnson entered the Oval Room, he returned the president's smile with a slight frown. No one pushed Kelly Johnson around. He had heard about this superspy project through his own spies in Washington, and he was, as he had heard pilots of the RAF say, "somewhat pissed." Why was his company the very last to be invited to the party?

Johnson was a heavy man with a round, rather underboiled face. Usually there was a twinkle in his intelligent eyes, but they were subject to instant change, and the look of agreeable mischief burned up in the fire. He was the first to admit that on occasion he could be iron-headed. You got things done by bulldozing the opposition.

"We're looking for an airplane that can fly so high no one can touch it."

"That's pretty high," Kelly said flatly.

"Can you do it?"

"With enough money, we can do anything."

"How about thirty million dollars?"

"That should be a reasonable ante, but who's going to be the boss? I don't like working with committees."

"It will be you, a few generals here and there, and the CIA."

"No dice, Mr. President. That's too many."

"Don't be so damned difficult. All right, you'll be the boss."

The final division of authority became less simple.

Defense Secretary Charles Wilson had to be included in the program. Then Allen Dulles made a call to the White House. Soon one of the most secret programs ever inaugurated by the American government became the CIA's "Aquatone." Then, for reasons now lost somewhere in the jungle of Washington politics, Richard Bissell, an economist with limited aviation background, was chosen as the operational chief of "Aquatone." Kelly Johnson discovered that what had originally been an air-force project had been commandeered by the counterintelligence agency. The funding for the entire project was supplied from the ever-deepening pockets of that organization, and the authority behind the money was Richard Bissell.

From the very beginning Eisenhower had taken an uneasy view of the whole U-2 project. He needed intelligence, but he disliked the means of obtaining it. Suppose a U-2 was shot down in the wrong place? The Soviets were so damned *unpredictable*!

The air force's General Nathan Twining tried to reassure his president. Reconnaissance flights into Russian airspace had been routine for the last ten years. Why should the Soviets retaliate now?

Eisenhower grumped about the U-2 for days before he reluctantly consented. Even then he insisted it should not be flown by members of the air force. "I don't want to take the chance of an American soldier landing in Russian hands."

As a consequence, the pilots who were to fly the U-2s were removed from the air force and became employees of the Lockheed Company. They were paid with funds supplied by the CIA, and there was some question as to whom this innocent corporate cover actually deceived.

Johnson, energized even beyond his usual self, led his "skunk works"* troops relentlessly, and the results were unique in aviation history. His unequaled reputation and enormous persuasive powers carried the design through frustrations that might have caused lesser men to surrender long before metal was shaped. At Lockheed the aircraft was often referred to as the "Angel." The CIA, bound to deny that such an item even existed, dubbed it the "Article"; that made it easy to hide in their inventory. Article? Oh, yes, Article Number 341? It could have been a computer, or an air-conditioning system. But once the tools and dies were ready for action and the first Article was actually under construction, something more had to be done about maintaining a low profile for such a high-flying secret.

Enter a man named Tony LeVier, Lockheed's highly regarded chief test pilot. LeVier was a man of chosen words, and those were delivered softly. Johnson told him to find an operational base, which must be "a lot of nothing. We don't want any strange noses in our business."

LeVier searched until he found an isolated area in Nevada

*Inspired by Al Capp's "Li'l Abner" comic strip.

known as Groom Lake. He warned Johnson that it was the biggest stretch of nothing in the United States. It did have a dry lake offering a similar surface to that of Edwards Air Force Base, where LeVier had made many test flights, and it was near enough to the Atomic Energy Commission's nuclear-test site to borrow their tight security.

Soon hangars, shops, and housing for personnel were built and a runway laid out on the dry lake bed. The desert heat gave a searing welcome to the first Article, which arrived in carefully shrouded pieces from the Lockheed plant. The assembly took a week, and the Article was ready to fly.

Kelly Johnson had modified his original presentation. The tips of the huge wings were now supported by the "pogo sticks" until the U-2 was airborne, and there was still some question whether they would drop away as intended. And the Article did now have landing gear, albeit only a pair of very small main wheels projecting from the middle bottom of the fuselage and another, even smaller pair beneath the tail.

As launch day approached, Johnson kept insisting that LeVier should land the U-2 "on the wheels" and nearly in a flying attitude. Patience fried on the hot desert griddle; an inevitable difference of opinion arose between two strong-minded men.

"Take a good look at your damned airplane," LeVier said. "Get your chin off the drawing board and look at what we really have. Landing in a flight attitude just won't work. This bird won't quit flying in anything but a stall landing. Otherwise it'll wind up in Mexico or Nebraska."

"Maybe I should find some guy who will do it my way. We can't afford the chance of a hard landing at this stage of things."

LeVier wiped the sweat on his forehead and squinted at the dazzling sun. Then he walked thoughtfully in a slow circuit around the Article, assessing its figure as a sculptor might regard the figure of a model for the first time. He had made this same encirclement many times before, because he knew airplanes usually flew the way they looked. He was having a hard time becoming acquainted with this aircraft, which failed to resemble any flying machine he, or anyone else, had ever seen. The fancy drawings were history; here was the fact.

LeVier paused on the side of the U-2 opposite Johnson. He was beginning to recognize those special sensations peculiar to a first flight. It did something to your guts no matter how many new planes you tried. The soothsayers with their computers were usually right, normally almost all the predicted numbers and events went as scheduled, but there was always the unforeseen. How many funerals had LeVier attended because some little detail had foxed the engineers?

The initial taxi tests had not been particularly encouraging. During one high-speed test the Article became airborne before LeVier had any intention of flying, and he'd had his hands full taming his charge. And he had complained of the runway, which had no markers of any kind to aid his depth perception. "It's going to be like landing on a glass plate with the sun in my eyes." Johnson knew very well he had the best test pilot in the world, and he wanted to keep him happy. "You must be getting old," he had told LeVier, "we'll put some markers out for you."

But Johnson had a way of not hearing what he did not want to hear, and despite his respect for LeVier, who now stood on the other side of the Article, Johnson was convinced that Johnson was right.

"Put it down on the wheels," he repeated. "Just fly it right on down. It's my airplane."

"It's my ass."

Considering the elaborate preparations that led to this momentous flight of August 1955—the consultation, planning, drawing, rejecting, funding, and politicking that had gone into the U-2 project—it was remarkable that no one found even an ironic simile when two of the aviation community's most respected members stood bickering so resolutely about how to land something that was not supposed to exist.

LeVier was still wary when he made a perfect takeoff and climbed for an easy altitude. There he checked all the systems, cycled the landing gear, felt out the stalls in various configurations, and generally acquainted himself with the flying temperament of this new airplane. Solicitous as a mother hen, Johnson followed his progress in a chase plane piloted by Bob Matye.

At last LeVier started his landing approach. Johnson's rasping voice sounded almost continuously in LeVier's headphones.

"Looking pretty as can be, Tony. She's just beautiful to behold from this distance."

"She's a nice lady. Somebody must have done something right."

"Modesty forbids my proper response to that. Now don't forget. On the wheels, Tony."

"I'll give it a go."

As LeVier descended toward the floor of the desert, he found he had even less depth perception than he had hoped for. The two parallel strips of masking tape he had placed across the windscreen were of some help, but he was still feeling for the ground when he realized the main wheels had touched.

Hello! He experimented ever so gently with the control yoke. The Article failed to display any notion of abandoning flight. It sailed right across the dry lake and kept on going without any significant loss of airspeed.

"I'm going around."

Johnson's voice climbed right along with the steep reascent. "You were going too damn fast!"

"I was right on the book."

Once more LeVier lined up for an approach and kept his airspeed according to drawing-board convictions. And once more he touched down so smoothly that only a miniature spit of dust beneath the belly of the Article confirmed contact. The Article bounced into the air and kept on flying.

LeVier swore as he aimed for the heights again. In his earphones he could hear Johnson discussing the situation with Bob Matye, who slipped the chase plane in below for a look at the Article's belly. Johnson wanted to be sure the little landing gear was properly extended. "Everything looks good, Tony. You want to try it a little slower this time?"

"Yes, by God. And it will be a full-stall landing."

"Ton-e-e-e." Johnson's voice took on a plaintive note. "That's not a flatiron you're flying. . . ."

"I almost wish it was."

LeVier was not happy. Something was wrong, if he was to believe the tingling along the back of his neck.

A third approach. This time for sure, LeVier was going to land this fine bird his way. He circled the landing area once and then settled into a long, easy glide, keeping the nose down until he was skating along the dry lake surface. The J-57 engine was throttled back as far as it would go. Then at last he eased the nose up and hauled the yoke back into a full stall. He felt the tail wheel touch an instant before the main gear and knew he was, at last, in charge.

LeVier's pattern for successfully landing U-2s became the pride and frustration of an entire generation of airmen. And no one, except the still dubious Eisenhower, had any idea that this strange flying machine would inaugurate a debacle and change the course of history.

❖

It was the first of May 1960 when Francis Gary Powers, an "employee" of the CIA, was flying a U-2 over Russia. There is still debate over the cause of the disaster that flight initiated.

Powers said he heard a thudding explosion and the airplane started to come to pieces. The Soviets claimed that one of their missiles had brought him down, but there was some doubt that they had such a missile then operational.

There was the very real possibility that the overweary Powers might have dozed off while the automatic pilot got him into aerodynamic trouble.

A U-2 at high altitudes has a very tender "throat" between stall and mach buffet, and a quick temperature change or turbulence aloft can induce either one. The result can bring about the very sudden destruction of the aircraft. No less than three U-2 pilots flying over the United States had experienced almost identical events; as their airplanes came apart, they lost control but ejected successfully.

Powers denied that an engine flameout could have been responsible for his crisis, yet it could have happened for the same aerodynamic reasons and he would have been obliged to descend to a lower altitude for a restart. He would then have been within range of Soviet missiles and even gunfire.*

It will never be certain why Powers was rather shy about the details of his catastrophe. He bailed out instead of ejecting because, he said, he was afraid with so much tumbling about, the choice of ejection might break both his legs. It is impossible to debate the wisdom of his decision or argue that he had one. Those who have experienced the enormous "g" forces in a tumbling piece of airplane know that survival of any kind is a matter of seconds, and reasoned contemplation is nearly impossible.

Yet Powers was a cool hand with an airplane, if not so much so with his marital problems. His rather stormy marriage troubled

---

*He bailed out at twenty-five thousand feet.

him, particularly on the morning he sat on the runway at Peshawar in Pakistan, waiting forty minutes for direct approval from the White House.

Eisenhower was still president then, and authorized each flight individually. When at last Powers was released, he left the boiling heat below and climbed toward his goal. He was to fly over Tyuratam, the Soviet cosmodrome and missile base, then on to Chelyabinsk, Kirov, Plesetsk, and finally to a secret landing base at Bodø in Norway. It was the last flight Eisenhower intended to authorize.

Powers knew before he suited up that he was in for a difficult day. An eleven-hour flight in one of the old pressure suits was an ordeal in itself, since they were much more primitive than those used today. Worse, that particular U-2 he was flying was known as a bad-luck airplane. It had several times proved itself an aggravating lemon.

And there was worse. Like the other military pilots "borrowed" by the CIA, Powers had seen glistening new Russian fighters climbing toward him and coming too close to his altitude for comfort. Additionally there were reports of new missiles capable of reaching U-2 altitudes and seeking out any intruders. The glory had worn off these missions, and it looked like reality was coming on fast.

While the CIA was delighted with the information the black planes had gathered regarding nuclear test ranges at Novaya Zemlya and Semipalatinsk, and such targets as the Alma-Ata weapons plant, President Eisenhower's balancing of risk against worth was as skeptical as that of the pilots.

It was all very well for people in Washington to suggest that in case of the "unfortunate unforeseen" (intelligence jargon for anything other than a peaceful flight), the pilot should throw one switch to arm the destruct system and a second switch that would blow up the Article. There would be a seventy-second delay while the pilot presumably departed. The glitch was that the scenario stopped there.

After separation of man from his machine, what then? While the pilot was floating down from seventy thousand feet to land, God only knew where, he would have plenty of time to contemplate his precarious future. Powers was no different from the others in his lack of enthusiasm for the CIA's solution if he landed amid a hostile society. He was supplied with a silver dollar that had undergone some meticulous restyling. It could be split into two pieces; inside was a small needle that in approximately one minute could spare the owner the agony of torture—or anything else.

On this last and fateful flight Powers took his dollar with him, and after the Russians captured him they injected the needle into a dog. Forty-five seconds.

Powers also carried a paper authorizing his entry into American military airports, which hardly surprised the Russians. So much for CIA covers.

What Eisenhower had most feared became a thundering reality. And it could not have occurred at a worse time, on the eve of a summit meeting in Paris starring Khrushchev, British Prime Minister Harold MacMillan, de Gaulle of France, and Eisenhower. The atmosphere just prior to Powers's fateful flight had been all lavender and rose; the president of the United States and the leader of the Union of Soviet Socialist Republics had become "friends," with laudatory pronouncements flowing freely between them. The Cold War was dead and all the world looked forward to real progress in disarmament agreements at the Paris meeting. Even a beautiful era of nonthreat was envisioned by the optimists in the diplomatic world. Alas.

Khrushchev was furious, and hollered that he had been personally betrayed by a man he had trusted. If Eisenhower was not responsible for Powers's flight, then who was? The evil American military was obviously running the country, and the president was but a figurehead. Khrushchev waved his fat fists dramatically and cried that Eisenhower must kneel before him with apologies and promises that such intrusions would never be repeated.

Khrushchev had recently paid a rather wild and woolly visit to the United States, and Eisenhower wondered why his new adversary had not brought up the U-2 flights during one of their meetings at Camp David. Now, Khrushchev had a great deal going for his side of the argument. "What," he inquired with justified sourness, "would happen if a Soviet airplane flew across the United States photographing Cleveland, Chicago, Denver, and whatever military installations happened to be along the way?"

The answer was known to everyone who had the slightest knowledge of the air-force defense system. It would be shot down the moment it entered American airspace.

The ebullient Khrushchev smelled blood, as well as treachery. He deliberately and vociferously destroyed the Paris summit, and Eisenhower, who had hoped in the last of his White House days to bring about a true détente, went home brokenhearted. Khrushchev continued the affair with relentless determination. He had a prize exhibit that he intended to exploit to the utmost. Here on the Soviet threshold, alive and breathing, was the worst of scoundrels, an American spy. Radio Moscow described Powers as the "bondsman of the Rockefellers and Morgans, who turn the tears of the mothers of the world into gold."

On his part Eisenhower admitted the U-2 flights were "illegal and in fact immoral," but he was damned if he would admit they were "aggressive." He canceled all U-2 flights over other countries.

While Powers's behavior before the Soviet kangaroo court was not that of a resolute martyr and since he did have a very human reluctance to be shot as a spy, he gave his captors information, though as little as he could manage. Since the revelation of American perfidy was so juicy and created such worldwide interest, Powers's trial was milked for months and was only terminated when the United States agreed to exchange a Soviet spy for their hapless aviator.*

The Powers U-2 affair caused even more rumples in the pages of history. In his memoirs Khrushchev himself said that from the day the black bird was shot down, he was obliged to share his powers with comrades who believed only in military solutions for international disagreements and he was never able to halt the trend.

That presumptive doctrine has been used for generations as an excuse for war.

If Eisenhower or any subsequent American president ever seriously entertained the hope of "open skies" over all nations, the concept now expired without an audible sigh. Soon satellites would make the sectioning of territorial air impossible. Whether we liked it or not, we were at last, from a universal peephole, one little world.

---

*Powers was not the luckiest of men. He was killed in a routine helicopter flight in 1977.

Three:

The Men

When a cabinetmaker draws his blade, lovingly, the sensuous feel of the wood beneath his calloused fingers gives him something he cannot explain. It is not so simple as pride in workmanship. A commercial fisherman sets his lines, and always does so expectantly, though he may be cold and sometimes not a little afraid; he has learned to mistrust the sea, and at the end of each season he swears he will never go near it again, and at the beginning of each season he is back. Likewise a farmer whose perpetual battle with nature is frustrated by the economics of his labors, or the endless demands of his place—he continues somehow a step or two ahead of foreclosure and he tells himself that he should know better because his father did the same and so did his grandfather. Some scientists are equally abstruse in their devotion, as are the majority of working artists; they continue to prostrate themselves until they can no longer see, or hear, or touch the ordinary in life.

They are obsessed, and it is a state that survives and even flourishes on denial. We cannot continuously lie with our love, because if we do the fire of enchantment falters and eventually becomes cold. All artists know this, and some aviators. A very few consciously seek a substitute, but the large majority simply allow a rival interest to take center stage now and then, providing the basic scenery is not changed. Yet although we may temporarily turn away from obsession, recapture is inevitable and tends to become all the more binding.

Flying is an almost fierce obsession. For the true believer it leaves only crumbs of the heart for other things. Old-timers smile wickedly and say it must have something to do with the grandeur of the view that inspires a sense of superiority.

Yet bluster is never acceptable in any air society. There is always a distinctive shyness to be found in good pilots and it was typified in Driskill, the commander of the 99th Squadron. He was a man who took all things in his easygoing, long Texas stride. "Hay-ell, what we do today won't make the slightest difference to anyone in the air force a hundred years from now." It was one of his favorite pronouncements. Laid-back, man. Guys who got excited were soon flat dead.

Driskill's brows were heavy and dark, overhanging porticoes transmitting their own signals on those rare occasions when he allowed himself to become riled. His heavy, gray-flecked hair was combed carefully over his right temple. Somehow his conservative haircut gave him an air of stiffness, which was the antithesis of the relaxed man wearing the olive-brown potato sack that the air force dignifies as a "flame-resistant flight suit." But even the drab flight suit failed to conceal Driskill's natural beauty. Although his features were somewhat heavy, his cheekbones and wide lips flanked perfectly white teeth. He was vaguely aware that his smile sparked warmth in both men and women, yet vanity was not in him. When there were moments to view himself in a mirror, he did so with purpose, not in admiration. Other matters were of much greater concern to Driskill.

There was, first of all, the everyday necessity of twisting his way through the wilderness of military bureaucracy. Better men than Driskill had been entangled in the vines of regulations; some he had known were never seen or heard from again.

One of Driskill's many escape routes from paperbound trivialities was his deliberate attempt to become a thinking soldier. He had read his Clausewitz many times, and while he frequently disagreed with that boy-soldier's dictums, he found him remarkably astute for his time. Why, dadgummit, the purpose of any military establishment had always been to win wars, but from now until a possible doomsday, its only excuse for being was to prevent war. Or so the high brass was fond of proclaiming. Nice bullshit, but at least it smoothed the ugliness of a missile or a belt of fifty-caliber bullets.

But for Lieutenant Colonel Larry Driskill there had never been any gain in brooding about the things he had seen in Vietnam. He was sure that hidden somewhere deep beneath every uniform was the ancient call of the warrior. Why, hay-ell, people just would not stop killing each other, no matter how much grief was involved. Even a dumb lieutenant colonel could see that.

Driskill's eyes ventured reluctantly to his "in" basket. Full. Goddamned paper-pushers destroying American forests just to keep a constant cover over their asses. You couldn't even take off these days unless the paperwork grossed out the same weight as the airplane.

There were times, like this morning, when Driskill wondered what he was doing in a windowless office, with government-issue air-conditioning that operated at either equatorial or arctic temperatures, never in-between. His office was part of the many in the enormous apricot-colored building wherein innumerable compartments and hallways, labeled by department, were supposedly keeping order in the air wing. Strangers, Driskill thought with a certain deep satisfaction at the incongruity of all government housing, could get lost in here for hours. This intelligence fortress was supposedly impregnable—not quite so, Driskill was often reminded. Entrance to the U-2 establishment was through black doorways secured by combination locks, which advertised that something very secret must be going on inside. Any half-resolute spy or traitor might sneak in at night and riffle through all the top-secret papers he wanted . . . if he could find any. And in the daytime, if you were not privy to the combination, or had forgotten it, someone with a better memory was bound to come along and let you in. There were no security guards, and a reasonably cautious visitor could spend an entire day inside without challenge.

Driskill crossed his long legs and allowed his mind to drift toward squadron matters. Should he send Fusco to Korea rather than to Fantasy Island? How about pulling Boudreau out of there a week early so he could be home in time to hold his wife's hand while she had their first baby?

The commander of the 99th Squadron waggled his head in a slow circle. Dadgummit, this flying a desk took away stiffness where a man should know it and as compensation gave him a stiff neck. If he didn't crash the desk, chances were he would make full colonel in another year or so, and that would do nice things to a pension. Carrot before the mule, air force style. As for ever making general? Forget it. General's stars were for West Pointers or Air Force Academy graduates, unless you got incredibly lucky . . . and who wanted it? Generals rarely found a chance to fly.

Driskill leaned forward and peered into his "in" basket again. His gesture was that of a man discovering a rattlesnake in its nest. Two hours' work right there. Two hours gone out of the life he had nearly lost so many times in Vietnam he had long ago lost count. The future then for a forward air controller (FAC) was about as dubious as a man could choose. Here today, gone to the morgue tomorrow—if they ever found what was left of you. Now, he was paid off in paperwork and a chance to fly. For that reward he was supposed to sit up like a nice little tin soldier and do the clerical thing. In addition, if you please, a squadron commander had to be a diplomat, an autocrat, and a laid-back democrat all at the same time. A whiz in a potato sack, playing father to young guys going overseas for their first time. He had the speech down pat now. A regular dadgummed litany. "You're going TDY.* Don't forget who you are. Before you fall in love or do something foolish, think a minute. Remind yourself that those pretty little faces belong to gals who are brought up in a different society. Bringing one back here might not work. They might be very unhappy as transplants, and they grow old just like the rest of us."

Driskill blew a large balloon of bubble gum between his beautiful teeth. And he thought, By God, no matter how you slice it, this was the greatest job in the air force and maybe the whole dadgummed world.

Hard by Driskill's office is the 99th's "Heritage Room." It shares the same eccentric air-conditioning system, and like so many other facets of the U-2 world, it is not supposed to exist. Despite its questionable reality, various aeronautical artifacts are there for the believers. On one wall there is a photograph of a church steeple complete with the ancient homily, "Son, observe the time and fly from evil." After certain overly festive occasions, various U-2 pilots are said to have stared at the photo long enough to temper their actions for as much as twenty-four hours.

Featured on a makeshift bulletin board in elaborate calligraphy is "Yea, tho I walk thru the Valley of Death, I will fear no evil . . . for I'm at 60,000 feet and climbing." Nearby on another wall, there is a large oil painting of a U-2 flying over what might be the Egyptian desert. Next to it is a clock with the hands set permanently at 1630, the usual quitting time for government employees, whether in uniform or not.

*Temporary duty elsewhere than assigned base.

One end of the Heritage Room is flanked by a bar, which is reminiscent of First World War squadron counters where dashing young aviators forgot their ordeals over the Western front. It is devoid of the usual accoutrements. As if to ease such austerity, someone has hung a large poster behind the bar that depicts the frontal area of a nude female in great detail. It is reversible, and the opposite side displays what was presumably the same lady's cream-puffed rump. That side is turned out before the arrival of visitors whose libido might be considered less than most U-2 pilots'.

Driskill has never approved of the poster. "It lacks class," he has been heard to say. Female officers and perhaps the occasional female guest might be offended by it.

When the poster first appeared, Millington, about to leave for assignment in England, dared to challenge him. "Since when is the torso of a beautiful female in bad taste? All the great artists have painted them since time began. If we can't afford a Rubens, we gotta settle for less."

"Because the rest of this world is not necessarily horny, like some people we know," Driskill slowly replied. "Ain't you ever heard of feminine liberation? They hate that sort of thing."

Driskill only used "ain't" during his deliberate down-to-earth moments, those times when it seemed appropriate to close the gap between himself as commander and the regular line personnel. He sometimes added an "h" to the beginning of his utterance, making a "h'ain't," which supposedly reassures the listener that he is really just a poor, small-town boy from Texas. The affectation is startling from a man otherwise so well-spoken—which is exactly the reaction he's after. There are many ways to capture a man's attention.

There is always beer on tap at the end of the bar, and normally there are two large boxes of peanuts within easy reach. The beer supply and meeting the enormous quantity of peanuts consumed daily (as much as two cases), are the province of the most junior officer in the squadron, whether he wants the duty or not.

Driskill's day terminated with a final flourish of paperwork, and he was usually expected to pause in the Heritage Room before going home. He leaned his long potato-sack suit against the bar, and one of his squadron mates handed him a beer in a paper cup. Driskill was then at least momentarily content. For here in this slightly muggy atmosphere he was surrounded by friends he knew well. Here, gathered about him and clad in identical potato sacks, were Fusco, Napolitano, Kelly, and Kishler of the training squadron, and Van Heeswyk, just returned from Korea, and Castle, Cross, George, and Marquardt, veteran U-2 pilots all.

Here was his flock, Driskill thought, as the first sip of beer tingled along his tongue. It was not his job to keep them out of trouble, but he must never refuse to listen to their troubles. As for close relationships, a good commander could go just so far before he had to turn his back. Having favorites was no way to run a squadron. The camaraderie was there, thank God, a powerful inner sense that could make guys endure incredible trials, but commanders did not have buddies. How satisfying it would be if he could tell someone of his own frustrations. But that would be inconceivable, of course. A commander did not have problems. The law of leadership said so. It also decreed that a leader be lonely and never discuss personalities, no matter what the temptation. Each man was part of the unit, and to compare one against the other, except in the most secret recesses of his mind, was the way to disaster. No mere squadron commander could bitch openly about the wing commander, who Driskill had long ago decided had an absolute genius for getting under his skin.

Driskill reached for a fistful of peanuts and found the box nearest him empty. "What the hay-ell is this?" He turned pompously on Hudson, the most junior of his officers. He arched his heavy eyebrows and allowed the timbre of his voice to suggest disgust. A sudden silence fell on the room as he asked, "Is there something I should know? Is it possible that the mess has run out of funds for the simple things in life . . . or have the farmers down Georgia way quit growing peanuts? Exactly how are you going to explain this situation?"

Hudson, a shy man with jowls, bowed his head as if in shame. "In five seconds, sir, the situation will change." He stooped immediately, brought up a large carton, tore off one end, and poured a cascade of peanuts along the bar.

Driskill bared his magnificent teeth in a forgiving smile. Little things, he thought, made for good squadron mates. And here in the Heritage Room, he reminded himself, a man could rest his soul in piles of peanut shells and go on and on with tales of his affair with U-2s. Here was the place to communicate with others in the same black business. He could lie outrageously and be understood, if not believed, and he could say things that could not be said anywhere else in the world, or in any other company, without risk of treason. For each man here carried a top-secret clearance, and each man, whether he liked it or not, was essentially a spy.

Driskill turned about and rested his elbows on the bar. His gray-blue eyes held a touch of weariness at this time of day—too much dadgummed paperwork again, but he took a nostalgic pleasure in surveying the memorabilia on the walls. There was the drag chute from a U-2 that had flamed out over Korea. The pilot had done everything wrong, then bailed out successfully, then went and got himself killed in another U-2 three months later. God had funny ways.

There was that life ring from a Cypriot-registered ship found on, of all places, a beach in Korea. There was the ship's bell with the rope fashioned of old squadron mufflers, beside it a photo of Tony LeVier (not sitting on the right hand of God, where he probably should be), and there was a collection of group photos from the past—old guys, some of them dead, some gone to staff jobs, some metamorphosed into civilians and fat.

Driskill liked the placard on the bulletin board, which exclaimed in bold letters, "It's tough to think about the future when you're so busy changing history."

This is home, Driskill thought, where the real world is kept outside the door. More guys were arriving to sip a beer before starting for their official domiciles—the places where they stashed wives and children while they devoted themselves to their unique jobs.

Now, easy of mind from the beer, Driskill asked himself if the men about him were aviators first and spies second, or vice versa?

One of the veteran citizens of the Heritage Room was absent that evening. Musholt, Driskill's deputy commander, was in the air on a routine test flight. A U-2 had just come out of overhaul, and all the systems needed checking.

Musholt was a big, quietly genial man with a passion for every variety of personal electronics. His large hands caressed the keys of a desktop computer tenderly, as if he would arouse some lovely creature within the machine and make her his own. There was always a pronounced shyness about Musholt that emphasized the contrast between his bulk and the cool dexterity with which he treated an airplane. And there was a certain ageless quality about him; his boyish grin obscured the fact that he was one of the older veterans in U-2s.

Musholt carried a certain detachment about him. It often seemed as if there was a flicker of melancholy in his soul, a longing he tried to shake off but could not. This test flight was a welcome change in Musholt's day; like Driskill and so many others in administrative jobs, he found even the anticipation of flight recharged his spirits.

Now, as the ocher disk of the California sun slipped behind a layer of stratus, Musholt made a normal takeoff. Since this was not to be a "high" flight, he was wearing the standard potato sack and an ordinary flight helmet instead of a goldfish bowl.

The U-2 accelerated as expected, and he eased back on the yoke for a conservative climb. Musholt knew better than to initiate the stunningly steep climb of the U-2 when it had just been taken to pieces and put back together again. Sometimes little things were overlooked by the most devout mechanics, and wise men do not provoke risk.

At twenty-three thousand feet Musholt found himself enveloped in an amber twilight gloom while all below was now in darkness.

He was high enough to begin the tasks for the flight. Aileron control? Elevator response? Rudder? All normal.

Musholt smiled as he eased back on the throttle, a fist-sized lever on his left. There was a nice feel to this airplane, and who would not smile when sliding so swiftly through this solitary world?

His smile faded. He pulled back the power to level off, yet the U-2 kept accelerating. Still 92 percent power? What had he eaten to suffer such a cuckoo illusion?

He retarded the throttle a trifle more. No change. Here now! A runaway U-2? Incredible.

He pulled the throttle all the way back, yet the U-2 continued a rapid climb toward the heavens. Hey! The power percentage gauge had not moved. Musholt shook his head in disbelief. Good-bye to twenty-three thousand. Hello, thirty.

Musholt's usual Buddhalike calm persisted, although his breathing rate increased slightly. He tinkered with the throttle. The lever was missing connection somewhere, but that discovery would not solve the problem.

And it was a problem. A vexer. A rock and a hard place, but then he had been in many sticky situations before; which was why he was the deputy commander of the 99th and a lieutenant colonel.

If he pushed the U-2 over into level flight, it was bound to exceed its design speed, which could be disastrous.

Discretion, he was reminded, is often just a lack of choice.

Doctor, lawyer, artist, farmer; there comes a time in every professional's life when previously reliable factors twist out of form and crumble. The surgeon operates on a heart patient. He is halfway through cutting the sternum, when his magic electric saw stops. A fractured wire? Here is a spare. The spare fails to work. A circuit breaker has tripped. Time passes until it is discovered, time when the patient's heart is exposed to the elements. The "snowballing" begins and may or may not become an emergency.

Musholt became stingingly aware that without a pressure suit or proper helmet he must soon stop climbing. He also knew that if he started a descent with the engine producing full power, it would not be long before his beautiful flying machine disintegrated. It would become a victim of "snowballing," one thing leading to another and all combining to produce serious trouble.

The U-2 was behaving like a bird escaped from a cage.

Like most professionals, Musholt was convinced that independence was holy. The first commandment of the flying faithful proclaims that you are your own savior when things go wrong. Calling for help is futile; no one except an overburdened God can reach out to help you. Radio can bring the dubious assurance of another human's voice and sometimes useful advice, but the ultimate performer is you.

Musholt frowned and pressed the microphone switch on the control yoke. "Oakland Center. Requesting a higher altitude." What else? There was no real choice.

"Name it." Oakland Control Center, which managed the airspace in the region, knew Musholt was flying a U-2 and had already cleared an area of sky for his testing. They expected him to operate above the usual airliner traffic.

"Request clear me on through to level four-five-zero. I seem to be having a little problem. . . ."

"Cleared to flight level four-five-zero. No significant traffic in your area. State the nature of your problem."

"Stand by."

The U-2 continued a runaway ascent. The throttle was useless. Musholt ceased experimenting with it. He was absorbed in finding some controlled escape. And as in all emergencies, things were happening just a little too fast. Here was forty thousand already and sailing right on by.

Declare an emergency? There was something that rankled about declaring an emergency. It stained the notion of independence. It implied that some stranger sitting before a radar screen could reach out and do anything at all about a problem that is all yours. Even so, he had best advise Beale Control; the duty guys there understood U-2s.

Musholt was aware of a slight catch in his voice. Time was racing. Here was an airplane taking command of the commander.

"I think the throttle connection is busted, or something has come unhinged in the fuel metering system."

"What are your intentions?"

"I'd like to make a successful return to earth." Musholt was puzzled at the sarcasm in his voice. It was not his habit. Was it because a whiff of fear had slipped into the cockpit undetected? Or was he putting on an act—which was also not his habit?

"I'm returning to Beale."

"Now?"

"Affirmative. Now."

Musholt was appreciative of Beale Control. They had not asked just how he intended to return, or how he would manage to make an airplane go down that did not want to go down. They had not tried to fly the U-2 from the ground. He thought Driskill would still be in the Heritage Room at this hour. Good place to be. This promised to be an experiment best reviewed after the conclusion.

Now, he must do everything right, else the snowball would become much bigger. Outside temperature minus 70 degrees. Cockpit heat to maximum while you still have power. Generator off and all unnecessary electrics.

Fuel off. Ho-ho! Immediate and not unexpected results.

A sudden silence except for the soft whirring of the slipstream. Flameout.

There were the lights of Beale—fifty miles or so toward the horizon. Nice night for soaring.

Beale Control on the horn. ". . . no reported traffic. The field is all yours. Do you request emergency equipment?"

There was that word again. "Affirmative." Never mind. The cat was out of the bag now. They would have sent it out anyway.

"You're cleared present position direct Beale."

"Roger." What other path was there available to a powerless flying machine? There must be no grazing about the black pastures beyond the windscreen. Home. Sweet home. Keep same directly ahead.

Musholt knew he was about to attempt something that had not been done before in a U-2 and probably would not be done again soon. He must glide fifty miles to Beale—powerless. Altitude was money in the bank. He must spend his thirty-nine thousand feet like a miser now, eking it out to maintain flying speed, and maybe, with a great deal of luck, have enough left for a few tentative approaches in the air. Once over Beale he must do everything exactly right. A hesitation at the very last could see him crunched into the old gold-mine trailings near the north end of the runway; or too much speed at the last could shoot him right across Beale with no hope for a second try.

Musholt squirmed in his seat. He was surprised and somewhat offended that he had allowed tension to build in his spine. It was so quiet. A man had no business in an airplane with so little noise. It was like being embraced by something that had died.

Check "tacan," which was announcing the distance to Beale. Forty miles. A strange time for a sudden sense of security. So far not even a thought of punching out. A dead-stick landing at night was not so special. And maybe less dangerous than becoming a decoration dangling from a California redwood.

He had made a decision he knew was final. He would ride the bastard down.

Now, time seemed to hesitate. Beale was enlarging, bright as a Christmas tree. He could see the end of the runway now, and the sweeping green-and-white finger of light atop the control tower. Home.

How much money in the bank? Eight thousand feet and only six miles to go? Plenty. But no squandering.

He found cause to smile. He was fat. With the airport directly below, he still had six thousand feet. The moment of truth was about to arrive.

He circled the expanse of Beale, one time around in a gentle bank. Feeling things out. Too much altitude?

Five thousand. Four thousand. There was the mobile car on the end of the runway, red lights flashing.

Driskill's voice on the intercom. "How y'all doin' there, friend?"

"Reasonably good . . . considering."

"Don't bother with the tower. Everything is cleared for your landing."

Airspeed 140 knots. Three thousand. No time for a second circuit. Start base right now. Gear down. Throttle back? Humph. Nothing from nothing leaves nothing.

Driskill's voice. "We have you in sight. Looking good."

The difference between this landing and every other night landing was its finality.

He smacked his lips and twisted in his seat to settle himself.

Driskill's voice. "Still looking good. About one-half mile from the threshold . . . quarter mile . . . you're right in the groove . . . slip down a little."

The U-2 flashed past the revolving red lights on the mobile car.

"Fifty feet . . . forty . . . miles of runway yet . . . twenty . . . ten . . ."

Musholt landed on the first one thousand feet of runway and turned off on a taxiway without using the brakes. When the U-2 came to a halt and the left wingtip dropped down to the concrete, he sighed. As advertised. No extra cost to the taxpayer.

Quiet here. Only the dying whine of the gyros.

The following morning there was a mighty embarrassment among the airmen specialists responsible for the maintenance of Musholt's aircraft. Someone had failed to secure a pin in the throttle-linkage mechanism, and it had fallen out. The possible consequences were reviewed in polished invective by the crew chief, and the maintenance hangar was pervaded by gloom and strangely subdued voices for the rest of the day.

At the same time the crew chief was lecturing certain airmen on their questionable ancestry and clumsy fingers, the regular "stand up" staff meeting of the wing's departmental officers and squadron commanders was already in progress. It was held as usual in a subterranean conference room furnished with a long horseshoe table, government-issue executive chairs, a podium, and a public-address system.

It was a pentagon-shaped room, and trios of miniature flags were posted at intervals along the table. The colorful bouquets were the flags of the 9th Wing and the Strategic Air Command, flanking the national flag. The temperature in the room, at the mercy of the government-issue air-conditioning system, was chill—"Just right for penguins," one of the officers grumbled.

The room was illuminated through small holes in the ceiling, which only enhanced the doomsday atmosphere. It was difficult to believe that anything but events of stupendous and very secret magnitude might be discussed in such a locale.

"As you may be aware, the air-conditioning is on the fritz again," Pinsky announced with a frown.

Pinsky was a full colonel, and the commander of the 9th Wing. This morning, as usual, he was not entirely pleased with the state of his world. Driskill was fond of saying, "Hay-ell, there is no way to satisfy that man. He wants every damn little old thing to be super plu-perfect."

This morning Pinsky was also tired, a condition Driskill claimed was unnatural to the man. Most of Pinsky's officers agreed that he was overenergetic and inclined to belabor the prod, but they were obliged to admit that he had somehow managed to win every honor in the air force for the wing.

Today Pinsky had risen at four, flown for two hours, and was back at his desk before seven. "The guy doesn't know how to sleep," Driskill often commented. Now, Pinsky's ordinarily sallow complexion was matched by a slight slump about his broad shoulders. There were even moments when his powerful jaw slackened and his eyelids drooped, as if to protect his sight from the light over the podium. Except for the flying at dawn, which had at least provided a sense that something was right in the world (after all, the sun had risen on schedule), everything else this day had brought frustration. There was a crisis at the hospital because the new budget had reduced the rescue teams by ten men and the doctors were screaming. The tankers often carried passengers. If one crashed at Beale, God forbid, how could they handle it?

Next he had attended a court-martial involving several enlisted men charged with possession of drugs and two with drunken driving. Frustrating. They were all unsophisticated kids trying to be part of what they saw as the national scene. They wanted to join their peers, but the military was a handicap. If they had fought their way up from poverty, holding two jobs the way he had while trying to get an education, they would know an opportunity when they saw one. So he had told their deaf ears.

Then he had reviewed and tried unsuccessfully to memorize parts of the weekly speech by the Commander in Chief of the Strategic Air Command. Good stuff—some of it.

Just after his flight, while he was still pulling off his helmet, he had been tackled by the base deputy engineer, who wanted to file a charge claiming someone had been altering his performance record. There was bound to be a long and intricate investigation. Sometimes it seemed incredible that so many distantly related factors were necessary to get a few airplanes off the ground.

Now, at the staff meeting in the room that so resembled a funeral parlor, Pinsky surveyed the attentive faces of his officers. All except Driskill, he noticed—as usual. The man was off on some other planet just when he ought to be listening. Driskill thought too much. A time-waster.

Pinsky sighed, a rare gesture for him. The Pentagon was in his hair again. This day, this very damned day, when there was so much else going on, they wanted a written review of his antiterrorist plans for the base. There was also a quarterly report on retention . . . screw all the airlines for swiping his pilots. The chain of command was inexorable. If David Pinsky failed to keep young men in the air force, the brass would find someone who could.

"Lieutenant Colonel Driskill? I passed your place on the way to the flight line this morning and what do I see? Two rusty parking signs. It makes the whole area look like a slum. Clean it up."

"Yessir." Driskill's voice was as cold as the room.

"For reasons I won't disclose now, we're going to need ten more U-2 pilots by first June. If they go to work today, we're already behind in their training. Why don't we have more applications? I see the paperwork, but something happens in between the time they apply and the time they arrive here. I want to see some bodies. What do you say to that, Colonel Driskill?"

"It's sort of hard to explain, sir."

"What do you mean, 'it's hard to explain'? They just don't arrive here and evaporate. Who's looking after them when they get here? Does anybody give them the time of day? The wing needs pilots right now, damnit, and I don't have to tell you we're losing guys every day."

Pinsky favored Driskill with his best frown of disapproval. At stand-ups Driskill always managed to find a place at the very back of the room and seemed to be pretending that the wing's problems had nothing to do with him.

Pinsky raised his voice just in case anyone missed the import of his message. "I want a solution for our retention problem . . . right now. Would you care to start, Colonel Driskill?"

Driskill hesitated. "Well, sir . . . I can't give you a solution, but one explanation could be the wives."

Pinsky allowed an even deeper cloud to creep across his face. Ridiculous. Here he was, now a full colonel, listening with great patience to a mere lieutenant colonel, and here was Driskill offering one of his smart-ass answers. It seemed to make no difference that they had both been forward air controllers in Vietnam—they just damn well did not get along. One of these days there was going to be a new commander of the 99th Squadron. Or would there be, even sooner, a new wing commander?

Pinsky's thoughts drifted. A reminder to tell Wilson, the base commander, that the street gutters over by the recreation building needed cleaning. Details? Damned right. A man had to get down to the details or the whole wing would fall apart.

Obviously Driskill was going to let his facetious comment stand without apology. He was standing there in the shadows, his hands folded in front of him, leaning against the wall, just as if he had said something sensible. He was the kind of guy who just never would understand how complex the job of a wing commander could be. "Well . . .?"

Tomorrow noon, Pinsky suddenly recalled, he was due to make a speech at the local Rotary Club. He would have to find a gracious way to remind them that the payroll to the local community was now $113 million a year on a $334 million investment. There was no point in telling them that a request to SAC headquarters for a seventy-nine-hundred-dollar copying machine had been turned down after six months of shilly-shallying. "What's this comment about wives, Colonel Driskill?"

"It's simple enough, sir. An applicant comes here and he gets all steamed up and ready to go into training. Then his wife finds out he's going to spend at least half of his year overseas . . . and without her. When she hears that, she remembers the bank clerk she almost married instead of her intrepid airman, and she lays down the law. She doesn't want her man gazing up at some foreign moon when she h'ain't around to supervise the activities."

A muffled chuckling followed Driskill's words. Pinsky allowed it to subside and forced a smile. "Are you trying to tell me the wives are running assignments in the United States Air Force?"

"Yessir."

Pinsky shook his head like a boxer recovering from a blow. He wanted to say he didn't know what the country was coming to, but decided against it. He had an uncomfortable notion that Driskill was laughing at him, and there was nothing to be gained by giving him a second chance. Why didn't everybody understand that this wing was the winner of every damned trophy the air force had for excellence, and the reason was because a certain person took an interest in every detail and did something about it?

Pinsky referred to the daily operational schedule, of which every officer had a copy. "I see here that Colonels Driskill and Hinkle are due to lead a sortie of six T-38s* tomorrow to Patrick. What is the purpose of that flight, Colonel Hinkle?"

Hinkle was the commander of the 5th Strategic Training Squadron, and was highly regarded by his peers.

"Familiarization, sir," he answered solemnly.

Familiarization with what? As if Driskill and Hinkle and those with them were not well acquainted with every air base in the country—that is, the pleasant ones. Curious how such flights were never planned to North Dakota in the winter. Or Alabama in the summer.

And where would Pinsky be? The guy who had to keep all this machinery going. Swallowing his envy at the Officers' Club, where a ten-member accounting team from the Pentagon would be expecting a hearty welcome. In full dress uniform. Maybe he could persuade them to come through with a copying machine.

When the stand-up was dismissed, Driskill walked back to the apricot building, routing himself by the longest route so he might breathe fresh air for at least a few minutes. He tried to use as much time as he could for the transit, but his natural pace and long legs covered the distance all too quickly. He passed two other officers, returned their salutes, and then a pair of enlisted men. None of the salutes, including his own, were as crisp as they might be, Driskill decided, but perfection in formalities was not the way of the present-day air force—if it ever had been.

Greetings passed between officers or even between officers and enlisted men were likely to be a single "hi" or a "howarya?" A

*A splendid little twin-jet fighter-trainer. When posted at bases like Beale, they are intended to keep pilots of bigger operational airplanes current.

part of this conduct, he knew, was the hidden fear of behaving the jingo, plus the natural consequences of all-volunteer forces. And maybe, he thought, some of the looseness was because of the traditional American antipathy toward soldiers of any description.

Driskill looked off beyond the flight line where he knew the neighboring towns of Yuba City and Marysville were located. It was remarkable how the local population could almost ignore the existence of a huge air base in their neighborhood, even though they might take their full income from it and send their kids to schools at least partially financed by base expenditures. The plumbers and doctors and printers and launderers and bankers would have a hard time making ends meet if not for the base . . . and yet the same citizens would drive by without so much as a sidewise glance. Did they want to pretend it just was not there?

Driskill stood outside the apricot building and breathed deeply. Air, by God! Real, dadgummed God's air!

No wonder there was such a retention problem. There were times like these, when a man could not avoid considering leaving the military and finding another line of work. Americans did not honor uniforms. In fact, enlisted men were sometimes taunted by the local hoodlums, and their patronage was not welcomed by the local bars and restaurants unless they were wearing civvies. The Soviets, where every male had to spend two years serving the military, took the opposite attitude. They were proud to be seen in uniform.

So much for a chestful of medals. Get on with the day. It was up or out in the air force.

As Driskill climbed the stairs to his office, he thought about Pinsky. There was a man so dedicated to the "up or out" system that he had trouble understanding people who refused to be ruled by it.

Maybe Pinsky had become so blind to anything but his idea of perfection, so wrapped up in the multitude of problems that came to every wing commander, he had forgotten what life was like among the troops? People wanted some kind of solidity. Had it ever occurred to Pinsky that the most ubiquitous sight on an air base was the moving van? Promotions meant the transfer of a man and his family to somewhere else. He and his family lived like gypsies, trying to put down roots at every new assignment and never quite succeeding. Sometimes the move was to a pleasant place, and other times to a "hardship" post. And may the fairy-princess computers of the Pentagon not send him off to a nonfly-ing job.

No wonder the temptations to become a civilian and start a life you could call your own were almost irresistible.

If a man joined the air force to fly, that's what he should be doing. It was one obsession that only made it tougher to take a desk job . . . which was "up." The higher the "up," the less chance for flying. Generals wept when they saw a young lieutenant blast off in a hot fighter—or almost any other kind of flying machine.

Still, it always happened. The pattern was unbreakable, dad-gummed hard-riveted. Sooner or later a bird found his flight boots crunching pebbles. His children, who once saw their hero taking off for the wild blue, now saw him coming home with the grumps. His flight suit hung mildewing in the closet, and the spark was gone from his eye. His wings were still on his uniform blouse, but they only reminded him of a life he had once known—a round of sunlight and rain and the inspiration of star-filled nights viewed from his very private observatory.

Driskill heard a quick series of steps on the stairway behind him. He turned to see Kinego, commander of the SR-71s.

"What's the hurry, friend?"

"I'm late and I've got a launch."

"Lucky you."

"Amen."

Then Kinego was gone, and Driskill understood his haste. It was tough luck that the SR-71s were so expensive to fly. The pessimists were predicting they would be mothballed in the near future.

Poor Kinego and all the others like him. He was on his way "up." Soon, too soon, he would be bound to some desk job with a pair of eagles on his shoulders. He would be rattling his chains and watching the clock and dreaming of his days flying a sled.

It was as the whore's mother once said, a fate worse than death. A perfectly good flying officer obliged to go home like any other government employee (right on the dot, ma'am, here I am), and he takes off his uniform as fast as he can because melting into the groundling routine is easier without reminders of a better life.

A man was never the same once he regarded the earth from very high altitudes. Kinego had forty years on him. If he survived to be at least eighty, what in God's name could he do with the second half of his life to match the first?

Driskill often scolded himself for not telling the full story to applicants for a seat in U-2s. He had never told any of them that after a few years flying he might be barricaded behind a collection of government furniture. When the applicant came to him, it was all happy soaring along the fringes of space; good talk between airmen, but where that would eventually lead to was just not mentioned. The 99th Squadron needed the best of available pilots. It was just dadgummed inconvenient the way everybody else, including the airlines, was crying the same song.

While Kinego brooded about the future of his expensive aircraft and Driskill schemed to find the best men available for his squadron, their ultimate executive authority remained with Jack Farrington, a genial, pipe-puffing two-star general. His office was in a spacious bungalow a few miles from the flight line.

Farrington was the son of a coal salesman, a onetime poor boy who, like Pinsky, worked his way through college and thence via the ROTC to the air force. His diction was that of a cultivated man, and there was not a syllable left on his tongue to suggest his Boston background.

There was also not a hair on Farrington's head, which gave him a remarkable resemblance to the late Yule Brynner. Fortunately he was not inclined to take himself as seriously as he did his job. Even so, Farrington was very aware that his two stars glistened with power only a little less formidable than his Maker's. He knew he could make or break an officer's career with a flip of his pen, and that enlisted airmen held him in such awe there was almost no relationship between his world and theirs. There was not intended to be. Democracy stops short of a general's flag.

Farrington was Pinsky's boss and Driskill's boss as well as Kinego's, Hinkle's, and all the other field-grade officers' on the base. That responsibility alone kept him reasonably busy, although he was not one to trouble himself with details. He was a "clean desk" man with a firm dislike of paperwork. "The only way the top brass can find to keep guys like me out of mischief is to do double time on the copy machine."

Despite his avowed dislike of matters in quintuplicate, Farrington was careful to keep himself informed on the infinite number of events going on around him. What the lieutenant knew, the captain must know, and what the captain must know, the major must know. Then the lieutenant colonel must know, followed by the colonels, until at last the general must know. It was unthinkable that the form should be violated.

Air force protocol says generals must know everything that can lead to some extremely embarrassing moments. Should a general of even more exalted rank phone Farrington and ask, "How are things going?," he must not stumble over an answer.

Today a crash truck turned over and injured three airmen. Why?

Today a tanker was late for a refueling rendezvous with an SR-71. What happened?

If Farrington found himself ignorant of troubles and said, "Things are just fine and dandy," he knew there would soon be another general sitting at his immaculate desk.

Farrington had an easy smile. "All military organizations are self-perpetuating," he was fond of declaring. "In peacetime the protection of an officer is based on the volume of paperwork per square lieutenant. All the military of every nation is a ponderous entity fearful of change. It was while the Duke of Wellington was fighting in Spain that he received a nasty note from the War Office in London. They had found he had not enumerated all the saddles, bridles, and tent poles of his army, and his accounts were one shilling and ninepence short. The old boy sent a letter back asking if they wanted him to train an army of uniformed British clerks, or see to it that the forces of Napoleon were driven out of the country."

Farrington had been in the spy business for a long time. He not only flew 154 combat missions in Vietnam, but was also involved in "sensitive ground missions" and "special operations," which is air-force mumbo-jumbo for intelligence work. He was a past master at playing "I've got a secret," and the noncommittal answer.

Like almost all air force generals, Farrington wore wings that announced that he had once been obsessed with flight. Pretty medals of all kinds proliferate in the air force, and tin stars do not always measure the true worth of the man who wears them. The wings do, and most airmen are convinced that anyone who has earned them can at least be trusted.

Although Farrington's trust in himself was obvious, he shared a perpetually nagging burden with the majority of other generals, particularly those engaged in the reconnaissance business. What if something really went wrong?

A fighter plane crashes? Regrettable, but part of the life. A tanker makes a wheels-up landing? Machinery can be repaired. A transport slams into a hill on final approach in bad weather? Terrible. The worst part is telling the families.

What must not happen was another sort of catastrophe. If one of the recce boys made a mistake . . . if somehow one of them strayed over the wrong place at the wrong time, then his error could develop into much more than an incident. It could conceivably change the history of the world.

This long-odds game put a special burden on all the young officers who might be involved, and remembering that each one was human did nothing to improve a general's sleep.

Farrington was acutely aware that there were good generals and bad generals. He also knew that the making of a general was unquestionably due to the staff he managed to assemble before a competitor took the cream. Once backed by talented officers, the drill was to appear extremely busy without actually doing anything drastic. In time of peace such ultraconservativeness was the signal of wisdom and perpetuation of self unto retirement. War might permit a bit more daring, but best leave the details to men like Pinsky, Driskill, and Hinkle.

For these and many other reasons Farrington accepted his role as a peace-keeper, a sort of referee between the numerous factions within the local military bureaucracy. There was the great god SAC (Strategic Air Command), which directly controlled the 9th Wing and the even greater and all-powerful god the Pentagon. All generals knew that if they seriously entertained the thought of bucking the system they would be chastised and thrown unceremoniously into the alien world outside.

Farrington is a good general because he believes in the code. And he keeps a constant guard against some high-in-the-sky lieutenant or captain provoking a calamity.

Because he is a squadron commander and so theoretically on

call at all times, Driskill is not permitted to live off the base itself. His residence is one of the reasonably pleasant little government-issue houses situated, along with many others of the same tract design, in the residential area of Beale. The kind of house any medium-level young executive might inhabit, although distinguished from its neighbors by a Texas flag at the front door.

As a squadron leader, Driskill had obligations other than his regular flying duties. He was not compelled but "requested" to host occasional social gatherings with his squadron mates and their wives, thereby fostering the philosophy that they were all one happy family. Although they were informal affairs, the successful mix of squadron members and wives called for delicate handling, if only because the gypsy life they all led made it difficult for the wives to establish enduring relationships with other wives. The estrangement was amplified by the fact that so many of them worked at jobs outside the home and had little spare time for extraneous social events.

Pinsky was not invited to this gathering because he was not strictly a squadron member. And certainly not Farrington, who was also required to live on the base, although in a much bigger house.

No soldier of any army or nation can relax with a general hovering in the background. Even if he is out of uniform.

The small living room in the Driskills' house was furnished mainly in neo–Grand Rapids. Adjoining the living room was a cramped dining area with a round table in the center of it; tonight the table was laden with munchies traditional to the American cocktail pre-dinner time, but there was no rush to consume them. People were nursing their one beer or white wine until the glasses became sticky. No one asked for or was offered a second libation. Two military generations back, the guests would have been appalled at such decorum.

Everyone present wore civilian clothes, a metamorphosis for

the men that included a marked change in mannerisms and language. Each was somewhat ill at ease and overattendant on his wife. Would she say the wrong thing? Would she talk too much about the children and so bore the be-jesus out of everybody within range?

It was very hard for a man to maintain his hero image after the first years of an air force marriage.

Driskill was sprawled in his rocking chair, his cowboy boots extending enough into the living room to make a steeplechase barrier for his dog. If he were not playing host, Driskill would prefer something with a bit more pizzazz than a beer, but now he must be the fearless leader, and the younger men needed to know a saint when they saw one.

Yet he was reasonably content. Here were his favorite people. They were his scouts, and he knew they were as dedicated to their jobs as were similar hardy men who always preceded the van in conquest.

It had occurred to Driskill that since ancient times the scouts had been among the bravest of the brave. Alone, they ventured beyond the horizon and brought back precious knowledge. Why, hay-ell, the squadron motto was "Toward the Unknown."

All of nature's beasts and birds and fish are careful to designate scouts for the anticipation of danger. Watch a herd of cattle and see one apart from the herd. The scout.

See one robin wait alert while the others of his flock gorge themselves on fresh spring worms. The scout must not be distracted.

Watch a school of porpoises allow one to go ahead. He will return to advise the others of his discoveries.

Now, Driskill sat like a tribal chieftain as one by one his emissaries came to pay him homage. It was so mellowing to sit back among such attention and unspoken honors, without the ingredients to make either a fathead or a worthy leader. It was up to the recipient to remind himself that the world could get along just fine without him.

Each of Driskill's guests came and said a few words and then went away to rejoin the twenty people who, he was amused to see, were not listening to each other.

He saw Laidlaw approaching him. Valuable man. Longtime U-2 pilot with an excellent record, but quite some hell-for-leather fellow on the ground. He was so blond and handsome Driskill had often wondered if he just might be the incarnation of a Viking warrior. Easy smile.

Driskill saw that his face was slightly flushed and he was working his powerful shoulders as if to relieve himself of an intolerable burden. Had he stopped off at the Officers' Club for a snort before he arrived here?

"Boss, I got to talk to you. You're so busy down at the squadron, there hasn't been a good time."

"Okay, shoot. H'ain't nobody here going to hear a word you say, and I'm not sure I can."

"I have a problem."

"What else is new?" Driskill was suddenly wary. Laidlaw squatted on his knees beside him and his eyes became strangely intense. He handed Driskill a small piece of paper. "Would you mind reading this?"

"Now?"

"Yes. Now. It's called 'Rainbow Chaser.' "

Driskill scanned the paper. On it was typed a poem . . . something about the dragon lady's song, which was a nickname given U-2s in Vietnam, and something about dusk and dawn.

"Very good. I didn't know you had such a way with words."

"I didn't write it."

"Ah," Driskill thought. His wife. She was standing at the other end of the room, a tall, willowy woman who was said to be a talented inventor of profane riddles. As a consequence,

Driskill knew, his own Patricia had a little trouble accepting her.

"A dancehall girl wrote it," he heard Laidlaw say. Then he added almost shyly, "I'm in love with her."

"Spare me," Driskill said softly. What was this? He spoke not to Laidlaw, but to the photograph of himself in uniform that his wife kept on a table next to the couch. Medals and all. Carry-the-flag expression. The man in that photo did not look like a father confessor.

Laidlaw reached into his hip pocket and brought out his wallet. His fingers searched inside as he glanced toward his wife. Then he held out a photograph of a young woman in a sequined dress. It revealed the very prominent mammalian features of her torso without actually baring them.

"Humph," Driskill said, wishing he could think of a better comment. Maybe Ann Landers could.

"Isn't she beautiful? You won't believe how much I love her."

Was this some kind of game? Was Laidlaw about to launch some preposterous joke? Maybe something had gone wrong on his last high flight. Oxygen starvation. Brain damage. Could it be that one of those strange illusions every U-2 pilot witnessed now and then had so affected Laidlaw's inner being that he could not rid himself of the vision and had therefore somehow lost a sliver of his mind? "Well . . ." Driskill said, "there's nothing quite like being in love."

"The trouble is," Laidlaw answered with clear but unhappy eyes, "she lives with her boyfriend, which I don't like, and I live with my wife, who of course doesn't know about this."

Driskill looked across the room at Laidlaw's wife. Suzanne? No, Sue was her name. Here was a flaw in the system again. Dadgummit, why couldn't Laidlaw just stick to flying airplanes?

One of the unfortunate twists of an air force marriage was the direct result of "up or out." All officers were continuous students, whether they wanted to be or not. If they hoped to survive, they must attend various schools and add further letters to their college degrees. Sooner or later they would win their master's degree and then at least start working on a doctorate. Many of the courses and associations would have nothing whatsoever to do with the military, and unless the wife trotted right along with such obligatory self-improvement, she was bound to fall intellectually behind and then the bloom would begin to fade.

Still, Laidlaw was far from an intellectual, and if reports on his wife were true, she was one very astute woman.

Driskill leaned forward so he could not be heard by anyone except Laidlaw. "I assume you are aware that one photograph can do more damage than a bundle of letters?" He wished profoundly that Laidlaw had come to him with some rational suggestion to improve the squadron or perhaps tell of his last view of an aurora borealis from peak altitude. Instead, here was this uninspiring triangle. "This poetess," he said, wishing Laidlaw had chosen a more appropriate time, if ever there would be one, "I must say, she does have imagination."

Laidlaw reached out and took a firm grip on Driskill's forearm. "You really think so? Can I tell her you said that?"

Driskill eased his arm away. This sort of man-among-men exchange made him uncomfortable. There were certain rules to impropriety, and discretion was one of them. If a man was having an affair, he should do everything possible to keep it to himself.

And yet when he met Laidlaw's eyes, he could not reject him. Who dared judge his comrade?

"Don't get the idea she's a prostitute! No, no! She works in a dancehall nights because that allows her to go to school days and get her college degree. She wants to be a dentist."

For an instant Driskill wondered if he should pull a supreme cop-out and actually remind Laidlaw of his marital vows. No. His tongue would refuse such pomposity.

"What do you think I should do?" Laidlaw asked, and his eyes were still pleading.

At least the Laidlaws were childless, Driskill reminded himself. But where in the lonely eyes of this immature husband was a decision that would hurt no one? "If she has a live-in boyfriend, why is she involved with you?"

"She loves me."

Was there something wrong with this beer? Had Pat slipped a jigger of vodka into it?

"Has she told her boyfriend about you?"

"Yes."

"And they're still living happily together?"

"Yes. But he is very unhappy and he's going to move out."

"And you're going to move in?"

"That's the idea . . . eventually."

Driskill took a long swallow of his beer. What in tarnation was he doing in this conversation? Laidlaw was serious. And he was not just some swaggering philanderer. In fact, his sincerity was embarrassing. What the hell could be said?

"Your Sue? She doesn't love you?"

"She says she does, but she doesn't approve."

"Of what?"

"My flying. The air force . . . especially U-2s."

"And the poetess does approve?"

"She's crazy about airplanes and anything to do with them."

There it was. Right there. The crux of the trouble.

"Have you tried to change Sue's attitude about your job?"

"A thousand times. She says she didn't get married just to become a widow or have a husband who was away half the year."

Standard case. A few different trimmings but the same old story. The air force was doing its damndest to educate the wives, trying to include them, trying through demonstrations to show them what their husbands did for a living, but it wasn't working out very well. Among other things, the air force was discovering how hard it was to persuade anyone flying was safe, especially if you had some reservations about it yourself.

Laidlaw was a victim of an old aviation conundrum—one woman saw him as a hero when he was doing what he loved to do and the other identified as a villain, bound sooner or later to destroy her family's future in a ball of fire. It was all too easy to envision Laidlaw's sequined woman listening in awe to his flying stories and then his wife Sue nattering about the evils of flying, while emphasizing the glories of civilian life.

Driskill took another long swallow of his beer and shook his head. He surveyed the room and stood up slowly. "Okay! Anybody hungry? I think Pat managed to find a can of Mexican beans, so let's have some chili!"

There followed an immediate rise in the decibel level as the guests started moving toward the kitchen. So he was able to say without caution to Laidlaw, "I don't know a hexameter from an iambic pentameter, but I think your friend should write some more poetry. And I think you're about due for some TDY on Fantasy Island."

Even if Pinsky had been invited to Driskill's squadron party, it was doubtful he would have accepted. He would plead another commitment, not as a deception but as a self-reassurance that he was utterly devoted to his job and no outside amenities should be allowed to dilute his enormous energies.

Once Pinsky was out of his baggy flight suit, he looked more like a West Pointer than a man who put himself through Rutgers by serving as a night watchman at Revlon's lipstick factory. His uniform always appeared to have been painted on him, his garrison cap was always precisely level, his tie knotted as if it were on display in a store window, and the crease in his trousers sharp-edged.

Both officers and enlisted men were inclined to be brisker than normal when they saluted Pinsky—for he was the walking portrait of a commander and a gentleman.

While Pinsky's appearance was martial and somewhat stiff, his occasional smile canceled the image of a martinet. And he was afflicted with a slight stutter. Just when he became the most uncompromising, just as he launched into his damn-the-torpedoes manner, he was almost certain to hesitate and catch at a syllable, and all offense became lost in a mild glottal shock.

The morning after Driskill's party was gray and limpid. Pinsky, driving toward his office at precisely the allowed speed for the base, found the heavy overcast erased any sense of the hour. It could be soon after dawn or noon, he thought. The weather clocks of California are not geared to the absence of sun.

Pinsky assessed the sky. It was a clam-chowder sky, with bags of cloud hanging down like drippings on a bowl. But it would do for the day—no sorties would have to be canceled.

Pinsky's route on this morning caused him to pass by the only U-2 that had ever irked him. The damn thing was perched on a cement pedestal, right in front of the headquarters building, calling attention to itself under the American flag. It was painted black, like all U-2s except trainers, and in Pinsky's opinion it was like standing some old woman on a box and taking her pants down to expose her parts.

He frowned at the thing on the pedestal. It advertised an imperfection and, he thought, there was no room for imperfection in this record-breaking wing. The people responsible for that absurd display were long gone into civilian life or transferred to the boonies. They could not be asked, "Why did you want to remind us of that unruly affair? Why should you want to glorify an abomination?"

Why didn't they give the damned thing an honored burial in the junkyard, instead of leaving it there as a symbol for all to see? It did not memorialize diligence, skill, courage, or tenacity, or any other attribute in the incomparable 9th Wing. Instead, it stood there smirking at those who tried to believe that a well-ordered life was the consequence of well-ordered planning. It proclaimed the incredible, a word that should not be in a recce man's vocabulary. Pinsky had looked at the offensively pickled U-2 so often that there had been moments when it seemed to speak out and address him personally.

It said, "What fools would presume to command me, when I can do quite well by myself?"

Pinsky looked away. He continued, jaw set, along the scrupulously clean street that led from the wing's complex of buildings until it joined the flight-line road. He consoled himself with the realization that there were no longer many people around who would remember Pomeroy or the reason that ghost of a U-2 was available for a decoration. It was more than that—it was a taunt. It was a monument to the unpredictability of events. It said, "What makes you think you can manage a vast organization when at any moment some sly freak can sneak in the back way, stick his finger in the machinery, and bring logic to a halt? No doubt the freak had laughed his head off while experts went around with long faces and tried to explain that it happened this way because . . . because it *just did*. Logic was castrated; a shoulder shrug was the only honest answer. Which was no way to run a wing.

Pomeroy had been the pilot of that U-2, and he had been a pleasant young man. Wherever he was now, he must regard himself as the luckiest human alive. He flew with the angels before his time.

Pinsky forced a smile and turned off the car radio. He wanted no distraction while he was compelled once again to recall the details of Pomeroy's mystifying adventure. It was all too easy, because he had played the tape countless times and had been so close to the investigation.

He fingered his freshly shaven chin as he remembered how everyone in the air force tried to pretend the flight never happened, even though it was like trying to conceal an elephant. It was not every day that a U-2, specifically that one on the pedestal, landed in a cow pasture.

No one seemed to have known Pomeroy very well. He was on a training flight, had taken off from Beale and had flown in a northwesterly direction until he completed his mission. Four hours after his departure he was returning to Beale and began his descent. He made all the customary reports to Beale Command Post and to Sacramento Approach Control. His call sign was Ginger 56.

Then, for a long time, there was no transmission from Ginger 56. Yet that was not unusual. He had a long way to come down.

Pinsky remembered the exact time when Sacramento heard some grotesque sounds on the frequency. At 1438 they said they heard moaning and what sounded like heavy breathing. The controllers thought it might be some radio nut, the jerk type who was prone to finish illegal transmissions whistling "Dixie" or a bar of any other familiar tune. When the eerie sounds persisted, the controllers became convinced they were listening to a very troubled human being. They called Ginger 56.

No response. Pinsky remembered there was a long blind spot on the tape.

They tried again and again. "Ginger Five-six? How read Sacramento?"

Nothing except the moaning and heavy breathing.

"Ginger Five-six. We seem to have lost communication. Try squawking seventy-six hundred."

They were requesting Pomeroy to set the standard "loss of communication" code into his transponder. If he complied, they would know that even if he could not transmit, he could at least receive. Meanwhile, his assigned transponder code for the flight was still on the screen. Four-two-two-five and the altitude read-out confirmed that he was descending.

"Ginger Five-six. If you read me, do a ninety-degree right turn for identification, and thank you."

Nothing. Nothing but the moaning and heaving breathing.

An Air Force T-37 was flying near Oroville, call sign Colt 24.

"Colt Two-four? Sacramento. We want you to look at a U-2 that appears to be in extreme difficulty. He's one o'clock about ten miles right over Oroville Airport."

"Sacramento, Colt Two-four. Can't see much over that way accounta' cloud deck."

"Can you get below it? Traffic is a Cessna 172. He's squawking VFR and is four miles west of the airport."

"Roger. Colt Two-four."

Minutes passed. Nothing.

Then the T-37. "Sacramento Approach. Colt Two-four has the U-2 at twelve o'clock."

"Okay. He's indicating ten thousand feet now and descending. Maintain visual separation."

Silence again. Then Colt 24 said, "We're closing on his left wing . . . we can see him just sitting there. He's wearing an orange flight suit. No head movement . . . no control surface movement. Do you know what his problem is?"

"No. He's out there . . . we can't communicate with him at all. He's just circling and descending . . . getting lower and lower out there. We dunno what the problem is."

Oakland Center came on the frequency. The curse of an aerial emergency, Pinsky thought, was the universal desire to partici-pate—vicariously.

Oakland said, "We think there's a health problem involved. We can hear him breathing and we heard some moaning on the frequency, but we couldn't tell anything about it. Are you still on his wing, Colt Two-four?"

"Roger that. He appears to be in a constant descent . . . about a thirty-degree left-bank turn. Sometimes he climbs a few hundred feet, then slides down again. I don't know whether he's going to try to put it down in the grass or what . . . Ginger Five-six! Ginger Five-six! Do you read Colt Two-four? Ginger Five-six! Come on, man. Fly the airplane!"

There was a long pause. No sound.

Both airplanes were now down to less than a thousand feet. "Oakland, Colt Two-four. There's one open field below, and it looks like he's heading for it. There's also some high-tension wires, and it looks like he can't miss hitting them. Now, he's in about a thirty-degree bank. . . ."

"It looks like he's flying it?"

"No . . . hold it! Stand by!"

A long silence then, "My God . . . I don't believe it!"

There were a lot of things not to be believed that day, including the investigating team who arrived all solemn and self-important and were soon disillusioned. How the hell, they complained, could you come up with a believable analysis for something like this? And, of course, everyone from the Pentagon to Pomeroy's family wanted some solid answers.

It is not the absurd that is impossible; it is often logic that runs for hiding, and in Pomeroy's case there was a lot of help from the angels.

As he drove on through the grayness, Pinsky decided he must be some new breed of aerial masochist to so often review that insane incident. Listening to the tape was addictive even though it gave him the willies.

The investigators could find nothing wrong with Pomeroy's slightly damaged U-2. It sat there in the pasture owned by a farmer named Carmichael, defying the experts, flopped into the grass and manure like a shot bird. With only a broken nose for wounds, it mocked the engineering minds who were so intent on proving Pomeroy had done something wrong, or the U-2 had betrayed him mechanically, or his oxygen system had gone wrong . . . or something. Anything but what actually happened, because investigative types do not believe in miracles. They just can't shrug their shoulders and say, "Well . . . there we are. What is, is."

That flight had been perfectly normal until the time of Pomeroy's descent, when he reduced power to idle. And because a U-2 is more unwilling to descend than to climb and is too fragile for a fast dive, Pomeroy should have followed the normal drill, lowering the landing gear, flaps, and raising speed brakes. He had no chance to do any of those chores. He had just throttled the engine back to idle when—oblivion. The real world ceased for First Lieutenant Pomeroy.

Now, the U-2 was on its own, trimmed for descent and holding a steady course for Beale. For reasons never to be understood, Pomeroy had not been using the autopilot during his initial descent. Aimed at Beale, the U-2 continued down in a long glide until some lower turbulence packed just enough force to lift a wing, or the fuel balance in the wing tanks, ever a touchy relationship, did the same thing. A spiral began . . . and steepened.

The helpless Pomeroy just sat there with the sun beating down on his goldfish bowl, his gloved hands still and his lips locked.

Flying itself, the U-2 augured down slowly, as if uncertain of a nest. Its moving shadow created a gracefully wavering pattern over the rising ground.

A series of 230,000-kilovolt power lines cut across the land adjacent to Carmichael's pasture. Supported by giant steel towers, the wires were two inches in diameter and were owned by Pacific Gas and Electric Company. Pomeroy's angels put them there. For the descent had suddenly become more abrupt, and the left wing went down. Logic called for the left wing to be the first part of the U-2 to strike the ground, and a cartwheeling smashup was inevitable. Logic called for flames to follow.

Instead, the U-2 glided down between the two towers and slipped beneath the first set of wires. The high right wing struck two of the last wires, and the impact pulled the wing down until the U-2 was in an almost level position. It collided gently with the ground and cut a long furrow across the pasture. The touch-down speed was eventually determined to be within a few knots of that specified for the gross weight at that moment, an extremely critical management factor in a U-2. Ginger 56 slid to a stop just short of a fence line.

A minute passed with Colt 24 watching from above. Sometime during this eerie stage wait, Pomeroy regained consciousness. He looked about unbelievingly and saw he was on God's good sweet earth. He also saw that some of that earth was on his lap, and there were clumps of mud on the nose of the U-2. Convinced he was hallucinating, he shook himself, then pounded the side of his helmet with his fist. No change.

He saw a white car racing toward him, lights flashing. He recognized it as a California State Patrol car, and thought he should get out of the cockpit.

He tried to open the canopy, but it would not unhinge. The hard landing had jammed the release mechanism. He was vaguely aware that the engine was still running, but now knew only an overwhelming desire to depart from the cockpit.

He began unhooking the tangle of wires and hoses. As he was peeling away his seat harness, he accidentally pulled the ejection handle. Three-tenths of a second later the rocket catapult fired and started the ejection seat up the rails. Simultaneously a sharp metal prod behind Pomeroy's helmet smashed through the canopy. That was what it was designed to do. That was logic. Yet because the ejection-seat railings had been crimped in the landing and were not in perfect alignment, the seat went up only with enough force to break the canopy and dump him, on his feet, just over the nose of the U-2. Time from punch-out to landing: about three seconds. He stood staring at the airplane and said, "My God! I've ruined an airplane. The air force will never let me fly again."

The patrolman arrived, but they could not hear each other because Pomeroy was still wearing his goldfish bowl and the engine was still running. The patrolman gave Pomeroy a boost so he could reach inside the cockpit and shut the engine down. It expired with a long sigh.

The patrolman asked what had happened.

"I don't know. Where are we?"

The patrolman was solicitous. He winked. "That's okay. I understand you spy-plane guys." He winked again. "You don't have to tell me anything I shouldn't know."

Total flight time since leaving the U-2: about two minutes. Total damage to pilot, one bruised chin and several chipped teeth.

Pinsky shook his head as if to cleanse his brain of such an aggravating paradox. He anticipated a busy day, and there were so many things to keep on track. Yet the ridiculous numbers would not be denied.

Pomeroy had escaped almost certain death four times—in thirty minutes. Once when in flight, the U-2 could have gone into a dive and destroyed itself; or it could have turned east and slammed into the mountains. Again, when passing through the cables; at best, Pomeroy could have been caught like a fly and electrocuted. Then the uncontrolled landing and, finally, the failure of the ejection seat to rocket him high enough to kill him but not high enough for his parachute to open.

So much for organized systems and mortality. And there was one final absurdity.

Pinsky was well aware that the air force physical exams were as thorough and demanding as any in the world. For those who hoped to become pilots, very near perfect health was mandatory, as many a rueful candidate had learned. Flunking a flight physical was about as devastating a development as a young man could know. Yet there could be no compromise. Too much of flight, especially military, depended on the harmonious synchronization of all the human organs.

Poor Pomeroy. He was a man betrayed by the very society to which he thought he belonged. Certainly he had never suspected that he might have a problem when he joined the air force—nor had his examiners. They could not have found the vaguest hint that he might suffer such a severe seizure, that he would remember nothing that happened before the instant his U-2 struck the ground and the moment when the eject system lofted him like a cannonball into a cow pie.

Pomeroy not only flew with the angels, he walked away from calamity—hand in hand with them.

Pinsky's office in the apricot building was far enough away from Driskill's to suggest two separate establishments. Pinsky's office was much larger and had a window. During the late afternoon he stood before that emblem of rank, watching the strength of the flat light fade, speculating on the weather of tomorrow. Like so many pilots, Pinsky was a practical meteorologist and had, to the despair of many professionals, an uncanny talent for accurate prediction. People who had long known Pinsky were convinced that he had some private understanding with the atmosphere.

Pinsky could not actually see the long runway from his office, but the sounds cued him to every activity. Now, a tanker was roaring down the runway, its old-style jet engines pounding the languorous air and smoking like four steam locomotives. The sounds always reminded Pinsky that one of the most expensive organizations in the world must often function with equipment older than the operators. The U-2s were designed in 1955, the

SR-71s in 1960, and the tankers in 1950. It would seem the extravagance of the military-industrial complex was going to some other place. Maybe more energy should be assigned to an acceptable division of the budget (acceptable to the air force, of course), and less to the invention and cooking of alphabet stews by the ever-productive gremlins in the Pentagon. Anagrams was the favorite game of the military. Catchword acronyms were apparently invented by people who had no notion whatever of simplicity in the English language. Among the current and countless number of jaw-saving combinations, there was "CBPO" for consolidated base personnel office and "FOD" for foreign-object damage to an engine, "RPV" for remotely powered vehicles (rockets), and "ADDISS" for advanced deployment digital-imagery interpretation system.

Pinsky wiped at his weary eyes. The prospective meeting with the Pentagon brass weighed on him; he was reasonably sure not much would be accomplished. Somewhere in the Pentagon, down some subterranean hallway, he thought, there must be a round dozen gnomes, with maybe a demented fairy princess in command, and all of them with extensive legal training. No other combination could create the esoteric subject descriptions that so tried the alphabet and a man's comprehension. Now, he thought, shoulders back while you say "PLSS" rather than precision-location strike system.

The air force flying world was peppered with linguistic experiments. A pilot no longer flew whatever it was, he "energy managed," be it a fighter, bomber, or transport. He "drove" it, a euphemism that meant his accomplishment was of such a snobbish and wonderful nature it must somehow be minimized and made comprehensible to those poor souls who are not fortunate enough to be doing the same thing. "Driving" had become a verbal pillar in the "aw shucks, I'm just a regular fellow" phraseology of modern military aviators.

Pinsky folded his hands behind his back and rocked on his feet. Visibility was deteriorating along the northern margin of the base; a haze was forming and would undoubtedly thicken with night. Never mind. Some of the millions of military budget dollars had supplied electronic systems to aircraft that made bad-weather flying much easier and safer than a few years ago.

Another tanker was just airborne. It would doubtless be gone for several hours and would find a low ceiling and poor visibility upon return. Rest easy. Nature was tamed. Or so some people who had not recently been scared witless were inclined to believe.

Pinsky smiled at the pallid view. If some of the romantic man-against-the-elements factor was gone from flying, then that was a very good thing. Unfortunately even the finest electronics could not forgive plain stupidity.

Pinsky's phone trilled. He moved to it quickly. It was always as if he desired to establish an instant link with the rest of the world and it must not be necessary to summon his attention a second, or (God forbid) a third time.

"Pinsky . . . ?"

It could be Korea on the line, or Mildenhall in England seeking more advice on the damage some peaceniks had done to the aerodrome fence.

"Driskill here, sir. I want to send Laidlaw to Fantasy Island rather than to Korea."

"Why?"

"It will just work out better for everybody, sir."

Pinsky hesitated. Was there something more here he should know about? No big deal, but it would mean his deputy would have to crank out a new set of orders. "When do you want him to leave?"

"How about tomorrow, sir?"

Driskill, he thought, was being might lavish with his "sirs" these days. "All right. I'm still waiting for a straight answer on our retention problem."

"Sir . . . I told you what I thought."

"That was an opinion, not a fix. My ass and yours are going to be in a sling if we don't come up with a practical solution."

"I'll think of it some more, sir, but if the airlines come along and offer a guy more than he can make as general, he's going to run away as soon as he can. Even so, we have two new applicants coming in next week."

"Keep me posted."

Pinsky hung up the telephone. The pilot-retention quotas in the air force were in real trouble. Where was the genius to solve it?

The phone again.

"Pinsky." It was the same statement of presence, deliberately curt.

"Operations here, sir."

"Go ahead."

"We're going to have to close the field, sir."

Pinsky glanced at the window. It was not exactly sunshine and flowers outside but it was flyable, and nothing is perfect. "Why?"

"Sir, a tanker just landed and the aircraft commander reported numerous ducks aloft, sir. The fucking ducks have come back."

An unhappy pause: It was that time of year. An air base employing over six thousand people, whose energies were supposedly devoted to the full operational status of a billion dollars' worth of flying hardware . . . all brought to a halt because a few migrating ducks refused to share the sky above this part of California. He had seen the invasion before. Squadrons, wings, armadas of ducks skimming above and below the low-cloud layer, disporting in formations any air-group leader would envy. Even a single duck colliding with an airplane in just the right way could cause a catastrophe. So much for air power.

"Very well. Close down. Let me know immediately if there's any change."

Pinsky replaced the phone. Just recently in Idaho, one of the new B-1 bombers, an airplane so expensive no one wanted to admit the actual cost, had been destroyed by a single bird. The lives of four top men were lost, along with at least $200 million.

Pinsky was still staring pensively out the window when his secretary entered. He turned and favored her with a wan smile. Because it was a Friday, he knew the folder she was carrying, for his study on the weekend would be the daily log of events at Beale. It would be worth what little free time he had if he could discover something in the résumé that would improve the wing the following week.

She handed him the folder, and he stuffed it in a briefcase already overburdened with paper. "There is one memo that's not in here, Mary," he said. "It should remind me that nature is not only wonderful . . . but is always victorious."

❖

Halloween crept softly over the rolling expanse of Beale Air Force Base. Apparently on a mass whim the ducks had departed, two days ago, but this night there were few takeoffs and landings of any type of aircraft. It was as if there were a secret agreement that flight activity be held at a bare minimum even though this was not an official holiday. It was an excuse for parties, and one was in progress at the house of U-2 pilot Hensley.

Mayfield came as a pumpkin and Winiger as an owl. There were two sheikhs, a variety of witches, and a pair of devils. Hinkle wore a German Luftwaffe cap equipped with miniature red and white flashing lights; and there was Napolitano in a trench coat, a nasty black mustache, dark glasses, and papers marked "Most Secret." He said right off he was a Soviet spy—in case anyone doubted. Driskill appeared as a caveman, complete with fur rug, beard, and club. Everyone hooted politely and said he was the funniest thing they ever saw, possibly because he was the squadron commander.

All holidays are taken seriously in the air force, and on this Halloween night those who were packed into the Hensley house were straining the bonds of nonfamiliarity. While the jack-o'-lantern flickered and the smell of scorched pumpkin pervaded the house, the decibel level was reflected in an aura of polite restraint. Even the yelps of recognition were subdued, because it was not a gathering of old friends. Elsewhere in the land similar parties were in progress and the decibels shook the chandeliers, but they were civilians who had known each other a long time, the liquor was hard and life was soft.

Here in the house of Hensley, the husbands knew each other although at most it would be for no more than a few years. The Hensleys had also invited as many SR-71 crew members as were available, and so it was a rare mix. The wives had a much more difficult problem, and the inherent defenses of female to female were a tough barrier. "Oh, yes, we've met before . . . or have we? I'm not sure because we've moved so many times I often wonder just where we are. . . ."

Because they were transferred so frequently from the hinterlands of Texas to the steppes of the Dakotas, the wives' basis for even a nodding acquaintance rested mainly on a common locale, their jobs, and the care of children. The coffee klatches that had once been the ceremonial introductories for newly assigned wives were still held, but not very often and attendance was poor. The main cause was outside work; a wife with a degree in nuclear physics was not going to sit around sipping coffee and making chitchat about children and promotions if she could find a job with a local computer company. And by the time she arrived home at night and took care of her household chores even halfway, she had little time for socializing with the neighbor up the street or even next door. At best there might be nodding acquaintances—on Saturdays and Sundays—but even if some sort of friendship was established, the duration would be short, for it was absolutely certain a transfer would come. The whole family could then enjoy the dubious pleasure of starting all over again.

The punchbowl at the party was patronized mainly by cats and tramps and softly giggling devils with masks. The males drank beer straight from the can. No one drank very much or displayed any influence from it. Hard liquor was not offered because of expense, and everyone understood.

A cat said to Cleopatra, "Where do you work?"

"Up at Pave Paws." That was the big gimmick on the hill with all the radars.

"Good heavens. That's very secret, isn't it?" The cat was practicing listening and finding the project onerous.

"That's it. Where do you work?"

"I just started teaching school down in Marysville. It's good to be back at it again, but I don't care much for the long commute."

"You're . . . Dan Kelly's wife?"

A polite laugh. "No. I'm Wendy Starbuck. We came here last May."

In civilian life this Halloween party might have been considered a bust, despite the jolly efforts of the hosts. But then something happened that no group of civilians could have arranged.

Among the guests was Murphy, the assistant deputy for operations. His costume was an ordinary sport shirt and slacks, because Pinsky was busy at the Officers' Club, entertaining the visiting Pentagon brass, and Murphy was automatically responsible for all that transpired. If the occasion arose, he could hardly show up on the flight line dressed as a gorilla.

Murphy was a huge man with a genial air and a tall wife to match his size. As a "sled" driver he was not quite one with the U-2 pilots, although they had generously offered to forgive his sins. He carried the "brick," a heavy hand-held radio, which kept him in constant touch with all that pertained to the 9th Wing, down to the most minor detail. Farrington did not like to be overly isolated, and Pinsky wanted to know everything that happened. Pinsky never liked surprises.

Murphy refused a beer. "Just my luck," he laughed. "Somebody has to mind the store."

During the early phases of the party Murphy spoke occasionally into his brick, but whatever he said was terse and unintelligible against the background chatter, and no one seemed anxious to pry. Then, later, when things appeared to be prematurely winding down, which was no place for a party to go so early on Halloween, Murphy waited for one of the too frequent gaps in decibels and said, "If anyone's interested, there's going to be something worth seeing outside." He turned to the twin doorways that opened on the side lawn, and some ten people followed him. Out of about thirty.

They stood expectantly while Murphy spoke to his brick again. The night was so clear even the Pleiades were each sharply defined. The chatter in the house was muffled here, and nearby a cricket called to a frog, who called right back. "Halloween," someone said quietly. `

Murphy spoke confidentially to his brick and looked west into the darkness where, a few miles away, the flight line stood. He was smiling—the big kid with a surprise. Soon his audience heard the rumble of distant thunder. It came rolling through the night, increasing with savage intensity until it was tearing up the still air.

They saw it, a cluster of tiny lights flickering between the stars followed by two white, flaming orbs. The lights passed Betelgeuse, then Rigel, hid Capella momentarily, then slid on toward the planet Jupiter, hanging like a signal beacon.

"One of our sleds," Murphy announced with the pride of a

salesman. "I asked him if he'd mind leaving his afterburners on."

Only a minute or so had elapsed since Murphy had led his audience to the lawn, but now nearly the entire party stood in awe as the SR-71 slipped rapidly away. Suddenly it was gone, and with it the sound.

Murphy listened to his brick. "He was at twenty-four thousand when he passed over us . . . two minutes after takeoff. He'll be in England in five hours."

A momentary silence. A few people whispered. Murphy, supremely smug, smiled down upon them like some master sorcerer. He shrugged his broad shoulders and said simply, "I asked him if he'd mind swinging by this way. . . ."

The effect was magical. The wary acquaintances, all determined on arrival to do the best they could in mixing with relatively new personalities and then sensing defeat in their attempts, were now bonded together by the echo of a thousand kettle drums. They knew how the earth had trembled beneath their feet from the sound of gigantic power, and they knew that two young men like their own were sitting just ahead of the flaming orbs, climbing very high toward their immediate destinies.

Now, very suddenly, the specific identities of the party became unimportant. Driskill, calling from behind his caveman beard, yelled "How about a bon-voyage toast?"

He raised his can of beer. At once there were many cans raised and voices rose increasingly against the soft night, until, from the fluency and persistence of their communion, they appeared to have known each other all their lives.

❖

Laidlaw was unable to attend the Halloween party. At the same hour it reached its social zenith, Laidlaw arrived in the Athens airport. It was early morning. Since there were no military aircraft bound for the Middle East at this time, he had been obliged to ride economy class on a commercial carrier, a journey shared with a vociferous rock-and-roll group, which did not improve his disposition. It was a long way from Beale straight through to Athens, he had been robbed of sleep, and he was missing his dancing poet. It helped some to resent Driskill for sending him off so abruptly, but it really had been an overlong spell since he had caught a TDY assignment. And Fantasy Island was where the action was these days. So it was carry on.

Laidlaw did not present a figure of military smartness on this steaming Greek morning. He was wearing civilian clothes, as directed for all American military personnel in the region (the premier of Greece was anything but an Americanphile), his shirt was wilting, and his suit creased with wrinkles from trying to sleep in an airline seat. The washrooms aboard had been so continuously in use he had not managed a chance to shave. The raucous commotion in the Athens terminal made him irritable, and he was anxious to pass through Greek officialdom as quickly as possible. When he reset his watch to the local time, he found that he had a bare half hour to make his connecting flight to Fantasy Island.

A Greek immigration officer frowned at his passport and gave him a cool welcome. Yet he experienced no serious delay until he encountered a sad-eyed little customs officer, who stared at Laidlaw's fair-complexioned bulk and wanted to know what was in the small trunk that was the principal part of his baggage. The officer stared in amazement at the spacesuit, boots, gloves, socks, two sets of long underwear, and a goldfish-bowl helmet. He wiped his hands on his striped shirt and took up the helmet. It obviously puzzled him.

"I have twenty-six minutes to catch my connecting flight," Laidlaw said, and tried to smile.

"What this be?" The officer pointed to the open trunk and

began rummaging through the space suit. Evil was obviously at hand.

"It's something I need for my job. It would take a long time to describe why." Laidlaw was vaguely aware that the Athens airport was a major transfer point for some of the world's most wide-eyed people, but he saw no reason to be concerned about himself. He was an American officer and could prove it. There was his name and rank right on the helmet.

The sad eyes became increasingly dissatisfied as the officer poked through the trunk. He shook his head and studied Laidlaw with open suspicion.

"I really must get a move on," Laidlaw said.

Sad Eyes made no move to close the trunk, but continued to examine Laidlaw as if he had just landed from another planet.

Determined to avoid becoming the Ugly American, Laidlaw glanced at his watch and summoned his friendliest tone of voice. "Look, sir, I have a problem, and I hope you can help me by clearing me through right now . . . because if I fail to make my connection, I may lose my job."

"You dive in the sea?" the officer said, fingering the space suit.

"No."

"Then what this for?"

Laidlaw knew his brain must be weary when he said, "I can't tell you." He knew it was a mistake the moment he uttered the words, and he mumbled something about time passing.

Ignoring him, the official left the trunk and a moment later returned with a colleague. The new man's upper lip was adorned with an enormous walrus mustache, and he moved with a certain unrestrained suggestion of grandeur. He also wore a uniform cap above his plump face, and a long cigarette dangled from his lips. He peeked into the trunk and regarded the space suit as he might a captive crocodile.

"How much costa?"

Laidlaw decided he was neither friendly nor unfriendly. Apparently he was some sort of supervisor, because Sad Eyes readily deferred to him and listened to a long speech in Greek, which seemed to be based on the conversion of dollars to drachmas.

Laidlaw could not imagine why his brain came up with such a ridiculous response to Walrus Mustache's question. He shrugged his shoulders, and an instant later wondered if it was his overwhelming fatigue that led him to say, "Oh, it only cost about half a million. . . ."

"Drachmas!"

"Dollars."

Walrus's vast chest emitted a sigh that sounded like a punctured truck tire. Then he launched into a voluble exchange with Sad Eyes, who seemed concerned with high finance.

Laidlaw glanced at his watch again. Twenty minutes. Unless something was settled immediately, the commuter plane would take off without him.

Suddenly Walrus Mustache glowered at Laidlaw and asked, "What you do with this? You wanna blow something up?"

"Of course not. Please . . ."

Walrus Mustache closed the trunk and came around the counter. He took Laidlaw gently but firmly by the arm. "Come," he said, "we go see boss."

Laidlaw abandoned all hope of making his flight connection. So he would be late reporting for duty and his excuse would be accepted without comment, but there would be, he supposed, some lingering doubt in Driskill's mind and in Pinsky's because of a few little insignificant matters in the past. They would probably convince themselves that he had been dallying with some pleasant companion when they should understand that he was entirely and forever devoted exclusively to his dancing lady.

Walrus Mustache was polite, although much too curious for

Laidlaw's comfort. He must bear in his tired mind that as far as his own government was concerned, he did not exist. At least for the moment.

"What you do with this thing? You make trouble? What you do for a living, mister? Your passport say nothing." Walrus chuckled and poked a fat finger into Laidlaw's waistline. "You be a loafer, yes? I no believe you. You fix ships that are broke? Tell me what you sell that thing for. Maybe we sell it to a rich Greek and you give me a little commission?"

Walrus roared with laughter, and Laidlaw managed a smile. He watched helplessly while the porter heaved his trunk and his canvas B-1 bag into a taxi. Walrus held the door and waved Laidlaw inside. Soon they were driving through Athens's eye-biting smog, then veered away from the center of the city toward a suburb. After twenty-eight minutes by Laidlaw's watch they stopped before what appeared to be a military compound. Were they going to throw him in jail, for Christ's sake? If he had to appeal to the American consul, he would hear the flak bursting all the way from Beale.

At the gate there followed a barrage of discussion with a sentry. He wanted to look into the trunk. When Walrus Mustache allowed him a brief viewing, the sentry gasped and closed the trunk as if it might explode. Terrorists, Laidlaw remembered, were all too familiar to the Greeks.

Once inside the compound, the taxi stopped before a stucco building. Mustachio smiled confidentially and said, "Come, my friend. You say to me what you do with the thing?" Then his face darkened. "You tell me or we have plenty trouble, yes?"

The hell with it, Laidlaw thought. He was going to have to say something sooner or later. "I can't tell you because it's classified."

"What this mean? It's very expensive?"

"Yes."

"Ah . . ."

For the moment, Laidlaw thought, Walrus seemed satisfied.

The procession with the officers carrying the trunk entered the stucco building, and after a moment's discussion an aged attendant led them to a large office. It was so deeply shadowed it was a moment before Laidlaw saw an officer lounging behind a huge desk. He was smoking a cigarette and was wearing a full uniform. He waved the cigarette lazily at a collection of demitasse cups on a small table standing against one wall. Behind them a pot bubbled on an electric heater, and beside it an old-fashioned alarm clock ticked resoundingly.

"You wanna coffee?" Walrus Mustache inquired solicitously.

"No, thank you." Laidlaw's decline was accompanied by the suggestion of a bow. Here, he was certain, was a face-saving situation, and he might as well play the game. He saw that Higher Authority was studying him. All right. As long as he had missed his flight anyway, he might as well reverse the field and show these gentlemen he had nothing to hide . . . well, not very much. "I am a pilot, you see, and I fly very high. So high there is almost nothing there. . . ."

Higher Authority nodded and took a long draw on his cigarette as he slowly closed and reopened his enigmatic eyes. The alarm clock ticked several times before he exhaled a cloud of smoke.

"If you won't give me back my trunk and send me on my way, I shall have to telephone the American consul."

Again the slow eye blinking. Laidlaw saw that the nail on Higher Authority's right little finger was left purposely long. Now he stuffed it into his right ear and twisted it carefully. He continued to regard Laidlaw with silent attention. Tick-tick-tick.

"A suit like this enables me to survive at the higher altitudes. It not only meters the proper amount of oxygen to my system, but prevents the expansion of gas in the gastrointestinal tract. . . ."

Laidlaw saw Higher Authority's attention was still with him, but was he understanding? He seemed to be falling asleep, or was there something about those drowsy dark eyes that was far from reassuring?

Higher Authority scratched at his heavy black hair and murmured something to Walrus Mustache. He held out his hand as Walrus brought out a printed form. Then he reached toward a Christmas tree of rubber stamps on the corner of his desk, and after what appeared to be careful consideration chose one. He smacked it down vigorously on an ink pad and then on the form. He scribbled a hieroglyphic for his signature, and smiling ever so slightly handed the form to Laidlaw.

Walrus Mustache took Laidlaw's arm and led him away. "Everything okay now. Everybody gotta good feel."

As they left the entrance to the building, Walrus Mustache slapped Laidlaw between the shoulder blades and for the first time displayed his mouthful of badly bucked teeth. "We feel good, no? We are happy? Now we go to little taverna, stay open all the time, and drink some retsina, yes? No problems. Maybe we sing a little. . . ."

Laidlaw hardly heard him. There was only one flight a day between Athens and Fantasy Island, and a taverna at ten o'clock in the morning was not the best place to catch up on sleep. Yet somehow he had developed a surprising affection for his two companions. Sad Eyes had not said a word since they left the airport, but there was now a certain sympathy about his attitude, as if he deeply regretted the fuss he had initiated. "Okay . . ." Laidlaw said wearily, "I'm buying."

As they bounced between potholes en route to what Walrus Mustache described as the best little taverna in Greece, Laidlaw glanced at the printed form. He remembered the ceremonious flourish Higher Authority had given his rubber stamp.

Here, on this form, was his passport to freedom and all was

well. The Greek print was a mystery, but there in violet ink was Higher Authority's elaborate signature. And then, slightly askew, below the signature, stamped in plain English, were words to warm any terrorist's heart. Higher Authority, fingering through his assortment of rubber stamps, had obviously chosen the wrong one.

IN-FLIGHT LUNCH NOT REQUIRED.

Laidlaw relaxed against the back of the taxi seat and closed his eyes. Never again, he thought, would he doubt the power and the majesty of higher authority.

❖

By the time Laidlaw had proved to his own satisfaction that he could drink as much retsina as any Greek customs officer, including Walrus Mustache and the man he now addressed as Sad Eyes, relations between the Greek nation and the United States of America were firmly reestablished. Laidlaw also tried to convince his new friends that air force pilots were lovers rather than warriors, a theory the customs officers found quite incomprehensible. They understood Laidlaw's occasional naps between dollops of retsina, but they had great trouble with the word "classified." It seemed that everything they asked Laidlaw brought the answer, "No, no, that's classified," a response that was not in their limited vocabulary.

After his tenth retsina Laidlaw admitted that he was a spy of some sort, confirming the first suspicions of Sad Eyes and Walrus Mustache. They protested that they did not care what he did, as long as Higher Authority had issued his precious chop. Thus all went well through the balance of the night, and when Laidlaw could hold his eyes open long enough, he found himself attempting an appropriate furtive look.

Each glass of retsina was served on a saucer, and as the stacks reached hazardous heights, Sad Eyes worried about Laidlaw's ability to match the final count with money. Walrus was more interested in Laidlaw's ever more frequent orations on a certain dancing girl. Perhaps he could trace his ancestry back to Demosthenes.

If she was indeed such a paragon of virtue, why didn't he marry her . . . or was it that spying did not pay enough to support a family? Only when Laidlaw confessed that he had a wife did the party become shadowed with distress; the Greeks shook their heads solemnly, as men who understood such trying situations. His dilemma, they insisted, was not uncommon in Greece, where most marriages were arranged along sensible financial and family lines. Romance, they declared, with solemnity, invariably brought trouble to a union.

❖

The curse of physically beautiful men is the sneaking sense that because they are so lavishly endowed, they must owe something to the lesser world. So, often they chew on humble seeds, hoping, like very rich men in poor company, that they will not be noticed and consequently isolated.

Laidlaw was almost totally without conceit, even though he knew very well that his striking appearance often caused comment. He reviewed his character often, trying to make the inner man match the impressive exterior—and always he was disappointed. Yet he persisted, and he found the long missions in a U-2 offered an ideal sense of removal. Night sorties were particularly favorable for such times of introspection, and sometimes he thought he might be quite another person.

Now, two weeks after his convivialities with the Greek customs officials, he had been sitting in his U-2 since just before midnight. It was already 0400 of the new day, and dawn should be along soon.

Laidlaw knew that the Mediterranean lay below him as it had

during much of his flight out of Fantasy Island. Far in the depths below were ships steaming for Suez, fishermen riding to their lamplit nets, and, Laidlaw mused, hanky-panky abounding. It was a pleasant diversion from self-censure to think about hanky-panky as it was doubtless being played out in Marseilles and Istanbul and Cairo, cities that had all been more or less just beyond the horizon during one time or another this night. Verbal vagaries? "More or less . . . one time or another." Neat indefinites as quoted by a "recce boy" with a top-secret clearance—just part of the language. Hey, Ayatollah! Wake up and watch the early bird.

The first hour after takeoff had been standard drill. Up onto an easterly heading with the stars hanging in the black sky like a theatrical curtain, like so many glow-plugs, Laidlaw thought, or a rock musician's hairdo. Oh, no, my friend, you can dream up something more appropriate than that.

When Laidlaw was aloft at night, he sometimes discovered deep within himself a twinge of fear. At such moments he found inexplicable comfort in thinking of himself as "my friend." Here, alone, man's best friend was himself.

The first hour was always just listen and verify, climb and adjust. Everything "copacetic" and the warning panel dark. Nightlife in a U-2 was less luxurious than a daytime sortie; there was no sun spiking on the old goldfish bowl, no need to take out a chart, fold it, and stuff it against the top of the canopy until it formed a nice little tent. Like down home . . . like a separate little room in the heights, a room with a hell of a view.

Nightlife up here was different from that known to any other men. It was a separate world. Hey, man! A lonesome cocoon floating in a black pool. A guy could feel closer to the stars than to the planet he left. Here was a wilderness populated by a single individual who had severed all connections to the human race. Which might be handy, considering wives who disapproved and dancing girls who didn't. No other man within twenty thousand miles. Son of the stars, my friend, have a look at those thunderstorms down in the basement.

He wriggled around in his space suit, trying to get as comfortable as possible and sort of get the feel of the airplane, which could change character sometimes right damn smack in front of your eyes. Sometimes during the first night hours a man would hear sounds he never heard before—little squeaks maybe, or a soft drumming sound that might be the canopy fan, which finally would go away by itself. Usually. Every U-2 was the same, but each one had its little idiosyncracies. A U-2 was more than just a blowtorch on one end of a tin can. If you spent a whole long night in one, it was as though the thing actually breathed.

By the second hour, the first way-points had come and gone on the computer, and he was ready to orbit over target. Then, according to the flight plan, he hit the right switches and all kinds of machinery up in the nose and in the belly started listening and sending out data in real time, which was difficult for the honcho in charge of the platform to comprehend. It was much easier to understand why the program had to wait for daylight before starting the cameras, despite infrared capability. The spooks wanted those early morning shadows to clue them in on something. Okay, but who was up to mischief in these parts at four o'clock in the morning? Hell, the muezzins hadn't even started climbing their towers.

And who was *they*? Who wound up with all the stuff coming out of Fantasy Island, who was the real dude responsible for keeping a reasonably good, not-too-clean American boy up here all night in a space suit while so much enjoyable hanky-panky was going on down below?

Anyway, God was in His heaven and it sure was beautiful. A man could reach out and grab the Pleiades as if they really were a bunch of grapes.

Then again, a man could also reach out and grab a few things if he were to spend a few hours on Nici Beach—south side of the island, if anyone needed directions. There, between flights, a U-2 pilot was free to roam through a personal harem whose members formed their own United Nations. Such abundance wore a man down.

This was the best job in the air force . . . in the world. Look at the navy down there somewhere, the whole Sixth Fleet with a bunch of fighter jocks cooped up in some rust bucket for months unless they were actually flying. And what did they do but practice, practice, with once in a while a little brush with the dudes in turbans?

Here was the real thing, but there were disadvantages. A letter from the dancing girl took three weeks to make Fantasy Island! And the wife's complaints about the quality of the TV shows she was watching came in one week.

The second hour up here was reading, writing, and 'rithmetic time. Everything had to be read out and put down on the green card. Cabin pressure. Suit vent checked. Oxygen pressure and quantity. Fuel counter, sump-tank cursor set sixty-five gallons. Autopilot just hanging right in there.

Rome had a good all-night rock-and-roll station he could pick up on the ADF . . . usually. Tonight? No banana. The eye-talians must not have paid their power bill. So here was the *Reader's Digest* with a lot of interesting stuff in it. He could sit back for a few minutes and read a whole story. Laidlaw's colleague Butch Hinkle says that before he became a schoolmaster, he read philosophy on some of his flights, and that he used to hook his tape recorder to the intercom system and play classical music. Okay for Hinkle, but thank you very much, Laidlaw will take hard rock.

Below, everything was black-black. A void. Okay, the flight plan said sunrise would be at 0525.

May the good Lord bless Pratt and Whitney. It was truly wonderful how that J-75 just kept humming back there. Suppose it didn't? Show me the pilot who hasn't given this matter serious thought. Like his best thinking. No way is anybody going to land this flying machine at any place they've ever seen before. Perish the thought, as they say. Laidlaw, you are a wit this morning. Right on, man. Slap hands.

Now it was lunchtime. Dress for same, that is stretch as far as possible, which isn't far. Flex the muscles. Give the space suit a tweak here and there. Ready to copy? Black tie, champagne at the ready.

The menu, if you please. Lay out the tablecloth, a nice clean paper napkin, and let's see, how about peaches through a straw? Or mulligan stew? Or chicken soup or broth, washed down with plain water? All sucked into the goldfish bowl. And après lunch? How about a crossword puzzle?

Why was it that at the pre-dawn hour of the morning in any cockpit of any airplane bound anywhere, the mind always went a little dingy? It wasn't exactly hallucination, but the cuckoo started chirping, and sometimes it was hard to stop. Fantasies churned around, and one might even suppose that a U-2 was over the Persian Gulf where, of course, one would never be, or over the Sudan or maybe alongside Libya or worse yet, right over Lebanon. A U-2 would never be sent within a hundred miles of those places, of course, but then that was the sort of wild speculation that came on while waiting for that first spray of light in the East.

The mission's fifth, sixth, and seventh hours were taken up with flight chores interspersed with short, undisciplined time zones that allowed the urge to take a brief nap to become almost overwhelming. Sleep, dear blessed sleep. Thirty seconds. One minute would be enough. Somewhere in the depths below, Walrus Mustache and Sad Eyes would be snuggling with their mates before setting off to work. That was as it should be—a life of peace and order. Elsewhere below, a few hundred million people were presumably engaged in the same drowsy activity. And Laidlaw . . . ?

Laidlaw was alone. Fighting a yearning to close his eyes—just for a moment. Just long enough to rest the irises. A sort of easy dive into limbo.

The sixth hour brought the sun into a blazing, milky sky, and the inevitable post-dawn battle against slumber became easier.

Now, as always, Laidlaw realized he was approaching a peculiar state of mental suspension, a sort of brain levitation that drew his attention from all earthly concerns and left him in a cramped little world surrounded by clocklike dials and flashing digits, all of which were trying to tell him something. And now he realized that his pissoir must be nearly full, and there were hints deep within his bowels that were difficult to ignore. But the worst was this itching of the beard stubble, which couldn't be scratched because of the goldfish bowl. By twisting his head in a certain way and wiggling it back and forth along the metal wing collar of his suit, Laidlaw was able to brush a very small section of his chin against it. A while back he blew up his suit until he sat there for twenty minutes like a trussed-up hog. He was not convinced the process relaxed his muscles.

He was reasonably awake, but he was bored with the orbit. A few minutes ago he thought he saw a flicker on the intruder-warning indicator, and that had sure as hell gotten his attention. Man! If some downright unfriendly dude down below decided he didn't like U-2s around here and launched a missile . . . by the time it got up here, it would be going ballistic and he could get out of the way—presuming he had enough warning and was paying attention. Fighter planes were about the same; the Soviets made a few that could get this high, but they also went ballistic at this altitude, and the theory was that since a U-2 could be turned and a MIG could not, one could just step out of the way. Presumably.

Sometimes, when all was going well and the mission was in the bag, the guys flying U-2s out of Fantasy Island contrived to lure units of the mighty Sixth Fleet up their way. Laidlaw smiled at the scene. He had been one of the originators of the game, and no action, not even that to be found on Nici Beach, delighted him more. The drill was to find a carrier, call its frequency, and challenge the navy guys to come get you in their hot iron fighters. The results were always hilarious. Up they would come zooming, all set for a mock kill. Then, about ten thousand feet below, they would start to falter, and with still five thousand to come they would fall right out of the sky. But the real bad guys weren't playing games.

The flicker had been a false alarm, which did happen now and then. Still, the dudes were down there somewhere—the somewhere being classified even to guys with top-secret clearance. What else could anyone expect with a nutty ayatollah on one end, a crazy colonel on the other; in between, people killing each other in the Lebanese sunlight, Israelis armed to the teeth and waiting to kill Arabs armed with rocks. People starving by the thousands in the Ethiopian sun, and people running for their lives in the Sudan.

There were a few pockets where people were not trying to kill each other, but not very many.

Seen from up here, the world looked different. Who owns that grain of sand? Who rules this one?

Laidlaw could see it now, the plaque hanging over his fireplace back in Happy Valley. It was one of those needlepoint jobs in colored thread. It read, "What the hell kind of world is this anyway?"

Suddenly he was sitting on a couch with the dancing girl at his side. She was listening devotedly while he described the unclassified details of this flight.

You're dozing! Whoops!

Here, dozing could kill him. Think of something. Quick!

Maybe people liked being terrified. Maybe deep down there was something that called out, "Salt me down with a little danger, man. I got myself infected with the misery of the ordinary."

Time to start the descent for home. Hello, Nici Beach.

It was interesting to speculate on the basic features of Nici Beach. Fundamental, you might say. There were so many vacationing females there, making sure not an inch of their torso missed acquiring skin cancer, it was hard to believe they did not exist. If the presence of Americans on that island was not supposed to be real, then how could the girls on Nici Beach be?

Sometimes it seemed as if this whole job were just part of a dream.

Driskill now, he would not exactly smile through his bubble gum at a man who would take even a short snooze up here. Even though he had probably done so himself. He knew that if a mission called for it, a man could stay awake for more than twenty-four hours. In fact, Driskill was no dummy. Who did he think he was fooling by sending a guy away on this remote assignment? Of course, he hadn't said anything straight out, but it had been pretty obvious he was not enthusiastic about the dancing girl.

All right, boss. When I get down from this one, I'll take the vows of chastity. I'll pinch off a little sleep first and write the wife a real husbandly letter. It will say in there somewhere that I thank God for watching over me . . . and for her.

❖

All human experiences are brought into balance sooner or later, and all of our trials and triumphs are best viewed from aloft. The perspective of altitude has a way of reducing all things to trivial proportions, which may account for the inner serenity of so many aviators and even explain their devotion to flight.

Yet life aloft is extremely temporary, and the ties binding the airmen to earth are all-powerful.

There is always the family, and there are the worldly plans common to almost any society; we work, we love, we worship, we give and take, and we lust. As we age, our pursuit of happiness intensifies; we try to compensate for what we are persuaded has been missed. Quick! We must see the world. Quick! We must play one more game, attend one more function, make that which perhaps may be a last journey. As the summation approaches, we gradually slither down from the heights, never quite fulfilled.

Our solace is in each other. At last it is society itself that binds us together, and in no other confederation is this more pronounced than in the flying military. So it is that the man you flew with today may be your companion tonight. Long before the uniform is put away forever, long before the vigor of middle age fades and allows even the thought of a natural death to sneak into our minds, the pattern is established. We are a recognized part of something, a tribe, a band of brothers, a community—and membership is still the most fundamental need of mankind. We must not die alone.

Even as Laidlaw was struggling with the composition of renewed sentiments to his wife, life at Beale continued according to established habits. It was Saturday, and for the majority of air-force officers it was the day at least partly reserved for personal pursuits. There were haircuts to be had, garden supplies to buy, cars to be fixed, golf to be enjoyed, and, in Driskill's case, time to work with his model airplanes. Saturday also offered a chance to renew acquaintance with his family.

There was Cory, his son, who was black-eyed like his mother. He was standing beside his father now in the garage of the house while Driskill worked on one of his model airplanes. This was a sacred place, he had once told Cory, who had developed a nine-year-old's tendency to pick up the wrong thing. His curiosity was unbounded, and he invariably brought questions to the sacred place, just when it was so necessary to make a minute adjustment in a wing sweep, or recut the tail feathers of a little bird that was bound to win the national championship.

Cory picked up a model of a Spad. "Did you fly one of these?"

"No, sir. That was long before my time." Driskill noted with amusement that he always "sirred" his son. He could not for the life of him understand why. It just seemed to bridge the gap between forty-five and nine.

"How about this one?" Cory held up a model of Nieuport.

"Also before my time. Those were First World War airplanes . . . slow, and I'd guess real clunks to fly."

Driskill cupped a magnifying glass into his left eye and tinkered with the mount for the tiny gas engine that would power his champion model. Being a good father and trying to concentrate, he thought, were the opposite poles of paternal life. He was not in the least surprised when Cory asked him why he had not flown in World War I.

"Because I wasn't even born yet, sir." He hesitated and waggled his heavy eyebrows. "Did I receive some wrong information, or isn't this your day to rake the yard?"

Cory took on his hard-of-hearing gaze with the ease of a professional. He had picked up a model of a P-51 fighter and had zoomed away to land far removed from the sacred place. "Did you fly one of these?"

"No. How old do you think I am?"

"Less than a hundred?"

"Thank you, sir. Now about the yard." When a man could only spend a little time with his offspring it was better not to overfill that time with unpleasantries. But then there was the need for some variety of discipline.

"If you didn't fly in the First World War or the Number Two, then when did you fly? How come you are the squadron commander?"

"Sometimes I wonder. I flew in Southeast Asia, if you're looking for a war."

Cory frowned. "Humph. Did you kill anybody?"

"Not directly."

"Did somebody try to kill you?"

"Yessir. Many times." It was one statement Driskill thought that he could make with absolute conviction.

"Why did they want to kill you, if you weren't killing them?"

Driskill took the magnifying cup from his eye and pretended to clean it. "I was afraid you were going to ask that."

"Well . . .?"

Driskill saw himself over the jungle in a little spotter plane. A forward air controller, like Pinsky, his job was to discover the enemy and bring in troops or aircraft to eliminate them. Eliminate . . . exterminate? Ugly words. Sometimes he had deliberately exposed himself to enemy fire, the better to spot their location.

At last he reinserted the cup in his eye and said, "I don't know, son. I don't know."

❖

This Saturday night at Beale would see the officers and their wives joined in the most important social function of the year. It would be the wing's annual "dining out." At various times of the year all of the armed forces had their own version of this gathering, and all represented an almost touching longing and respect for tradition. There is also an annual "dining in," which is confined to officers only and surrounds the participants with an atmosphere of gallantry and romance. In a sense both ceremonies are a revival of those long-ago times when the life of a warrior was the only honorable profession for a gentleman. Now, female officers are invited to attend the dining ins, which has softened the language if not the exchange of barbs. At the dining outs the sparkle and ambiance of the evening provided by wives and sweethearts is all the more picturesque, and at both affairs full dress uniform, complete with medals, is mandatory. Formal gowns for the ladies is also an imperative.

This night Driskill, Pinsky, and Farrington were present, along with all those wing officers who were not on duty elsewhere. The large, candle-lit room at the Officers' Club resounded with multiples of conversation, and there, bobbing like corks on a sea of white tablecloths, were the familiar faces of Fusco, Napolitano, Hinkle, Kinego, and Bozek, among many others. All wore dark blue dinner jackets, cut away at the waist in the style of eighteenth-century uniforms. Their wives, most of whom had devoted hours to preparing for this event, were radiant. Here was their man as their little-girl dreams once portrayed him, now come very alive in an almost Napoleonic aura. Here was the hero at last personified as he was in the photo at home. Here was the one night of the year when military panoply was shared with them.

It is said that the basis for these functions began with King Arthur, who sought to create greater harmony among his knights by throwing them together in a formal party where they could brag at will and become aware of each others' feats of arms. The Knights of Malta gathered on similar occasions, and our own ceremonies are based almost exactly on the protocol of the English Royal Air Force.

Tonight, according to custom, a small collection of outside dignitaries had been invited. There was Bevequa, a physically powerful man of Sicilian descent, who flew U-2s in the days of the Cuban missile crisis. There was Halloran, a dashing ex-general and U-2 pilot of the same era. He was still regarded with great respect by the relative newcomers to high-altitude flight. And there was Orville Wilbur Tosch, a man of such vast proportions he would have the greatest trouble fitting into a U-2. He was invited because he was known to be obsessed with flight in any form and because of his impressive record bush-flying in Alaska.

As commander of the wing, Pinsky was automatically president of the mess—a job he executed with relish. Soon after the party assembled, he abandoned his usual intensity and surrendered to the gaiety of the evening. Tonight there was a new snap to his normally weary eyes, and from his elevated position at the head table he actually smiled upon Driskill, who, combed, polished, and bemedaled, sat beside his wife. Separation of mates during dining outs was almost unthinkable. The institution of marriage took its place along with all the other traditions.

The toasts were rigid protocol, the first "To the Colors," next "To the president of the United States," then "To the chief of the air force," and finally, "to our fallen comrades."

Bonsi, a stock block of a man, was among those at Driskill's table. It was Bonsi who experienced the second U-2 explosion just after takeoff in Korea. When the tail blew off, the aircraft became unmanageable "in a hurry," as Bonsi put it, and he ejected. Because the U-2 was starting to roll on its back, the ejection system fired him off at an angle almost parallel to the earth's surface. Five seconds later he was looking down at a rice paddy and trying to maneuver his chute so he could avoid landing in one. "They use human fertilizer over there!"

A poor man staring death right in the eyes only three seconds before had the gall to think as a rich man and presumed to choose where he would land.

Plane to paddy—a total of eight seconds. Major Bonsi logged a total flight time of two minutes and fifteen seconds, which was probably giving him a few seconds unearned. His report was traditional. "The airplane exploded, that's all. The whole tail blew off, so of course I thought it best to depart."

Of course.

The rules covering a dining out are specific and vigorously enforced through a series of "penalties." One rule states, "Thou shalt not murder the Queen's English." Another, "Thou shalt not laugh at ridiculously funny comments, unless the President first shows approval by laughing." There are countless other infractions, which first must be called to the attention of the vice-president of the mess, an officer appointed because of his recognized wit and ability to think fast on his feet. He is addressed by all members of the mess as "Mister Vice."

"Mister Vice! Point of order! I call your attention to Major Napolitano, who has arrived at this function with lint on his left shoulder board. I protest that this is not a minor infraction and possibly is an insult to the mess."

Mister Vice then addresses the president, who considers the matter and sentences Napolitano to "one trip to the grog bowl."

The entire mess expresses their approval of the sentence by banging the table with their spoons or glasses and waving their red napkins. And there is considerable cheering as Napolitano proceeds to the large silver bowl filled with a combination of alcoholic liquids. His behavior before the bowl is full of pitfalls, and he will be called to account for the slightest error in protocol. He must first salute the bowl, then fill a cup, perform a smart about-face, and toast the mess, saying, "To the mess!" He must drain the cup without removing it from his lips, turn the cup upside down over his head, about-face again, place the cup on the table, salute the grog bowl, and return to his seat.

Since this whole ceremony must be done smartly and in exact sequence, errors are inevitable and become more frequent as the evening progresses. Some officers are obliged to repeat the sequence several times before they execute all perfectly. For once in the year the junior officers are able to momentarily humble the higher ranks.

During the meal the big room became somewhat subdued, the candles flickered highlights of beauty across the young faces, many now slightly damp with the heat of each other and joyful excitement; conversations became a low mumble, punctuated with occasional yelps, chirps, and the tintinnabulation of silverware, crockery, and glass echoing across the clustered tables.

At the dignitaries' table, surrounded by a spellbound audience, Orville Wilbur Tosch held forth in the style of a man who values attention. Squirming uncomfortably in a rented tuxedo, mischief shining in his merry eyes, Tosch spoke of another time. The normal rasp of his voice disappeared as he pushed an invisible fur-lined cap back on his head. Here was a bank of fog smothering the Aleutians. There was the tundra unending and the Arctic wind screeching across the snows.

"I was flying an airplane that was so slow a moose could trot in its shadow," Tosch announced. "Hauling a load of fish from Naknek see, and all of a sudden the goddamned engine packed up and quit. I landed in sort of a dry marsh a hundred miles from nowhere. . . .

"I am about to get out and see to the damage when I realize I'm not alone. There is this brown bear waiting for me . . . big guy, looks just like my uncle Victor. And hungry. He just sits there outside waiting, and I just sit inside waiting, until I figure he must be hungry, which is not good for brown bears. They get antisocial. So I thought to throw him a fish. So I do, see, and then I throw him another . . . then another. He swallows fifteen fish and stays right there waiting for more . . . or me, I can't be sure. Comes twilight . . . never gets real dark up there except in winter, and this here bear starts looking offended when I stop throwing him fish. My supply is going fast. He's looking more like my uncle Victor all the time, so how can I shoot him?

"Then another bear comes by, and obviously wants some of the action. I throw him a fish too, hoping they'll start a fight among themselves, but they just wait for more. I don't know what to do. So you know what I done?

"We always carried a gallon can of gasoline in our emergency kit for starting fires and the like, if we had to camp. So what I done was pour some gas down the throat of the biggest salmon I had left, then I climb outside very slowly, light a match, and drop it in his mouth. Boom! I singed my eyebrows before I could toss the fish away, but you should have seen them bears take off. They never come back, and I had a nice restful night sleeping between the fish and mosquitoes."

Tosch has little interest in his credibility, and his stories are often careless of time and place. Yet he holds that anything could happen in Alaska, goddammit, and he had certainly earned his right to indulge an audience via fifty years of losing dear friends to the elements and tiptoeing past death himself countless times. He realized that this unusual mixture of sour-dough flying and the hush-hush atmosphere of reconnaissance flying was not as odd as it seemed. He understood the compulsion of his hosts to fly U-2s, and they understood his lifelong obsession.

While Tosch was exceptional in his way, there are still hundreds of his kind frequenting the smaller hangars across the land, returning to their devotion as pilgrims do on a holy day. There is something fundamental in their subjection, some inexplicable mystique that involves far more than merely riding in a machine.

Man has been dreaming of flight since history was inscribed on the walls of caves; for thousands of years this great accomplishment awaited our own time.

As the jubilation of the dining out washed about them in waves of laughter, Tosch knew—and Driskill, Hinkle, Pinsky, and even

Farrington, the general, knew—that flying is a release of the spirit, an extraordinary human experience that somehow hoists men or women far above themselves. Aloft the spirit sings without a sound, and no true airman ever regrets himself.

The obsession with flight invokes an ever-deeper compulsion, and it is unexplainable. There is the lure of a chance to be taken, especially when we have convinced ourselves that in no way can it go against us. All of us have a highly private pact with death, and our curiosity about the nature of our personal climax leads us into trouble—even if we win a postponement. In a few of us the urge to tease death without actually kicking it in the snout becomes almost irresistible.

When the roast beef arrived, there was a temporary lull in the conversation on the dais. General Farrington, resplendent in his medals, and Pinsky in his, had exhausted safe subjects except for flying, and even that was difficult when seated so far apart. Like Driskill, Hinkle, Kishler, and others of the Vietnam era, they wanted to avoid being yesterday's heroes, fighting a war their nation would never understand. Instead, Pinsky, known during his forward air controller days as Cobra Four, munched on his roast beef, smiled at everyone whose eyes he could catch, and nodded knowingly when someone on the dais said something he really didn't hear because of the noise.

Driskill's medals and Farrington's and Hinkle's and Pinsky's were more than "good boy" awards or acknowledgment of services rendered. They were symbols of discomfort and longing, fear and escape from death. There is no adequate recompense for being shot at, or worse, being hit. Their medals were also a reminder of another man, who had lived and fought with the zeal of youth and then perished little by little over the years.

The glitter of a dining out is like a tribal dance, which gathers momentum as customary decorum is put aside. More and more outrageous accusations were made to "Mister Vice," and this night even Pinsky became a target. His gentle stutter failed to excuse him from the charge that in returning the salute of a grog-bowl visitor, he had allowed his fingers to curl slightly.

Driskill was appointed temporary president while his wing commander made his trip to the grog bowl. Amid howls of delight from his junior officers, Driskill sent him back a second time for executing a clumsy about-face. Joyous pandemonium ensued when Pinsky saluted the bowl before, rather than after, placing the empty cup on his head. Savoring his opportunity, Driskill sent him back for a third round.

Pinsky, normally incapable of bending to the pleasures of fellowship, soon acquired a rambunctious group of supporters. For the great man had been humbled, and he took it well.

So, amid the smell of perfume and powder and flowers, the scent of whiskey and wine, the bloom of young cheeks and fine teeth, and hearty laughter along with talk of diets, so surrounded by all the accoutrements of the privileged American, the spirits of a few long-ago heroes were revived.

Four:

The Man

Employing the handy excuse of duty to his squadron, Driskill managed to be one of the very last to leave the dining out. As a consequence, he complained of a certain biliousness throughout the following Sunday, but on Monday morning at seven he strode into his office and declared himself "fully operational." Even as he entered his office, he was reminded that Pinsky was right—something had to be done quickly about the drainage of air force pilots to civilian life, and new replacements were sorely needed. The challenge was to find the best and avoid those who emitted even a whiff of the mediocre.

There was, as he expected, a young officer waiting for him. He appeared as crisp as the California morning.

Driskill flashed his finest early morning smile and crossed the office to his desk. He pretended to be searching for a certain paper while he adjusted his reactions to the bewildering passage of time. Was the air force now spawning a new type of child, or was too dadgummed much paperwork aging him too rapidly? The looks of this youngster who so-help-him-God wore a captain's bars was enough to drive a commander straight to section eight.

The blue nameplate pinned above the captain's right blouse pocket identified him as Hopper. According to the personnel file, his first name was Cecil, and Driskill saw that he was trying very hard to appear casual and eager at the same time—standard performance for young officers from other units who suddenly developed a yearning to become one of the "recce boys." They came from bombers, fighters, transports, and the training squadrons, and eventually only about thirty percent of the applicants could cut the mustard. The fact that all applicants must be experienced aviators did not necessarily mean they could master the eccentricities of the U-2 or tolerate the woes of high-altitude flight.

Driskill shuffled through Hopper's personnel file, which lay before him in a manila folder. A lifetime here—short to be sure, but nevertheless the record of the man almost since the day he graduated from diapers. What the file did not say, Driskill was amused to observe, was that Candidate Hopper had the damndest collection of freckles he had ever seen. Like confetti across his nose. Nor did the file describe his flaming red hair, or his alert eyes, or such details as Hopper's nose, which turned up at the end like a munchkin's. In fact, Driskill thought, there was a considerable amount of the pixie in the way Hopper held his head. He suddenly recalled that the last time he had seen a face like Hopper's had been while he had been reading a children's book to his son. One of the elves had been peeking around a tree.

"So you want to fly U-2s?" Driskill fingered the folio, which he had already inspected, but now he pretended to read parts of it again. He wished he could stop thinking of the captain as Huckleberry Finn. This choosing a pilot for the 99th was a very solemn business. A yea or a nay could alter the course of the captain's young life, and it was always a sticky business playing God.

"Yessir. Very definitely. I want to fly U-2s."

"Why?"

"I like the idea of flying alone. And I'd be doing something real instead of just practicing."

"Humph." Huckleberry Hopper had given a standard answer, while somehow Driskill had expected more. The applicant was going to be entrusted with a lot more than an expensive flying machine; brains, instead of daring, was the key to the right type.

Driskill frowned at the manila file, but he was really watching Hopper attempting the impossible—trying to find a comfortable position in a government-issue lounge chair. He was wearing the standard blue air force uniform, and his black leather shoes were almost a reflection of his polished face. Was this the sort of person other men would want to go to war with? That was a factor never to be ignored.

"You have considerable flying time for a guy your age."

"I've been lucky. You build it up fast in MAC."*

Driskill reached behind his chair and picked up a small white packet. Suddenly he pitched it at Hopper, who caught it in midair.

"Glad to see you're awake," Driskill drawled as he favored his guest with a slight smile. "Did you know bubble gum costs three cents each? If you buy a whole box of three hundred, you get forty pieces for free."

He watched Hopper fingering the packet and saw his cobalt eyes go hunting. He was obviously puzzled. How was he going to handle this priceless bit of information?

"Never would I want to miss a bargain, sir. . . ."

Better than most, Driskill thought. At least he hadn't sat there with his eyes fixed on the rubber plant in the corner, trying to hide the fear that he would be rejected before he even approached a U-2.

*Military Air Lift Command, the transport arm of the air force.

"It says here you lettered in basketball. How come? You're not very tall."

"I hid behind the bigger guys, sir."

"National Honor Society. You're smart then?"

"How I wish . . . sir."

"Air force ROTC program . . . Commander of the Arnold Society? Congratulations . . . Worked as night chef to help pay tuition at University of Nevada. You were a chef?"

"The term is a slight exaggeration, sir. I fried hamburgers at McDonald's. My hours were from ten at night to two in the morning, and by that time most people just don't care what they eat."

"Do I gather your heart wasn't in the job?"

"I haven't been able to eat a hamburger since."

"I see you're not married. What's your career goal?"

Hopper hesitated. "Well, sir . . . I don't necessarily want to be a general."

"Why not?"

"Because they don't get any flying . . . at least not very often."

"Is that why you joined the air force?"

"Yessir."

"So did everybody. Including me. I suppose you're the world's greatest pilot."

"Yes, sir . . . with the possible exception of yourself."

Driskill found himself beaming. This freckle-faced kid had spoken the God's truth even though it was deflating to realize that every other career pilot was under the same delusion. A chestful of medals was usually a matter of luck combined with some skill in staying the hell out of harm's way. Some guys diluted the bitter taste of Vietnam by forcing themselves to believe they really were extraordinary.

"I like your attitude," Driskill said.

He scanned a letter from SAC headquarters. The brass there

bossed the whole wing and many others. "It says here that Captain Hopper performs his ground duties with zeal and enthusiasm. Seems like the guy who wrote that has a zeal for redundancy. It also says you were nominated three times for junior officer of the quarter in the last six quarters. What happened? Why were you not elected?"

"I was . . . sir."

"Then why in the hay-ell don't they say so?"

"I guess that fact got lost in the redundancy, sir."

Driskill was pleased. Hopper could play mental Ping-Pong. Except for actually flying with him, he now knew more about Hopper than he needed to know. From this day on, the determination of his future would be in the hands of the training squadron, and they had callused hands. They would take him to pieces, and hopefully put him back together again.

"Go see Butch Hinkle tomorrow. He'll set you up for a flight. We'll see how you and a U-2 like each other."

Hopper almost leaped to his feet. "Yessir."

"Better take your gum out before you talk to him. Hinkle is a jelly-bean addict."

After Hopper had departed, smiling all the way, Driskill folded his hands behind his head and swung his feet to his desk. He stared thoughtfully at his heavy black flight boots and found himself satisfied with the way the morning had gone so far, even if fresh air and God's sun were hidden behind concrete walls.

Why was it, he wondered, that almost every pilot he had ever known was a devout self-deprecator? It was a fetish. No aviator in his right mind would say he had just made a perfect landing. It was always a "bit ragged." Combat with a thunderstorm was "panic time," when actually there had been no fright involved. Bob Hoover, the pilot's pilot, had been doing an airshow in his P-51 when he inadvertently struck a high-tension line with one wingtip and removed two feet of the span. He completed the show, and after landing successfully, he just smiled, tweaked his guardsman's mustache, and said, "No one told me I had to crash. So there was really nothing to it."

Of course not, Driskill thought. There is not all that much in putting your life on the line, if over a long time your brain has been conditioned to believe that nothing really nasty could happen to you. No one ever took off in an airplane with a solid expectation that he might not come back in one piece.

It was curious how Hopper lingered in his mind. He seemed to know what he was getting into, which was more than most applicants learn for starters. He knew that, except for overseas assignments, pilots of the 99th had an easy time living with themselves, because they were not just practicing for a war that might never come. They had a sense of immediate purpose that was impossible in other units, and it was a good idea to remind them every so often that while Pearl Harbor happened long before most of them were born, there could be other surprises. A guy got dadgummed weary perched up there in a U-2 all by himself for ten hours. Eisenhower must have been briefed by someone who knew what he was talking about, because Ike once said there was no glory in espionage. He said if you were successful, it couldn't be told.

And if you are caught, Driskill remembered ruefully, your own people never heard of you.

In the whole vast and incredibly complex American intelligence machine, one human spy was no more than a rivet; in fact, he mused, one of the main projects in the Far East regions was code-named Rivet Joint.

All right. Young Hopper seemed to have absorbed the message naturally. But the next applicant who came into this office was going to hear a short address on how just one guy flying alone could bring about an international catastrophe.

Driskill smiled at his boots. The guys had a phrase, the creed they flew by. "Oh, God, don't let me be killed . . . but mainly don't let me fuck up and live!"

❖

Tuesday Captain Cecil Hopper rose before dawn and started his twenty minutes of calisthenics. He rubbed the sleep from his eyes, did forty push-ups, twenty hand-toe bends, and five minutes jumping to the rhythm of an imaginary rope. Afterward, his breathing barely faster than normal, he shaved carefully, then showered, and finally donned his class-A uniform—blouse of air force blue, black patent-leather shoes, dark blue tie, and light blue shirt. He had spent his first night in VIP quarters, something Driskill had arranged. "Hay-ell, you might as well be comfortable. Just don't get too used to it."

So Captain Hopper, whose rank barely entitled him to crumbs and water in the military world, luxuriated in a one-bedroom apartment perched on a hill with a pleasant view of the surrounding Beale acreage. There was even a brace of wild deer reflected in the hall mirror as he passed his own inspection. He adjusted his garrison cap squarely on his head. It would never do on a day like this to allow even a slight tilt to his cap. That would speak of cockiness or, worse yet, an ingrown rebelliousness, which probably were not qualities Lieutenant Colonel Hinkle, who commanded the training squadron, was looking for. This was Squaresville.

Hopper was full of bounce this Tuesday morning. "You are the answer to their prayers," he said to the mirror. Maybe he was the youngest applicant they ever had, but this day was going to see a little old Albuquerque boy win all the marbles.

Although he had allowed himself much more time than he needed, he half ran to a lump of Dacron cloth that covered his most treasured possession—a double-X Camaro with dual carburetors and a voice like thunder. Painted Rolls-Royce gray.

Don't touch, if you please. When he pulled away the cover, he knew again the exquisite pleasure of viewing the car's pearllike finish, a job he had carried out himself. There she was in all her glory, the most beautiful Camaro in the civilized world. Why, hay-ell (as Driskill might say), time spent on the Camaro was better than women.

The air policeman at the flight-line gate proved to be a man of taste. He was big and black and wore his beret pulled down to a fraction of an inch above his eyebrows. He hardly glanced at Hopper's identification; his eyes were fixed on the Camaro. "Where you want to go, sir?"

"Fifth Strategic Reconnaissance Training Squadron." Might as well give him the full mouthful.

"Sir, that is some vehicle. You like to sell it?"

"No." A smile. This morning the world was full of intelligent people.

"It is extremely cool. Someday . . ." The policeman allowed his voice to fade away. He took a brace and saluted smartly. Hopper returned the salute and drove through the gate. He saw the apricot-colored building in the distance and felt a tightening of his stomach muscles. Being the new boy on the block was sure a lonesome business.

He found a parking place near the apricot building and stood watching the activity on the flight line, because his watch told him incredible news. He was nearly an hour ahead of time for his appointment with Lieutenant Colonel "Butch" Hinkle. Even the sound of his name was a bit nerve-racking.

He could see only a part of the flight line. He counted twenty four-engined tankers opposite the apricot building, and in the distance a pair of U-2s.

He heard a roar, then saw a tanker taking off, huffing and puffing beneath a heavy load of fuel for some unseen pilot who would rendezvous perhaps five hundred miles away. Pity the tanker guys. They flew airplanes built before most of them were born. Hours and hours of dragging around the sky so some hotshot could stay up there.

Hopper entered the apricot building, checked his watch again (only two minutes had passed since the last time), and came to a halt in the outer corridor.

Here was a bulletin board. He found it strangely comforting. All new guys on the block began by reading bulletin boards, right?

The wags had been busy here. Notes scribbled in various hands.

> Put out my hand and touched the face of God just before I yelled, Bombs away! . . . And watched 30 acres of jungle and huts go up in smoke.

Below it was another note.

> You are sick, sick, sick, sick—and my hero.

Hopper swallowed. What kind of ape cage was he getting into? Another note: "U-2s refuel satellites."

Next to it was a photo of Muammar Qaddafi sitting on a tractor. His printed monologue insisting terrorists did not train in Libya was augmented by a hand-written quote.

> Promotion boards are pig-fuckers. I didn't make General because my turban was dirty. May they all eat camel shit while I ride my John Deere over Mediterranean waters.

Hopper saw that the paper notes were yellowed, and decided they had been written long ago. There was also a photo of a crashed air-force jet of which almost nothing except ashes remained. Beside it a printed legend declared that the plane had crashed and burned, but was 90 percent intact and according to an army spokesman would be flying again by Friday. Below someone had scribbled, "Go Army! Go!"

Hopper went over his "in-processing" list just to make sure this momentous day would come off per regulations. New boys in any school, he thought, find comfort in regulations.

He checked his watch again. Only another two minutes gone? For the love of God, what was he going to do with the next fifty-six?

He went outside and watched another tanker become airborne. He would not mind at all if someone came along with a plateful of hominy grits and sausage right now, maybe with a side order of eggs and rye toast and gooseberry jam like they had back at the Plattsburg airbase, where he had been stationed for a while.

No, breakfast would have to wait. Hunger stimulated the brain, someone said, and a full belly was not going to impress a guy people called "Butch." Long, lean, and mean was the ticket. Forty-eight minutes to go.

He opened the brown manila envelope he had been carrying and confirmed the contents for what he supposed might be the tenth time.

Okay, ancillary training records filed. Fact sheets, personnel folder. Line badge already pinned to his blouse. Hometown news release—told not necessary here. Naturally. These guys were sort of spies. Even if they had a public-affairs officer, what would he say?

Air-force form 942, record of evaluation and several form 8s. Copy of official photograph—damned freckles looked like spattered paint. Officer personnel brief. Last monthly flying printout. Applicant copy of same. Form IAW AFR 36-20. Check.

Hopper watched a group of officers, all wearing flight suits, enter the apricot building. They were jovial and loud and laughing, and Hopper heard one of them say he was never going to lose weight unless he stopped eating so much breakfast.

Which one was Hinkle? They had all looked right through him. Had he suddenly become invisible? And breakfast? No one had thought to tell him where to find it.

He saw one of the officers poke at the combination lock on the back door. When he opened the door, the others followed him, and Hopper decided to do the same. He was supposed to be welcome here, but they had not exactly given him the key to the city.

While the others continued down the hallway, Hopper paused before an assembly of portraits on the wall—U-2 pilots all smiling the word "cheese." Which one was Hinkle? There was Driskill near the top row, and here? This was Hinkle? Jesus! That was not exactly the kind of face a mother could love. Hinkle had a jaw that said, Don't tread on me, even if he was smiling, and he had a pair of eyes that seemed to stab right through the glass on the portrait.

Hopper spent nearly half an hour studying the photographs, which were divided into the 99th Squadron members and the 5th Training Squadron. He tried to memorize several of the names and fix them to their faces—Lindeman . . . Kishler . . . Sherwood . . . Van Heeswyk . . . Weissenbuehler. What was this, the Luftwaffe? Some mix. Here was a black—George Marshall. As it should be.

When at last the hands of the watch stood one minute until eight, Hopper presented himself to the doorway he had reconnoitered at least fifty times. He smiled a nervous good morning to the civilian woman who apparently was Hinkle's secretary. "You're right on time," she said, as if surprised. "Would you like some coffee?"

He declined. He had never been a coffee drinker, and at this moment his heart was going fast enough without outside help.

He heard a burst of heavy laughter from the adjoining office, and the loneliness came rushing back. This new-boy business was the shits.

"Greetings," Hinkle said as he returned Hopper's salute, stood up, and extended his hand.

Hopper was relieved by his appearance. The gray eyes were disconcerting, but the twist in his smile created an air of warmth. He was a short, compact man with a bristle of black hair.

"Remove your cap and sit down. We're not very formal here."

A silence followed, which Hopper found almost intolerable. Those eyes were measuring him, bone by bone, he thought.

He saw Hinkle reach for a plastic container, meticulously pry off the top, and offer it to him. Jelly beans. He took one. This was breakfast?

The silence persisted while Hinkle selected a jelly bean for himself, popped it into his mouth, and replaced the container top. "Well . . ." he said at last.

Hopper's eyes abandoned his control momentarily. They ran away to the walls of the windowless office and halted on a plaque. It was obviously Oriental and depicted a willow tree with a small bird perched on a branch. Below the branch was a legend printed in English.

How can a bird, which is born for joy, Sit in a cage and sing?

"That's me," Hinkle said. "Got it in Korea."

"It's very nice."

"It gives me comfort."

Hinkle chewed thoughtfully on his jelly bean a moment, then he said, "I've been going over your file. I guess you know it looks pretty good. . . ."

"It could be better, sir."

"This is a different business. We have to be very careful who we take into the program. I'm not going to give you a lot of chaff about how special our airplanes are. You'll find that out soon enough."

Another silence. Hopper wondered if he should say anything at all or keep his peace. "The trouble with this recce business," Hinkle said without a smile, "is that one stupid mistake can do so much damage. Your first name is Cecil?"

"Yessir."

"Family name?"

"An uncle."

"Albuquerque your hometown? I haven't been in Albuquerque for years."

"It's still there . . . basking in the sun."

"I often wonder why we don't get more applications from guys born back East . . . Vermont or Maine or someplace back there. There must be something wrong with our demographics. I see you're still single? Then I assume you won't mind being sent TDY?"

"No, sir. I'd enjoy it."

"Maybe . . ." Hinkle said slowly. "You have to be at least a little peculiar to be in this business."

Hinkle folded his hands behind his crop of spiky hair and slid so far down in his government-issue chair he was almost prone. His eyes searched the ceiling as if he might find a bundle of words there, suspended and ready for plucking. He was silent for so long Hopper wondered if he had gone into some kind of military meditation.

"Last year," he said at last, "about Christmastime, Driskill called a meeting of the whole squadron. "He said, I have a real shitty job. I need a volunteer, and you can't even ask where the job is. I don't know when you'll get back home . . . and there's a chance of never. I can only tell you this much now, and that is that this is the worst TDY that has ever come our way. . . ."

Hinkle slid back to an erect position and leaned across his desk. "Guess what?" he asked.

"Everybody volunteered?"

"You got it. Each one was telling the other guy why he shouldn't go . . . their wives were pregnant . . . you'll get a divorce . . . you shouldn't miss Christmas with your family. On and on . . ." Hinkle studied the bird in the willow tree as if he were waiting for it to fly out of the plaque. "Why do you think they would do that?"

Hopper made a sound that was no more than a clearing of his throat. How the hell could he answer such a question?

"Love," Hinkle said firmly.

Hopper was sure he was hallucinating. He had better get some food in him soon. Here he was just after eight o'clock in the morning, listening to a guy named Butch talking about love.

"If you had been in Vietnam, you would have seen it ten times a day. Any war, for that matter. And maybe you have somewhere in your travels. I'm not talking about homosexual love, although basically I suppose it's about the same thing and has been going on for just as many years . . . like since the first two guys threw spears at two other guys. Our guys love each other and they love the job and they call it camaraderie, which is something their wives have a little trouble with. So do I sometimes, but it's there and we might as well have the guts to recognize it."

Hopper tried to smile as he told himself that his original impression fostered by the bulletin board might not have been as far off the mark as he had supposed.

"You ever fly a tail-dragger?" Hinkle asked suddenly.

"No, sir."

"Ever fly an airplane with a propeller on it?"

"No, sir."

"You are in for some surprises. After Bowen briefs you tomorrow, Napolitano will be your instructor. He'll take you around the patch a few times to see how you like our kind of flying. We lost two U-2s not so long ago. Exploded on takeoff. The tail. The guys weren't hurt. So if Napolitano says bail out, don't just sit there with your thumb up your ass. Pull the ejection handle and sing loud and clear . . . 'Nearer My God to Thee.' Any questions?"

Hopper stood up. The interview was obviously over. Did he dare ask a mundane question of this man who talked about love in a barren office?

"Sir . . . ? Is there a place around here where I can find some breakfast?"

"Next building over. Walk three miles down the corridors, get lost four times, and you're qualified. Then turn left, then right, and the cafeteria will be straight ahead of you. In the recce business you learn to find your way by yourself. If you make it in this outfit, you'll be one of the few guys in the air force who flies alone. Might as well get used to it."

❖

Reconnaissance pilots must accommodate their bodies to great heights, and at Beale their education was supplemented by a shaggy-dog-humorous man named Bowen. He was the civilian manager in the physiological support division, and knew as much as anyone about the practical business of keeping the human body healthy on the fringes of space.

Bowen was utterly devoted to his work, which he was more than willing to discuss. He often left his listeners sucking at the surrounding atmosphere like beached fish, wondering how they had survived so long.

At the moment his bright eyes were fixed on Captain Cecil Hopper's red hair. "You inherit that rooster brush from your mother or your father?"

"Both."

"Sisters and brothers the same?"

"Close."

"Holy mackerel! When you went to church, your family had their own torch parade. Anyway, welcome to the upper atmosphere."

Bowen's English always smacked of mountain bourbon, and there was a special lilt to his diction as he screwed his puckish face into a marquetry of expressions.

"We begin," he smiled at Hopper. "I guess you already know that Fart's Law is not to be laughed at? Just keep in mind that your 'lil old gastrointestinal system starts to expand even at twenty-five thousand feet. In that overfed belly of yours you nurse a variety of gases . . . oxygen, carbon dioxide, nitrogen, and hydrogen sulfide. Those vapors expand at altitude and can interfere with your breathing, because the digestive organs push up against the diaphragm. We can't have you swooning like a Victorian lady, because there's nobody up there to give you smelling salts. So lay off the onions, cabbages, raw apples, cucumbers, and the like, or I guarantee you'll be beggin' God to forgive you and you might even fuck up the mission."

For a man who cared little for ceremony and even less for pose, Bowen could present a surprising portrait of the professor who takes himself too seriously. "The ancient Egyptians believed that the circulation of blood by the heart was not only vital to life, but was the seat of our personality. So the heart was the only organ they left in the cadaver during the process of mummification. Likewise, we have to keep your pump going or we lose an expensive man damn quickly. The answer is our pressure suit and fishbowl helmet. If they fail, just remember you are no longer there. Instantly."

Two hours later Bowen was still warming to his life's dedication. "Be advised that when you get your space suit, you just don't sit there and suck air and decide that's all there is to it. The flow of air in your lungs operates in a sine-wave fashion. Even mild exertion will more than double the need of air, so you gotta learn to relax. Don't hyperventilate, no matter how many things go wrong with the mission. Are you still with me?"

It was obvious to Hopper that Bowen didn't care if he was with him or not. It seemed as if he was carrying on a campaign within himself and nothing would stop him.

"Now we've had an occasional problem with our U-2s, so you should give some thought to the ejection procedure. A' course Pinsky and company will never forgive you if you abandon one of their flying machines, but it's better to be trigger-happy than dead, as the sheriff in my hometown used to say! If you decide to depart, remember your head goes all the way back until your helmet is against the back of the seat. Elbows in. Feet back and knees together. Pull yellow handle and think sweet thoughts . . . same as in any other flying machine. The difference here is the possibility of ejecting at high altitude. You could have a free-fall of as much as fifty-five thousand feet. That takes a long time . . . like eternity, and meanwhile your l'il ol' body is subject to oxygen and pressure starvation unless all the systems in your space suit are working."

Bowen's eyes lit up as if he were appreciating the prospect. Then he added dubiously, "Course your space suit is geared to deploy your parachute automatically when you get down to sixteen thousand five hundred feet. It will let you drift back to earth like a gentleman . . . if everything works the way it should."

When Bowen was finished, he escorted Hopper to a locker room that reminded him of his basketball days. He was greeted by a young blond corporal who handed him a suit of long underwear. The corporal looked uncomfortably similar to his expensive friend Cindy, who swallowed almost as much of his spare cash as the Camaro. Same wide mouth. Same smile. Same bangs. He wished the resemblance were not so striking.

"You're not really going anywhere today," she said brightly, "but you might as well play it like you are. Put the underwear on inside out. That way the seams won't bunch up and pinch you."

She handed him a long, tubular sack shaped like a condom except that in the end it had a fitting for a small drain line. "Here," she said, unsmiling. "You won't need this because you'll only be suited up for a few hours, but you might as well put it on anyway."

Hopper knew his freckles were now dissolved in one great blush. He was supposed to walk around in long underwear, with that thing hanging out? In broad daylight? In full view of women? With maybe other guys watching?

Hopper heard himself say, "Yes, ma'm," and could hardly believe his ears.

The corporal showed him an empty locker and said she would see him shortly. Then she disappeared into the adjoining room.

It was a large room, about one hundred acres, Hopper thought, when he was obliged to cross it in his long underwear and with this pisser hanging out for all to see. And all were many.

Bowen himself was waiting with two sergeants, a pair of airmen, and the blond corporal. Hopper tried to pretend she was not so visible, but he failed. She seemed to be everywhere.

"Now," she stated crisply, "the fun begins."

She indicated he should seat himself on the edge of a large reclining leather chair. Then she knelt before him. She was joined by an airman first class, and together they shoved Hopper's feet into the legs of a yellow space suit. They yanked upward none too gently. "Stand up, sir."

Hopper complied. At this point he would stand on his head, if ordered.

At once he was attacked by the sergeant and the airman, who pulled his arms into the suit, then zipped up his fly and chest. The suit was overtight, because it was ownerless and used for transient pilots only.

As the dressers worked over Hopper, tugging and yanking until he was tightly zipped into his new cocoon, Bowen offered him a patronizing smile. "If you get the job, you'll have your own suits. Two of 'em. Made to measure, no less."

The circular wrist fittings of Hopper's suit were metal, somewhat like an old-fashioned deep-sea diving rig. The dressers slipped his hands into a pair of gloves and snapped them into the metal wristlets, making the arms airtight. Next a vest containing some of his emergency survival gear was added. Then his flight boots were laced up and sealed off like the wristlets.

Hopper's eyes, surrounded by constellations of freckles, became apprehensive. Ye gods! His bowels were reacting to all this attention. He couldn't ask these people to undress him and start all over again. And yet . . . ?

After a moment the sensation subsided. He aimed a small prayer of gratitude in the general direction of the ceiling, as the dressers eased him back to the reclining chair. They lowered a goldfish-bowl helmet over his head. They fitted it to a metal ring around the neck of his suit, twisted it into retaining slots, and snapped the security triggers shut.

Silence, except for his own strangely audible breathing.

Hopper had a sudden notion that death must be this way. Silence. No . . . there was the sound of his own breathing.

Cool air rushed about his face, and he inhaled deeply. Despite the presence of others, he knew a strange sense of isolation, almost as if he were alone in some eerie territory, floating comfortably through a long dream. Someone tipped the leather chair back to full reclining position, and there was a voice in the helmet. The blond corporal.

"You hear me all right, sir?"

"Affirmative."

"Feeling okay?"

"I feel like I'm a UFO." No microphone to pick up. It was part of the helmet. No headphones. Luxury.

"We're going to blow you up to check for leaks, then let you down again."

"Um-m-m." Was she talking about him springing a leak, or the suit?

Now, he felt the suit swell and embrace every part of his body. Pig on a spit. The corporal "chef" was fussing with a set of dials on her pedestal and an airman was checking sections of his new skin. Ready for basting?

"Looking good all around, sir."

The suit deflated. The corporal's clear voice again: "Everything seems to be working okay, sir. You go to the pressure chamber next. We'll leave you in place for about forty minutes to get rid of the nitrogen in your blood. We wouldn't want you to get the bends when you come down, would we, sir?"

"No, we would not."

"Okay. You're on a hundred percent oxygen now."

"Many thanks."

"Just sing out if you feel any discomfort. If you're too hot or too cold, just turn this little knob."

"Oh? I will, I will."

This was like going back to the womb. Why hadn't he noticed that there was now another man being suited up? He could see him on the other side of the room just above the perimeter of his faceplate, stretched out in the same way. His hands were crossed over his belly and he appeared to be sleeping. He was probably going on an actual flight rather than just to an altitude chamber.

Now, Hopper existed in a nylon-and-matting world. His silicone-rubber oxygen hoses, wire-wound and nylon-covered, contained a pressure-opening check valve to prevent reverse flow. There was one hose for his suit and one for his helmet, and a mechanical controller would maintain absolute suit pressure even if he was suddenly exposed to decompression. A dual helmet regulator not only provided oxygen on Hopper's personal demand, but maintained a slight positive pressure within his oral nasal cavity. An aneroid assembly allowed for his exhalation of gas into the suit, and yet another controlled the pressure regardless of outside pressure or lack of it. All of these systems had backup systems; all were machined to extremely fine tolerances and were very expensive.

Hopper closed his eyes and made a deliberate effort to review his situation. Whatever had given him the notion to apply for this sort of flying? Maybe it was too late for an assignment to fighters, but there were always bombers and transports. And Airlift Command, where he had just come from. At least that had been *comfortable* flying.

His thoughts turned to his good fortune in life. For sure he had been lucky. Never any real financial worries. The air force ROTC had even paid for his college education. Then, after four years of keeping chin in and shoulders back, he was commissioned a second lieutenant. Base salary $1,410.30 per month. Next it was off to flight school, where he was paid an additional $370 per month for "flight status." Then, first lieutenant at $1,850.10. Now, captain at $2,308.60. All of these rewards supplemented by housing allowances, insurance, and a someday pension.

Hopper squirmed in his space suit. According to the clock on the wall, he had to remain here another thirty minutes.

"How you doing, sir?" The blond corporal appeared in his faceplate, then moved out of sight again. He could look at her all day.

Indeed, this was the good life. During vacation leaves, he could ride free of charge on air force transports to places ordinary tourists dream about. Big plus. But maybe he was spending too much money on girlfriends. Did a man need three? Two were

"G-U" (geographically undesirable), but the third, Cindy . . . was right in San Francisco and liked expensive restaurants. And then there was the Camaro, polished with money. Gobs of it for those monthly payments. But class!

Lying here like a baked sausage afforded a perfect opportunity to consider the options. Some guys who had graduated in the same class had served their hitch in the air force and gone straight to the airlines. They were making a bunch of money, but they sounded unhappy. Some of them were honest enough to say they should never have left the air force. They said the life was awful and the flying was like tapioca. It was the union that dictated who actually did the flying and who rode sidesaddle. Screw it.

Hopper was dozing when he felt a gentle tugging at his shoulder. The corporal. Her voice dominated the interior of his helmet. "All right, Captain. Nap time is over."

She fussed about his various connecting cords, straightened his chair, and handed him a small metal briefcase. She said it contained his life-support system. "You're on your own now, sir..Just like you're bound for the moon."

Hopper was tempted to say something about how fine it would be to go to the moon with her, then changed his mind. This was not the time for that sort of thing.

With an airman on one side and the corporal on the other, he was led down a short corridor. He was guided into a large room occupied by large, circular tanks and a varied display of control valves. He was led to a small cell-like structure near the center of the room, which he immediately decided looked exactly like an execution chamber—gas or electric, it made no difference. There was even an aircraft-type chair inside, complete with what looked like restraining straps.

Two new airmen accompanied him into the booth. Both, he noted, wore oxygen masks.

Hopper's movements in the space suit were still so clumsy he had to be helped into the chair.

This was really claustrophobia alley! He had been in other pressure chambers during the course of his regular flight training, but this one gave a guy the willies.

While the airmen were strapping him into the seat, he discovered an observation window on one side of the booth. Two black sergeants were behind the window. They smiled at him. Then he recognized Driskill standing behind the sergeants. He waved his hand casually. Then Bowen appeared beside Driskill and the two laughed about something. They were watching him as they might regard a fish in an aquarium.

The voice of one of the black sergeants in his helmet: "Sir. We're going to take you up to twenty-five thousand feet and check everything before we go any higher. The two men will remain with you until that time. How do you feel?"

"Super." The biggest lie I've ever told, Hopper thought.

"Then we'll take you up to fifty thousand and stay there for a while . . . until you get used to things. See that little canister of water by the window?"

Hopper looked about frantically for a canister, and finally located it on a shelf about a foot below the window. If he was supposed to drink it, how was he going to get it inside his helmet?

"Sir, that water will begin to boil at about seventy thousand feet. The same thing would happen to your blood if it weren't for your suit. Understand?"

"I am impressed." Hopper hoped his voice didn't sound as agonized as he thought it did.

"Okay? The two airmen will leave you soon. You'll see by the altimeter you're already at twenty thousand . . ."

Altimeter? Where was any damned altimeter? Ah, there, in the window. This suit had to be the most uncomfortable contraption known to man.

The airmen departed through the small pressure-lock door. There was silence except for Hopper's own breathing, which he thought was excessively loud. Sounded like a draft horse plowing a field, he thought.

He watched the altimeter. Spinning now. Fifty thousand feet already? What was the hurry?

"How you feelin', sir?"

"Fine . . ." Liar.

The suit was beginning to squeeze him slightly. It was a strange yet not uncomfortable sensation. The altimeter was still winding around . . . sixty-five thousand now. Much higher than he had ever been.

"Sir. See that little green ball down on your right side? It has a lanyard on it. Can you reach it?"

Hopper fumbled along the right side of his suit. He was surprised at his clumsiness. Where the hell was that little green ball? He could not feel a damn thing through these pressurized gloves.

"There you go. You got it, sir. Now, we're going to take you up to seventy-five thousand feet and put you on hold for a minute. Understand?"

"Affirmative."

There followed an echoing discussion between the observers. It was not loud enough to understand what they were saying, but he was sure they were not addressing him.

"Still feeling okay, sir?"

"Never felt better." Lie three.

"Okay. The chamber is now at seventy-five thousand feet and your suit is keeping everything nice and comfortable, we hope?"

"Sure. Fine. I could spend all day like this." Lie four.

"You just might, sir. Now, we're going to simulate a pressure-system failure in your aircraft. It will be sudden, understand?"

"Roger."

"When I say so, you yank the green ball. It's your emergency oxygen system."

Hopper saw Driskill and Bowen watching him. Both had sly smiles. Their eyes said they were waiting.

"Ready, sir?"

"Roger." If he squeezed the green ball any harder, some sort of juice was bound to come out of it.

"All right, sir. Pull the green ball."

Hopper yanked. Instantly he was seized by a giant hand hugging his entire body as he had never been hugged before. For a moment he wondered if his heart had stopped. He seemed to be paralyzed.

The bottom rim of his helmet faceplate was jammed up hard against his nose. It was very painful.

"There is a white ball right at your chest level. Pull it down now, sir."

He sought frantically for a ball on his chest. Any ball. Never mind the color.

When at last he found it and pulled hard, the rim of the helmet came down. His nose was back on his face again. He was able to see directly through the faceplate, and there was the water—boiling.

His suit was fully inflated now, and he could barely move his arms.

"You have just experienced a pressure-system failure, sir. Now, reach down and put your fingers around the ejection handle."

He bent forward to grasp the yellow handle between his legs. The effort required to make the slightest move was enormous. This is U-2 flying? I'll take the train.

"Of course, it will probably never happen to you, sir, but now you know what it's like if it does. We'll bring you down to earth now, sir. Let you down real gentle, like."

"Thanks."

Where were Driskill and Bowen? They had disappeared. Where were Driskill's gleaming white teeth . . . and Bowen's mischievous eyes?

No smiles now. He was no longer a curiosity. Didn't anyone give a damn that he had done everything he was told to do as promptly as humanly possible? There were just the two black sergeants in the window, and even they seemed to have lost all interest in him. It looked as if they were doing paperwork.

The altimeter read ten thousand feet. The water had stopped boiling in the canister, and the two airmen entered the chamber. They went about the business of unstrapping him without saying a word.

What Captain Cecil Hopper did not know was that his behavior in the pressure chamber was monitored with great interest. Some 50 percent of the applicants for the U-2 program revealed themselves as unsuited in the pressure chamber. The claustrophobic effect of the space suit, exaggerated by the chamber itself, often proved just too much for many men. Some detested the experience so deeply they decided the life was not for them. Others became overexcited and sometimes incapable of following the most simple instructions. A few panicked and the simulation was abandoned.

When at last he was relieved of the pressure suit, Hopper was not told the score of his performance.

This was the recce business. It was one of the many things he would not be told.

❖

Hopper had no way of knowing if he had passed his altitude chamber test until that same evening when he was watching the Monday night football game on the ancient television set provided for his quarters. Major Napolitano had called. The ringing of the phone was such an unexpected break in his loneliness that he was long in reaching it.

Napolitano said, "You must have been out in the back forty. Or do you have a party in progress? If so, I would hate to interrupt with a call to duty."

"No, sir. I was watching the game."

"It looks like you're my next victim. I'll meet you in Operations at zero nine-hundred tomorrow. We'll go for a ride in a real airplane. Now go back to your box."

"Yessir."

Hopper heard a click in the phone and nothing more. Now where the hell was Operations?

❖

The next morning he rose abruptly as if a powerful trigger had propelled him out of bed. His first conscious reaction was common to all aviators. He inspected the sky. What sort of day was it going to be?

He found the limpid gray California sky uninformative, and went directly to the shower. There he tried to find some easy reason to commend himself. His morale, he thought, was sorely in need of a boost. He had been flying for eight years now, and no one had to tell him that flying was not just another way to make a living. What was it now that intrigued him so?

Later, as he dried himself, he thought that maybe this could be the most important day of his life.

He reviewed the possibilities.

Both Hinkle and Driskill had told him in no uncertain way that they would have no place for a man who just "gets along." And they didn't want blowhards. Hinkle had been especially basic on the problem of hiring applicants. "You hire the guy and he turns out to be an asshole. You know as well as I do that cashiering an officer out of the air force takes a court-martial . . . practically an act of Congress. So what can you do? With a great deal of time and effort and squeaking around corners, you finally manage to get the asshole transferred to some other unit. . . ."

Hopper remembered how Hinkle had put his fists in his piercing eyes and twisted them slowly, as if to rid himself of a terrible injustice.

"You know what happens," he said. "A few years pass, and you think all is well. You'll never meet that asshole again. Wrong. One day you look up and there he is again . . . only now he's moved up in rank and he's your commanding officer. That's why we don't take on assholes around here if we can help it."

"All right," Hopper said to his image in the mirror. "You are the most rum-tee-de-dum, hoot-and-holler, yank-and-bank aviator they can ever expect to meet. You are ice-nerved, wise, daring, and conservative. No U-2, or any other flying machine, can bug you."

He trotted to the window for the tenth weather observation since he had opened his eyes. Overcast, ceiling about four thousand . . . hard to be sure. Visibility . . . good. And good morning, God. Please give your boy Cecil the benefit of the doubt today.

As he slipped into his flight suit, he suddenly had trouble driving away visions of defeat. Fly a tail-dragger? This was going to be a whole new world.

For a moment he saw himself bouncing across the California landscape trying to make a U-2 stay put while all the world laughed . . . or they sent the ambulance. Was it a handicap to be, as Hinkle pointed out, the youngest man they had ever considered for the job?

And how about the instructor pilot, Napolitano? His photo in the hallway of the big building showed a man with very bright eyes and the usual half-sick grin. The choice (as if he had any) could have been worse. Some of the other guys had a sort of restrained nausea about their smile. Not exactly cruel, but no friend to a camera. Of course, being the new boy on the block was bound to charge the imagination.

❖

Operations, 0900 hours on the mark. And here was Napolitano, a major, a big man with a huge, warm grin and bundles of words fired so fast they could be coming from an automatic weapon.

"This morning we'll just work around the pattern, so you can get acquainted. Not to worry. Can you swear?"

"Yessir."

"You may feel like expressing a few opinions before this morning is over. Just call me Nap, and remember, I'm only along for the ride. You fly the U-2, don't let it fly you. We used to have a lot of carnage during training, but not so much anymore. Can you cry?"

"I guess I still can."

"Good. Because you may want to shed some tears of frustration. Don't let it discourage you. I'm accustomed to anything, and no student has managed to kill me . . . yet. You look in good shape, which is fine, because you'll need to use quite a lot of body English. How's your sanity?"

"I suppose about average."

"Then what in God's name are you doing here?"

Napolitano laughed mightily and gave Hopper a solid punch on the shoulder. "Okay! Let's go defy the elements."

Even before they reached the flight line, Hopper decided that Napolitano was one of his favorite people. He chuckled frequently, and his eyes danced as he told of his private war with a man named Carmody, Lockheed's senior technical representative at Beale.

"Carmody is some kind of man," Napolitano said, laughing. "He thinks all pilots are airheads and says so. I tell him his bloody airplane won't do something, or it's broke, and he claims I don't know what I'm doing and do it this way. His way. He talks with his pencil and gives me that down-home manure-kicking smile and says, Can't you read tech order seven-four-nine dash-two, page eighty-one? Then he says he does not tolerate fools."

Napolitano's continuous enthusiasm was inspiring. Here was a man who loved his work.

"Carmody is a beautiful man. You tell him your airplane is broke and he'll say it just ain't so. What you gotta do, he'll say, is figure the adiabatic lapse rate and multiply by the soaker's onion, then make sure you reeve the gangling over the sheaves and pull it through the lower fistula and you got it made. And you know what? Right away the airplane is a go."

The airplane was waiting for them on a broad expanse of concrete, and on the way Nap continued his fractured lecture. "Lucky thou art, Cecil, for this flight will be just up and down around the pattern until you get the hang of a U-2. No pressure suit to cramp your style, and no fine scenery to distract you. We'll just tiptoe through the tulips for about two hours, and then you may change your mind about getting into the recce business. It appeals to a certain sort, you might say. . . ."

The plane crew looked diminutive as they fussed about the U-2, which struck Hopper as being much bigger than he had realized from a distance. Unlike the black operational U-2s, this one had an upper cockpit on top of the fuselage for the student. The instructor occupied the lower cockpit, which was in the usual place behind the long nose.

Hopper was deeply grateful to Napolitano for lightening the forbidding aura of this morning. His jollity even carried through the sight of a tall and lean figure waiting at the bottom of the howdah. It was, God forbid, Driskill.

"Mornin' . . ."

At least he was smiling. And he directed his smile at Hopper.

"Nervous?"

"No sir . . . I mean, maybe a little."

"Good. I'd worry about you if you weren't." Driskill moved back a pace as if to give himself a better view of an airplane he must have seen hundreds of times. He cocked his head and said, "I think they look real pretty painted all white like this, don't you?"

What did a man say? I prefer them black? A nod. Did Driskill or Napolitano have any idea how many thunderstorms were going on in a man's stomach? And the color of this strange-looking bird was of no matter.

Twenty minutes later Hopper was enthroned in the upper cockpit. He was trying desperately to acquaint himself with this strange new cubicle that enclosed him so tightly. Everything was in a different place than in the airplanes he had flown except the throttle. At least that was reassuring, but the size of the control yoke was very sobering. Was it going to take the strength of Superman to get some response?

Napolitano had disappeared, presumably "downstairs" in the forward cockpit. Now, his voice was on the intercom.

"You hear me okay, Red?"

"Fine . . ."

Red? It was the first time he had been called "Red" since he had joined the air force. The nickname had always been like a screaming banner during his school years, but somehow it had become lost in the intervening time. He had always hated the name "Red," but now, with Napolitano, who obviously said whatever he pleased, it sounded comforting. Yessir, "Red" Hopper was going to conquer all these new whistles and bells.

He sat with his arms on the cockpit combing, while the plane crew made the final check of his strappings and hooked his flight boots to a pair of spurs, which would keep his feet back if he had to eject. As directed through the intercom by some unseen aide (it was certainly not Napolitano's voice), he closed and locked the canopy. Then he waited while he heard the whine of a jet engine starting, and all the instruments before him began to dance with life.

Hopper spied the oxygen control and turned it up. Maybe it would make him feel better if overdone. The plastic helmet he had been issued was the wrong shape for his head. Bowen had said that it was a fine fit. Well, it was not. It pinched him along his brow and squashed his ears unmercifully. Why hadn't he complained? Because his instincts at the time were to be agreeable, no matter what. The new boy in school again. Go stand in the corner, Hopper. Yessir!

Nap's voice. "Taxi on out and take it easy. You can get in more trouble on the ground in a U-2 than in the air."

As he advanced the throttle, Hopper was vaguely aware that Driskill was following in an air force–blue sedan. He had said he was going to escape his office for a few hours and be the mobile officer for this flight. Now there was a nerve-racker. The boss watching every mistake.

A truck with four of the plane crew in it was following behind Driskill.

"We sure have a lot of people following us." Now why had he chosen this moment to say that? The need for communication with someone was very powerful, and during the past long two minutes Napolitano had remained silent.

There he was, sounding as though he were mumbling the checklist to himself. "Canopy closed, check? Interphone, check . . . Oxygen quantity, check . . . Circuit breakers, eenie-meenie-miney-mo . . . Pitot heat off . . . ADF, TACAN, ILS . . . on."

At the end of the runway Napolitano began calling off more of the checklist. "Pitch trim set point five degrees nose up . . . continuous ignition on . . . flight instruments check . . . tee block . . . one notch open . . . just absolutely nothing to it, Red. Now, watch Driskill. He'll give us a thumb up to tell us our tail section is set right. I forgot to show you . . . the whole thing is movable in a U-2, and when two little white lines are as they should be, then we're a go."

Hooray! He forgot something, Hopper thought. Napolitano was taking his place among the lesser gods.

A feminine voice from the tower. "Lasso five. Cleared for takeoff."

Lasso five. Their call sign. At least he knew that.

The intercom: "Okay, Red? Don't forget to use your feet. The U-2 takes a lot of rudder sometimes. The airplane is all yours."

That, Hopper knew, would be far from so. Unless Napolitano was out of his mind, his hands and feet would be bare millimeters from the controls until his student got his hand in. For if anything went wrong, it would be the major who was held accountable, not his student.

Hopper took a deep breath and shoved the throttle forward. He felt a trembling in the seat of his pants as the engine spooled up. Then the runway started sliding backward at an astounding speed.

"Pick up your left wing." Hopper sensed that Napolitano had already given him an assist. Long before he was ready, the U-2 became airborne.

"Hold a hundred and sixty knots. Retract."

Oh, yes! Up gear handle. Damn near forgot. "Ye gods!" Hopper's eyes had been fixed on the airspeed indicator. Suddenly he was astounded to discover that he is climbing at a sixty-degree angle. The damn thing was going over on its back!

"Easy . . . easy." Napolitano's voice was soothing.

"Mama mia!" Hooper was in a semitrance. Now why would he say that aloud? Influence of the invisible Napolitano?

Hopper recommenced his breathing sequence. He saw his altimeter climbing through fifteen thousand feet, and the runway was still below.

❖

Driskill lounged in the mobile car. He would judge Hopper's approaches and landings each time as he followed the U-2 down the runway. Waiting now for Hopper's first attempt, he considered the relationship between "the recce boys" and the Strategic Air Command (SAC), which owned the U-2s, the SRs, the tankers, missile squadrons, countless bomber squadrons, and all the assorted hardware that went with them.

Maybe the bomber men had too much clout in the organization? At headquarters, where military politics were always in a stew, it often seemed as though the recce boys were left out of the funding gravy, and even the missile shooters did better.

Maybe it would be better if the CIA came back and took over the U-2 business once more. But they were soured on actual operation of U-2s. And no wonder. A long time back, when they were engaged in monitoring the nuclear tests at Lop Nor and the work on intercontinental ballistic missiles in Communist China, they had lost eleven Chinese U-2 pilots. The operation turned out to be a little war of its own.

Driskill was ill at ease with this morning. Something had to be done about Laidlaw and his not-so-private soap opera. Sending him away to cool off was one solution . . . if his dancer held true for six months, then maybe . . . ? Or was it any business of a squadron commander at all? Pinsky would understand. He might ask why Laidlaw was being sent to Cyprus when another man had just been sent as a replacement, but he would understand because he knew that an outfit took care of its own.

Driskill smiled at the sky. There were many good things about Pinsky to balance his perfectionism.

Driskill leaned back in his seat and studied the overcast. It was not exactly the ideal flight day, but good enough for Hopper to make it around the Beale pattern several times and do a little low-level air work.

And where was Lieutenant Colonel Driskill while young Hopper and Napolitano were enjoying the best things in life? Well, the next-best thing. Driskill was sitting in a dadgummed automobile waiting . . . and watching a piece of sun the size of a Mexican bean trying to poke a hole in the overcast. A guy sat here in the grayness and watched his spirit melt. He began to have morbid thoughts about stuff that just could affect his work if allowed to take charge. Like suppose there was a war. Would it be a terminal calamity for both adversaries? Or a half-assed victory for one or the other? Was salvation to be found in deterrence, as the brass was so fond of preaching, or was there another way? Along came that old goat Clausewitz, who said, "A nation that finds itself on the brink of an abyss will try to save itself by any means."*

Had the world changed enough since Clausewitz's time—to prove him wrong? Of course, we fought only holy wars, against communism, fascism; and now, terrorism was bubbling in the kettle. All very moral—our wars. At bomber bases around the country guys were still on alert, ready to go twenty-four hours of every day. They could be aloft and on their way in minutes.

Driskill frowned at the overcast and slipped a piece of bubble gum between his fine white teeth. He chewed reflectively. Hay-ell, it was a near miracle how a bomber flown by nice young guys, like Hopper, could become an instrument of morality.

❖

Two weeks of almost continuous schooling passed before Captain Cecil Hopper was scheduled for a "high flight." All that he

---

*In early 1988 Gorbachev stated, ". . . the Soviet Union is on the edge of an abyss."

had absorbed since his arrival was focused on this important event, and a full day before the ascent his belly reflected the turmoil of his mind. This was the real thing; this was what U-2 flying was all about, and he must not fail.

Again the flight was scheduled for 0900 hours, which meant that Hopper rose long before dawn and, acting as casual as he could manage, appeared at the physiological unit at 0530. Here, in a small snack bar, breakfast was served to those bound for the high altitudes.

Despite his outward calm, Hopper was so nervous he had trouble swallowing his food. Joining him for breakfast was Jinneman, a graduate of the Washington University School of Drama, who was scheduled for a refresher flight, and Muus, who would serve as Hopper's mobile officer.

Napolitano, effervescent as ever despite his claim that a good book had kept him up past midnight, was also present. He would shepherd Hopper through his first high flight. "Just to make sure you don't go back to sleep."

Hopper was tempted to say, "Fat chance," but decided smart-ass remarks to his flight instructor were not the best way to start the day despite his longing for some kind of levity. He was having trouble with his concentration just now. It seemed to have escaped him entirely. What were the others saying?

The menu on the wall made no sense at all. It displayed a dreamlike quality by ignoring the inflation of the last fifty years. Steak and eggs . . . fifty cents. Any eggs . . . fifty cents. And the wine list was also haunting. Gatorade . . . pink, five cents. Gatorade, green . . . five cents. Could he still be asleep? Rip Van Hopper?

He watched as his companions were apparently capable of eating in a normal fashion. They were so casual, just as if this were not an extraordinary day. They talked about everything but high flight—Jinneman expounded at length on his collection of old gramophones and cars. Napolitano did verbal gymnastics with labels the Pentagon brass had tagged on various coming maneuvers.

"Gypsy Fiddle" . . . "Olympic Star" . . . "Fire Fly" . . . even one called "Toy Soldier."

"Pure genius," Napolitano said. "The guys who think those things up should be working for Disney."

Two SR-71 crews were taking breakfast at the only other table in the room. They were scheduled for a 0930 hours launching, and the backup pair announced joyfully that they were ready to sacrifice their morning and take over the mission if the doctor found the primary crew with so much as a hangnail.

Reaching beneath the table, Hopper took his pulse. Normal. How could that be? The mere mention of the word "doctor" had sent his heart pounding. Was it possible for a man his age to have a heart attack? Out of flying forever?

When breakfast was finished, they went in company to the locker room. There, the staff doctor held a brief interview with each man who would fly. He looked into Hopper's preoccupied eyes and asked, "Have a good sleep last night?"

"Yessir." Lie . . . lie. Monstrous lie. How could a man dope off to sleep when *the* day was here? The big day. The high day. The make-or-break day.

The doctor took Hopper's blood pressure. As the pump hissed and exhaled, he shook his head in disapproval. "All you young guys are alike. Dead on arrival. But I guess the air force will be glad to get rid of you."

The doctor greeted Napolitano with a cheery, "How're you doing today, Crash?"

Crash? Then the doctor pulled down Napolitano's lower eyelids and said, "Boy-oh-boy! You must have had a wild night. How can a guy live the life you do and expect to fly the next day? What's her name? Come on. Share the wealth. We're all little

Napolitanos at heart . . . handsome . . . dashing . . . and a poor risk for high flight."

"You really start a guy off with a bang," Napolitano smiled. "I knew I shouldn't have had that glass of vodka before breakfast. I just can't break the habit."

Hopper was careful to pull on his long underwear insideout, as he had been instructed on his first day. He slipped on his pisser and followed Napolitano into the dressing room, where the same blond corporal greeted him. This time he hardly saw her; she was a person in khaki uniform, along with all the other dressers. She was, he thought, a person who was about to help him reach heights he had never dreamed of, and for that alone he was grateful.

Once in his space suit, Hopper was guided to a reclining chair next to Napolitano, already stretched out and gone into his private goldfish-bowl world. A moment later Hopper sensed the arrival of pure oxygen in his helmet. He closed his eyes, and it was as if he had slipped into a trance. He knew the drill now—he was no longer the new boy in camp.

He thought of that glorious day only one week ago when he had soloed a U-2. Only around the patch of course—up and down for some ten landings and takeoffs, all under the encouraging radio voice of Napolitano.

Afterward there had been the customary celebration party in the Heritage Room, which he had shared with Marshall, the first black U-2 pilot, who had soloed that same afternoon. The room reverberated with hooting and hollering and words of congratulation. Nearly every officer in the 99th who was not away on TDY was there to shake their hands and watch them suffer continuous ribbing as they tried to drink the traditional yard of ale. They were condemned loudly for spilling ale on their flight suits, and as the laughter bounced from wall to wall, Hopper decided that he had never known a happier time. Then at last his tongue contacted a pair of black metal wings at the bottom of the yard-long beaker, and he knew he had won his first battle with a notoriously difficult flying machine.

Eyes closed, now utterly relaxed in his space suit, Hopper allowed his mind to drift as it pleased. He thought of "g's," the force of gravity multiplied. The most he had ever known was six g's, which meant that his 170-pound body weighed a 1,020 pounds—momentarily. Fine for the yank-and-bank boys in fighters, but no thanks for Cecil Hopper. It had pulled his balls right down to his knees.

No problem in a U-2. At the most two g's. But other things? Napolitano had planted a whole garden of warning seeds, based on his own experience and gatherings from old-timers in the flying business whose confidence he treasured. He spoke of old trickeries and deceptions that could kill a man. Some had been handed down by men who flew in the childhood of aviation— legendary men who flew mostly by the seat of their pants. All colorful. All disappeared from the skies. Caperton, who hid his whiskey in the toilet tank to avoid combats with his wife; Turner, who flew with a lion cub; and Kalberer, who would drive nothing but a tulip-fendered Pierce-Arrow fit for a monarch. Old pelicans. Men with style.

Life aloft had its little quirks, and the legendary men were the first to learn about something called oculogyral illusion, caused by overstimulation of the semicircular canals in the ears. A target seen moving to the left would gradually become motionless, and might even start moving to the right. It could wander back and forth for half a minute. Confusing to the eye and the brain unless you recognized it.

Now was a good time to review other illusions, "wrinkles, swindles, and snares," according to Napolitano, who warned they could lead to very serious trouble at high altitude in a U-2.

Something called somatographic illusion? A sensation compounded when the aircraft accelerated forward, and even in level flight could persuade a pilot that he was in a nose-high altitude. But it might be a lie. Do not believe the hairs in your ears. Believe your instruments.

Somatographic illusion could also occur during deceleration—a sudden reduction in engine power or use of speed brakes, or both.

A voice in his helmet roused him. The blond corporal. Definitely not an illusion.

"Having a good snooze, sir?"

"No. I'm thinking."

"Bad for the liver. Relax for another ten minutes."

A total of eight hours now flying the U-2. Barely enough to visualize the major cockpit details. Let alone recall instantly the location of every button and switch. An ancient layout compared to modern aircraft. The U-2s looked fine in their black paint, but the cockpits were showing age. This was an airplane built originally to last only forty flying hours. Some had more than fifteen thousand.

It was difficult to be sure why it was so pleasant in his cocoon. A return to the womb? Great place for undisturbed thought . . . like memorizing the performance figures for a U-2. And the cockpit layout? Circuit breakers actually behind the pilot, barely reachable for a man in a space suit. Fiddling around with your fingers hampered by those clumsy gloves was frustrating. The navigational computer was stuffed into the only space remaining . . . like an afterthought.

Napolitano, who claimed several direct conversations with God, said that flight in a U-2 at night was a preview of heaven. "The ghosts of old aviators are riding right along with you. If there's a moon and you don't turn your head too quickly and scare them away, you can see them sitting on the leading edge of your wings."

Some illusion! Napolitano also said that if the weather turned sour, night flight in a U-2 could be an introduction to hell.

"Time's up, sir. Have a good flight."

There was nothing deceptive about the corporal.

One hour later Hopper's eyes were fixed on his altimeter. Seventy thousand feet. Not space, not even as high as the "sled" flew, but it was a hell of a lot higher than most humans ever achieved.

There was this sense of elation. So powerful and all-prevading he had to bring his thoughts back to Napolitano's voice. "How you feeling, Ace?"

Ace? It was a term used only in derision—unless you were a squadron commander or a Napolitano, in which case almost anything was allowed.

"I'm doing fine."

"Can you put a bit more emphasis on that *fine?*"

"Yessir."

"When are you going to cut out the sirs and call me Nap? You're one of us now."

"Okay . . . Nap. This is some view. I'm bug-eyed."

That planet down there is revolving and we're still with it, Hopper thought. And take a fast look all around. The human eye was just not accustomed to such a vast expanse of real estate.

Above was dark ultramarine—almost black. A band of viridian stretched along the curvature of the earth.

North out of Beale, the mountains had flattened to mere corrugations, the mighty rivers had become trickles, and the bays reduced to inlets. Now, far below, there was a dusting of tiny clouds strewn like granules of salt across Puget Sound.

There was no sound now except the exaggerated noise of Hopper's own breathing and the small electric fan blowing on the left-side canopy window—to prevent it frosting over, he had been told. Could he actually hear that fan, or had his imagination gone wild? Another illusion?

He could not hear the giant J-75 fan engine just behind him because there was almost nothing for the engine sounds to reverberate against. Almost nothing. This was the land of nothing, presided over just now by twenty-nine-year-old Captain Hopper of the space cadets. "Greetings!"

"Did you say something?" Napolitano's voice rattled in his helmet.

Hopper was amazed. Somehow he had managed to forget that he had a chaperone.

"You've been mighty quiet," Napolitano said.

"Would you like to know that this is the sexiest thing I've ever done?"

"I hope not."

"Well . . . you know what I mean."

"Amen."

"I could go on like this forever."

"Pretty, huh? Wait till you try it at night and look down at a star."

"I'm hooked."

"Of course. You hungry?"

Hopper took a moment to consider the state of his appetite. Food of various types was available just near his gloved hand. A tube of soup, applesauce, goulash, peaches . . . all to be taken through a plastic straw. There was a small valve in his helmet located just below his chin. He could insert a straw through the valve and have a banquet . . . including Gatorade, man. Phooey. Too much sodium, even though they had diluted it.

Water perhaps? No food.

Right now, the U-2's tender throat was more important. The airplane was responsive enough to his control, but seemed unwilling to stay put.

At these high altitudes even the U-2 became unstable, and so operational missions were flown using the automatic pilot. Napolitano would have none of such indulgence. "Right now, I want you to fly her manually just to get the feel of the old girl."

The feel? Come on, Nap! There is no soul here. Only metal and petroleum. And yet—?

Regard the two "barber pole" needles on the airspeed indicator. They had gradually converged as the U-2 gained altitude, and were now fickle and demanding. Between them was the airspeed needle, and the game was to keep it there. The reasons were imperative, and Napolitano had been adamant in his instructions.

"Keep that little mother right between the poles, no matter what. Pretend the world can't get along without thee and me. Because if your nose gets up a bit and you go too slow, we stall out, and that is something this airplane at this altitude is not meant to do. It might come to pieces before you recover and it might not. Let's not research the matter. Let us just take it for granted that the main reason we can get up this high is because we're in one of the world's lightest and most fragile flying machines."

Now, Nap warmed to what was obviously his favorite subject. "The other pole is your mach buffet indicator, and you don't want to slip beyond it or we'll sure as hell come to pieces. If you let things get away from you up here, it's hard to tell the difference between stall and mach buffet, and nasty things can start happening very fast. So keep your ass in between the two barber poles, no matter what. The hands of a surgeon, man."

Okay, sure, maestro. Certainly, sir. We wander. We slide up and down. We come very close to violating both barber poles. We are riding a drunken whale.

"You're doing quite well. Getting tired?"

"Negative." Lie, lie.

"You will be soon. Remember, every little exertion takes something out of you because, in spite of everything, your body is still at twenty-nine thousand feet. You're climbing Everest. During a real mission you're up here for ten hours or so. Now, make a gentle turn . . . not more than a ten-degree bank . . . and let's go home."

Home? Maybe, Hopper thought, home would never seem the same.

❖

Usually the apricot building was barren of activity on weekends, but this Saturday morning found Driskill arriving at his usual hour. An urgent request for a replacement pilot had come from Detachment Two, and Driskill thought he knew just the candidate. After two months of training, Hopper was supposedly qualified.

U-2 pilots are not expected to bring back any secrets that cannot be seen from on high with mechanical eyes, or with their own. They do not slink along wet cobblestone streets or hide behind picturesque lampposts. Their modus operandi is made up for them and comes out as a computer card, a flight plan with a soul of its own. It is designed to guide them to a precise spot above the earth where their target can best be photographed, or heard (electronically), or sniffed (electronically).

The limitation on the pilot's "need to know" is carefully evaluated lest he fail to come home to roost. Over the years a considerable number have not. Driskill knew that most of those pilots had been killed in training accidents, but there had been more than a plenty who never returned from operational missions. There were Primrose and Hyde and Snider and Henderson and Anderson and Locock, among many others. All killed in the line of duty.

Driskill remembered that U-2s had been particularly cruel to Chinese pilots who were allotted several when China was in an uproar and determined to wipe out all but Maoist-Leninist culture. The United States was condemned as a deadly enemy, and the CIA thought American pilots should not be employed in the reconnaissance over a nation then so violently antagonistic. They had employed Chinese pilots for the job. Shang Shi-hi, a Chinese captain, clobbered two U-2s before retiring from the scene, and Colonel Chen Wai-sheng and Captain Fan Hung-ti were killed. There were some who said the Chinese were having trouble transferring mentally from the water buffalo to aircraft, which was nonsense. In 1913, while aviation was still an infant and the rest of his immigrant countrymen were pounding spikes into railroad ties or running laundries, a young Chinese named Lim flew a Curtiss Pusher from San Francisco well over a thousand miles to San Diego. After his feat, the same Lim returned to China and became a general in the air force.

Driskill understood the paranoia of secrecy that continued to obscure U-2 history; it was not generally known that more than fifty had crashed during the program. The number of survivors, he thought wryly, remained "classified."

Still, the air force did not regard either U-2 or SR-71 flying as a high-risk job, nor did the pilots, who would all like to know more about their operational missions. Of course, Driskill thought, when a man takes off from Patrick Air Force Base in Florida, he does not expect to be routed over peaceful Bermuda. He is not at all surprised to find himself sliding along the coast of Cuba or almost any coast in Central America.

Those who flew out of "Det Two" in Korea did not expect to find themselves over Taiwan, Iwo Jima, or Hong Kong.

England was a grab bag. Good morning to Poland. Good evening to Hungary. The detachment in England could take full advantage of the U-2's enormous range.

Those who flew out of "Det Three" on Fantasy Island hardly expected to look down on the French Riviera or the boot of Italy. They were very busy with the eastern shores of the Adriatic, the

Middle East, and the Persian Gulf. And then, of course, there was Libya.

Driskill parked his black Mazda in its usual place near the entrance to the apricot building. He pulled a soft rag from beneath his seat, left the ignition on, and polished the black hood while he waited for the tape of "You don't have to call me darlin', darlin'," to finish. He had deliberately chosen black as the color of his car, as had many other members of the 99th. Black was their symbol, black their airplanes, and black their work.

The family, he decided, was in good health just now. Little things were the evidence. In fact, the sense of family was demonstrated yesterday afternoon. Becky Stone, one of the pilot's wives, had called the squadron, instead of a garage man, when her car refused to start. The squadron duty officer had then called Driskill, who had in turn called Weaver.

"Becky Stone can't get her car started. And she has to pick up her kids at school at three. One of them has a dentist appointment."

Weaver was the Stones' nearest neighbor and, because he was family, he would know that her husband was presently flying U-2s out of Guam and could not be of much help. "How about going over and giving her a hand?"

"I don't know anything about Hondas."

"You've been to Japan, haven't you?"

That was enough. Weaver would find some way of starting that car. The honor of the family would be at stake.

Driskill smiled as he remembered his own last absence on temporary duty. His wife, Pat, had locked the keys in her car not once, but twice. Both times a squadron member had come to the rescue. The fix, whether emotional or mechanical, was a family affair.

Driskill climbed the steps to his office reluctantly. It was such a beautiful day, and he was not supposed to fly his desk on a Saturday.

When was the air force going to come to its senses and adopt the policies used by many other air forces? Keep those who want to fly . . . flying. Maybe they would never be promoted beyond major, but they would be happy and all the more proficient with experience. It seemed that the high brass never would understand obsession any more than they could conceive that an officer might not want to become chief of staff or make general.

Driskill had thought the building would be deserted, but while he was unlocking the black door to his office floor, Hinkle came up behind him. "Only rascals smile when they go to work on Saturday. What's up?"

"I was just wondering how a certain freckle-faced guy is going to get along with the Irish of the Orient."

"Have you sung *Madama Butterfly* for him?"

"Not yet. He's had his mind on flying. I want his full attention."

As he opened the door, Driskill glanced at his watch. It was strange, he thought. He was about to send Hopper off to an assignment where inevitably there would be a certain amount of danger, yet he was more worried about the young man's exposure to earthly temptations.

It was ten o'clock. Precisely. Hay-ell, it was much too early to worry about freckles and Koreans.

Driskill entered his office, flexed his arms, and then made a slight obeisance to his desk. He would fly it for no more than an hour. He would fly the goddamned thing even if it didn't have any wings. And right now, he would ask himself why, if he must be paperbound, he had not chosen a more lucrative profession. A lawyer?

The paperwork realities of the air force were staggering. General Electric built engines for the air force. *Four hundred and fifty* "inspectors" were assigned to make very sure every engine sold to the air force was as nearly perfect as could be. The identical engines manufactured by the same company for use in civilian aircraft required no inspectors. The resulting contrast in useless paperwork effort was a disgrace to the senile bureaucracy that demanded such nonsense. Lockheed, a hard-trying company that was still building U-2s as of this very day, had been "audited" seven times in as many months by squadrons of bureaucrats, most of whom knew far less about building aircraft than the most humble employee. The wasted time, effort, and loss of creative production required to satisfy such audits was incalculable. There were enormous warehouses jammed with papers recording such activities that no one would ever see again, let alone read.

Driskill sighed.

Yet Monday. Ah, Monday! For the deprived squadron commander, for that sterling-silver soldier who was developing a tendency to feel sorry for himself, there was a U-2 flight scheduled. High flight. Idaho area and return.

He circled his desk like a circus animal trainer wary of a snarling tiger. And then there was Hopper, who had come in silently behind him, standing now in the doorway, his freckles shining, his eyes aglow, his nose polished until there was a little highlight on the tip, standing in parade-rest posture, expectant, waitin' on his destiny. There he stood, fixed as a pillar, a sort of sheepish grin on his face, a different Cecil Hopper from the young man who had stood in that same place only two months ago. Hopper the short basketball player. According to Hinkle, he had mastered the temperamental nature of his craft and had completed his training in communications, chemical warfare (for God only knew what reasons), escape and evaluation, life-support training, mission planning, survival training, tactical doctrine, and reconnaissance procedures. He had also been briefed on how to react should he fall into the hands of the bad guys. He was not expected to remain silent under torture. Nor would he be issued a "sudden death" needle in the style of the old U-2 drivers. Thanks to the ordeal endured by a young colonel named Mahurin in the hands of the Chinese during the Korean conflict, the air force had come to its senses about prisoners of war.

Driskill said good morning and took his time lowering himself into his chair. No sense in strapping himself in any sooner than necessary. Maybe the desk and that "out" file full of paper would go away by itself.

Hopper's orders were in a brown manila envelope on the desk. Driskill picked up the envelope and tapped it lightly. "I don't suppose you know why I sent for you?"

"No, sir."

"You're going TDY. Any objection to Det Two?"

Hopper's freckles chased each other into a grin. "I've been hoping for Korea."

"Why?"

"Isn't that where the action is?"

"There's action elsewhere."

Hopper accepted the envelope, handling it as if it were a live grenade. "I've never been to Korea."

"You're leaving on a tanker tonight."

What a dull collection of words, Driskill thought. What a mundane way to tell a young man that he will soon be on his way to a great adventure, perhaps more than he has ever reckoned for. No matter what happens, his entire life will be changed again by this simple assignment. And there is always the possibility that it might mean the end of his life. Shit happens. If it does? The man who sends him away cannot escape wondering what he might have been.

Driskill pulled out the top desk drawer and fumbled around inside. He came up with two pieces of bubble gum and tossed one at Hopper. He deliberately made an easy pitch, not the hard-to-catch shot Hopper had received during his first interview. That would be in Hopper's previous life. Now, as he would soon enough discover, he would belong to Detachment Two, and particularly to Horton, the commander.

Even the thought of Horton was enough to light a smile on the face of anyone who knew him. Willie the fox. Very little transpired in the air force without Willie knowing about it. And there was very little Willie might want that somehow he wouldn't manage to acquire, or with various discreet convolutions arrange to have assigned to him. Willie was renowned for his barely legal mischiefs, all carried out with apparently easygoing aplomb, all reflecting in some way to the benefit of his detachment and incidentally to its commander.

"Your boss will be Willie Horton. Listen to him. He is very wise."

Still grinning, Hopper said, "I guess I'll get to meet Oscar."

"You can't miss. Oscar runs Det Two. He can do no wrong."

It was obviously not necessary to tell Hopper that Oscar was an extremely autocratic cat who, except for one incident with Willie Horton, ran his life exactly as he pleased. And everyone else's. It was not just a coincidence that the shoulder patch of the 99th was a black cat, and Oscar, under the dedicated agent-managership of Horton, had achieved worldwide fame. It was Horton who had declared that if Oscar was to be adopted as a mascot, he must qualify like everyone else. He must make a flight in a U-2. And he did.

Now for *Madama Butterfly.* "When you get over there, don't forget who you are."

Driskill saw Hopper's face take on a puzzled look . . . as they all did at this farewell moment.

"I'm not sure what you mean, sir?"

"This is your first overseas deployment. Things are different over there. You're a bachelor. . . ."

"It so happens, sir."

"The Korean girls are very attractive."

"So I've heard."

"Just remember they can grow old just like anybody else."

The grin was still there, but he saw that Hopper was doing some accelerated thinking.

Driskill could not remember how many pilots he had known who had brought back Oriental wives. There was certainly nothing wrong with it as long as both parties understood they were trying to mix two vastly different cultures.

"Some guys fall in love over there and bring home a bride. It doesn't always work out very well."

"I understand, sir."

"Then get out of my hair . . . and good luck."

There followed the traditional handshake, which always left Driskill in a state he identified as "a tad melancholy." There was so much more he wanted to tell the new men he sent away, and yet there was always the danger of sounding the old windbag, trying to tell someone who was already sitting on top of the world just how to live his life.

After Hopper had departed in an obvious state of euphoria, Driskill slipped into the chair behind the desk and swung his flight boots up on the corner. He fixed his eyes on the ceiling, where a fat fly was posing an age-old aeronautical question. Did he reach that inverted landing position out of a half-loop, or roll into it?

He had said the right things, which translated into not having said too much. Hopper should not be burdened with a load of verbal lard to weigh on him while he sat through the long hours on a tanker. He knew he was bound for a non-war where medals were few and far between, and thus far, so were casualties. But would he eventually become complacent? Would he forget that his war was not so much with a single and obvious enemy as with forces more easily ignored? Once aloft, he must never relax entirely. He would be fighting in an atmosphere that had a density of about 3 percent of sea-level air. His engine, rated at seventeen thousand pounds thrust, would only be developing five hundred pounds of thrust when he cruised into his job. At this point Hopper was supposedly a psychological and physiological masterpiece, a bright and nearly nerveless young man devoid of hang-ups, very exceptional in his work. So his reports read. But a night on the town in Osan or Seoul could lead him into serious trouble.

Driskill blew a large bubble with his gum. Forget it! Hay-ell, if he fretted about every man he sent away . . .

His eyes came to rest momentarily on the volume of Clausewitz, which somehow always seemed to find a place on the small coffee table against the far wall. Funky old Clausewitz. What would he think of young Hopper and of *maskirovka?* After his education in the 99th, Hopper would know that *maskirovka* was the Russian term for concealing the real strength of Soviet bloc forces, but he would learn a great deal more when he was flying operational missions. Sooner or later he would also learn that *maskirovka* included scattering discontent through the defenses of NATO. And he might begin to wonder if there ever would come a time when neighbors could be trusted.

Or did we have to wait until there was nothing left to conclude? Maybe the two thousand or three thousand survivors, if there were that many, would be so frightened out of their wits by existing in desolation they would reach out to each other. Or maybe their experience would just magnify their mistrust and they would chase each other through the rubble until there was no one left at all. Jesus. Was it just that this office was deserted on a Saturday morning . . . or did the commander of the 99th need a visit to a shrink?

Sitting here alone in the unusual silence, with all the staff gone off to better things like golf, tennis, or becoming reacquainted with their families, made this office seemingly an island floating in the big apricot building, with a single castaway reviewing the peculiar situation. Here, on this Saturday morning with the rest of the world elsewhere, it was inviting to remember that for more than seventy years the Soviets had been busy trying to spread their faith all over the world—and trying to hide their activities. Hopper would be but a nit in their hair. He would be alone with *maskirovka* whether he flew out of England or Korea, or Fantasy Island, or anywhere else. When he joined the air force, he could not have had the slightest notion that he might be one of the fifty-odd men who were unique in the spy world. It was even possible that he might discover the "bad guys" were keeping their agreements instead of breaking them.

Driskill shoved his chair away from the desk and stood up. Enough of this brooding! Consider how luck has contrived to keep the rain off your head and the sun from blinding your eyes. It took years of work to attain a dungeon for an office. And the job? All other military flying was practice. This was the real business every day and night, and *maskirovka* was a game to be played for keeps.

Don't you forget it, Cecil Hopper.

❖

Lieutenant Colonel William (Willie) Horton was his own SCI, a man to hint of secrets but never reveal them. As commander of Detachment Two stationed at Osan in South Korea, he enjoyed almost a free hand—and used it.

Horton was a smiler. Why frown when a mere baring of teeth could accomplish so much? Add a touch of humility and a dash of innocence—"Why . . . I didn't know that!"—and insert some soft-voiced dignity. Then the Horton ensemble would begin to play, but the music was not a military march. He ambled, his shape suggestive of a concerned penguin surveying his territory. What remained of Horton's hair was carefully gardened, and his broad face, with alert and inquisitive eyes, had a Buddha quality. He would appear quite at home sitting cross-legged on a pedestal surrounded by half-asleep dragons, snakes, and other Oriental software.

Horton was inclined to slough through the English language, and his honey-and-grits accent left no doubt of his Carolina heritage. He was also capable of adding a conspiratorial undertone to his speech, which sometimes slipped into pure theater. Horton was so renowned as a mischievous and inventive wag that people were drawn to him just to see what happened next.

Horton's dedication to his job was always extraordinary. When Hopper's tanker finally arrived at two in the morning, Willie Horton was there to meet it and reach for the baggage of his very junior officer. "Welcome to Osan and Detachment Two! Y'all must be sleepy and hungry. Everything here is closed down tight at this hour, but I just happen to have . . ."

What Horton just happened to have in his simple, motellike quarters was a can of Beluga caviar, which drew an enthusiastic comment from his new flying officer. "Sir! Never in my entire life have I ever tasted anything like this! And you say it's fish eggs?"

"Russian ambrosia," Horton answered, with his most engaging smile. "It is part of the Gorbachev–Horton treaty . . . absolutely top secret." He placed a spoonful of Beluga on a cracker and offered it to Hopper. "Go ahead. Betray your country. Guilt is part of the taste."

Horton also "just happened to have" the makings of an exotic "submarine" sandwich: a certain Boursin cheese of Swiss make, an extraordinary Polish sausage, "made of tiger tails," as he described it, and some fine German beer to wash it all down.

Hopper was impressed. "Where do you get all this stuff, sir? I heard this was a hardship post."

"You will learn. In this business you develop some very valuable international connections."

Hopper did not learn, nor did anyone else in Detachment Two ever discover, the sources of their commander's exotic supplies. They were certainly not available on the drab post of Osan, where the personnel was inclined to wear full battle dress at all times. There was enough barbed wire about the perimeters of the base and enough camouflaged concrete and netting to assure any drop-in inspection team that all the proper preparations had been made for attack. The daily charade at Panmunjom was still going on, but no one dared suppose that true peace between the North and South Koreans was an actual possibility.

Horton, employing his most solicitous tone, explained the situation to his new pilot. "You'll probably not fly until next week. Give you a chance to settle in and get to know the guys who have been here on the job a while. First, study the Koreans. They're great people to get along with and good allies. More important, they like us because we keep the North Koreans from eating them for breakfast and we spend beaucoup dollars here.

"For amusement you can either go to the Officers' Club, which serves fair meals along with too much hard rock for me, or you can go to one of the joints in town. It's just over the hill. They offer fair beer, rotten whiskey, and expensive girls. Otherwise, there's always church or the library. Do you have an iron gut?"

"Sorry, sir?"

"This is no place for a delicate digestion. Some of the guys do their own cooking. You're safe enough eating at the Officers' Club, but watch it at other places. Until you've had the Korean curse, you don't know what agony is. Any questions?"

Hopper was emboldened by the beer. "Sir? When do I meet Oscar?"

"As soon as you knock off a good night's sleep. You may need it.

"One more thing. I am aware that you are the world's greatest aviator or you wouldn't be here. But while you're flying out here, just never forget you're in humble country. Things happen here that never seem to happen anywhere else. You already know how a U-2 can bring a proud man to his knees, so stay alert and no matter how tired you are, never forget it's the things you can't plan on that happen. Now off to the sack with you."

It was typical of Horton that he failed to reveal he would have only two hours' sleep himself. For at five in the morning he would be down on the flight line watching the launch of the daily sortie. It just wasn't right for one of his pilots to go aloft without anyone except the immediate airplane crew around to say goodbye.

No one who belonged to Detachment Two could be sure when Horton slept—if he bothered to at all. Day or night his round, smooth-shaven face would appear on whatever occasion was most vital to the group. He often said that he lived U-2s—"Why, all kinds of people would pay just to do my job. Of course, what we should do is sell tickets. Can you imagine how many customers we'd have if we took just one little old U-2 and advertised, 'Take a ride in the upper atmosphere for only a thousand bucks? See the world from afar!'? Why . . . you'd have people lined up for miles . . . even if you told them there was a chance they would never come back. They'd be scalping tickets. It's in the nature of people."

Horton had been a student at the Air War College when a prominent East Indian was invited to address the officers of his class. The guest was an eloquent speaker and knew his facts—all of which were to the detriment of the United States. He outlined poverty, crime, racism, and corporate greed in such a compelling fashion that there were murmurings of assent from his audience and on a few occasions outright applause. He finished with a scathing attack on the president of the United States and bowed expectantly.

There was silence. No one moved. Finally, the officer whose job it had been to introduce the speaker rose and murmured the routine words of thanks for this appearance. The East Indian bowed again, and still there was silence.

At last Willie Horton, then a major, rose and said, "I think our honored guest should take something away with him. Many of us obviously agree with some points he made, but I suggest that if he has gathered the impression we're divided . . . he might think again. He should realize that no matter who the president of the United States might be, if he orders us to go into battle . . . we'll all go."

There was immediate applause, and every man in the audience stood up. In so carefully preparing his address, the distinguished visitor had neglected to study the total conviction of his listeners . . . and the possible presence of Willie Horton.

Although Detachment Two of the 99th Squadron was resident on a very large base, the activities were relatively limited. The pilots lived in what might pass for a second-rate motel of the 1950's. Each man had his own room furnished in Spartan style, but it made little difference, because the rooms were rarely occupied for anything other than sleep, and the occupants knew their assignment to Osan would be over in a few months.

The quarters were located on the main street of the base, which was always noisy with the passage of military trucks bound for warehouses, the defense perimeters, or the airfield itself. This was a "presence" post, an infantry command, and U-2 activities went almost unnoticed beneath the overall might of armor.

There was a PX on the same side of the street as the detachment quarters, and the Officers' Club was on the opposite side. Now, in winter, whirlwinds of dust were everywhere, doing nothing to enhance the dreary atmosphere of functionalism common to military bases abroad. The Korean sun was pale, and the air cold enough to vaporize the breath of people passing by.

It was on such a chill morning that Horton called an urgent meeting of Detachment Two. Some forty men crowded into his office on the flight line, noses dribbling and hands reddening from sudden exposure to the heat of the interior. They snorted and coughed and unzipped their olive jackets. They agreed that they had never been so goddamned cold and somehow managed not to sound as if they were complaining. "It's the wind," they kept saying, as if to forgive the actual temperature and the Korean peninsula itself.

The enlisted men were present because they spent so much time with Oscar the cat, and Horton was a stout believer in ignoring rank when personal problems were involved.

"Gentlemen," Horton began in his best voice of the Confederacy. "You should recognize our new flight officer, Captain Cecil Hopper." He nodded a smile at Hopper, who stood as inconspicuously as possible near the doorway. "Although our names are somewhat similar, I doubt if we'll have any confusion." He nodded again at the appreciative rumble of amusement that swept across the assembly of faces.

There was a leather couch opposite Horton's desk, and two pilots sat on it. There was room for a third person, yet in spite of the tightly packed office, the space remained unoccupied except for Oscar. He was a very black cat with harvest-moon eyes, and he sat erect as a sentinel in the very center of the space. He was indifferent to all those about him and viewed Horton with what could easily be identified as marked displeasure. Captain Welby, a talented artist with his pen as well as with a U-2, had done several portraits of Oscar when he was in a better mood.

Horton cleared his throat and was satisfied with the immediate silence. He folded his hands behind his head and his office chair squawked as he leaned as far back as it would go.

"Gentlemen," he began slowly, "our problem for today is extremely serious, and somewhere among you I've got to find at least two volunteers for a demanding and very delicate mission."

Horton waited until he was sure his words had registered. These were his brave troops, but he was not at all sure he would gather the necessary number of volunteers. He suspected that there were many males who believed that on such a mission a hex might befall them.

Horton stared at Oscar and wondered who would blink first. If he understood English as well as some people claimed, those yellow eyes should at least narrow.

"The behavior of our squadron members is not above reproach. We all know those certain pleasures to be had in Osan, but the majority of us remember flag and country and are at least discreet. And there are others . . ."

Horton watched the mixture of curiosity and confusion among his audience and was pleased. He had their attention now—so necessary to this trying situation.

He allowed just a hint of urgency to salt his Carolina drawl. "I like to think if any of us observe a squadron mate in trouble or even heading for it . . . that any one of us will try to rescue him. And that is exactly what is happening, so something must be done. I am informed that this unfortunate person does not spend his nights in quarters; indeed, he roams the base and has been seen even in the streets of Osan after dark. He is looking for . . . shall I say, companionship? Yet such is his horniness, it could be the death of him. I fear for his life."

Horton searched the familiar faces before him and answered their questioning eyes by twisting in his chair as if he were enduring great physical pain. He sighed very heavily and said, "I refer, of course, to our friend Oscar, a man who has done so much for the morale of this detachment. His wanton expeditions have got to be stopped. You know the local roads . . . he just can't be seen. He melts into the night. If a car doesn't kill him, some Korean is going to put an end to his howling with a bullet. We must make a nasty decision. It's only a matter of time before he buys the farm—if he continues with his present routine."

Horton brought his hands from behind his neck and spread his palms upward as if offering something tangible to his audience. He saw much shaking of heads.

"Of course . . ."

"Can't we come up with something else?"

"What must be . . . must be."

Horton bowed his head. "It is written. . . ." he said softly. "Very well. I need two volunteers to take Oscar to the hospital. The rest of you can send your sympathies."

Horton looked at Oscar, who had not blinked. Instead, there seemed to be a new imperiousness to his stance.

"I will remind the volunteers now that they are going to be dealing with a tiger . . . and I suggest the heaviest gloves you can find. . . ."

Sergeant Trundy and Airman First Class Brockaway raised their hands.

"Very well. You two have it. And if Oscar gets really tough and you are wounded on this mission, I'll put you both in for a purple heart. Oscar's jewels will be delivered to this office . . . suitably preserved in a glass container. They will be enshrined on the shelf above this desk, and fixed thereto will be a brass plate engraved as follows . . . 'Oscar,' in large letters. Then, 'Lost in the line of duty—Searching for the unknown. With appreciation for a courageous comrade from the members of Detachment Two, 99th Squadron, USAF.' "

· ❖ ·

A few days after Oscar's shame the threat of a typhoon charging up from the South China Sea caused the crew of an SR-71 to decide against returning to their regular base at Kadena on the island of Okinawa. They landed instead at Osan, Horton territory, assuring themselves it would be a good choice to spend a comfortable night. There they could wait for the weather to improve. Wearing their most haughty smiles, they brought their great bird to a halt directly in front of Horton's office, and they were not surprised to see him waiting on the concrete when they shut their mighty engines down.

The pilot and the backseater of the SR-71 were known to Horton, and although the fixed antipathy between the two types of recce airmen could not be entirely disregarded, he displayed no hesitation in providing them asylum for the night. He arranged for the best quarters available and even took them to the Officers' Club, where he insisted on picking up the check for drinks and dinner. "It's our pleasure," he said in his best homily style. "After all, we're all in the same business, and who knows we may come to visit you folks in Kadena some time."

During the balance of the evening Horton played the magnanimous mint-julep host, and managed to conceal his true feelings until he saw them safely to bed. His evening of fraternization did nothing to change his conviction that the arrogant sled drivers were all alike. They had the gall to patronize the U-2s, and incidentally the men who flew them.

They said, "Oh, sure, you guys do a hell of a job considering what you have to work with, but don't you get tired of steering those old cows from A all the way to B?" They said, "We hear they're about to phase out the U-2s . . . or have they already started?" And as they warmed to Horton's liquid hospitality, they said, "Well, it takes all kinds, you know. We've heard you have solved the pilot-retention problem. Is it true that in the Mediterranean you have a new squadron flying U-2s, and they're all little old ladies in tennis shoes?"

Horton resolved not to trade insults lest he be carried away. The rivalry between the two types was ridiculous anyway, worse than the Hatfields and the McCoys, he thought. Determined to remain the gracious host, he took his guests by his office and among other objects of interest showed them a pair of North Korean pilot's wings, which he had obtained through sources he did not care to disclose, and an exquisite local carving of a U-2 ascending through mahogany clouds. With such trinkets, he declared, did men who were long from home and family brighten their days. The SR-71 crew expressed their sympathy and understanding in such a sincere fashion that Horton lowered his voice to a conspiratorial tone and said he would show them something that would interest them even more. "You both have top-secret clearances, so I have no hesitation in showing you certain items with which you may be concerned. . . ."

Horton unlocked his metal file and brought out a manila folder marked TOP SECRET. He flipped a few pages of the contents and began to read snatches and occasional full sentences covering future plans for SR-71s and their crews.

". . . all SR-71s except two now stationed in England will be redeployed to nonoperative status at Luke Air Force Base. . . .

". . . pilots will be reassigned to transport units at Travis AFB until such time as. . . .

". . . navigator officers will be reassigned to staff positions at either Elmendorf AFB or possibly as deputy commanders at North Dakota missile sites. . . ."

Horton shook his head mournfully. "For God's sake, don't tell anybody I let you in on this," he moaned, "or for sure I'll be in the stockade for the rest of my life."

As if to dismiss the whole incident, he quickly returned the folder to his file, locked it, and at once provided a distraction by showing them Oscar's jewels. When he placed his hand tenderly on the glass jar, he declared that Detachment Two not only had a symbol that would go down in recce history, but the former owner himself was present to greet them. He reached beneath his desk and brought out Oscar, who obligingly snarled.

Horton was convinced that the evening came to a very satisfying end. He had demonstrated beyond any doubt that Detachment Two held no petty prejudices toward those lesser mortals whom he had seen safely to bed, and he could hardly wait for the reverberations from Kadena once the rumors of what he had quoted from his confidential files spread with the speed of their ugly sleds. The results should be particularly interesting, he reasoned, since he had made up the quotes as he read along.

Horton slept for three hours; then, according to his fixed belief that he should be the one on hand for every mission launch, he followed its progress until it took off. When he confirmed that the pilot was well on his way, he went back to bed for another three hours, and at six in the morning was present to make sure the SR-71 experienced no problems in their launching toward home base. While the farewells were not exactly tearful, there was much comradely pounding of shoulders and hand-shaking in the suiting-up trailer, and punch lines that had been successful the night before were repeated along with mellow touches of sincerity. "Y'all drop in and see us again. . . ."

"You just come our way and we'll show you the joys of Kadena. No question, we have the most beautiful base in the world."

The SR guys, Horton thought, would naturally have the best of everything. Possibly they had for once spoken the truth, and in the spirit of the moment he would forgive them their intolerable smugness.

Finally there were the usual wishes for a good flight. Horton waited dutifully until the SR-71 had roared off into the dawn, then went to his office. He drank coffee from a paper cup, which he decided tasted like bird's nest soup, sat down at his desk, and steered his imagination toward a letter to his wife. He sucked on the end of his pen after he had achieved his usual "Dearest Sylvia . . ." and swung around in his chair. It always helped the composition of a husbandly letter to face a blank wall for a few minutes.

It was not until he had come out of deep meditation that he noticed Oscar's jewels were missing.

A corporal on duty in the operations office, which was some distance down the hall, heard what he later described as the howl of a wounded coyote. He made for his commander's office at a full run.

❖

After the departure of the SR-71 and the woeful discovery that a crime had been committed, Horton spent the balance of the day investigating the calamity that had befallen Oscar's pride. And gradually the evidence sorted itself until there was little question as to the identity of the thieves. Vengeance clawed at Horton's mind. He could find no mental peace except in the well-oiled machinery of his detachment, yet the finding of what had become the detachment's symbol seemed impossible. Arranging retribution was difficult when the supposed villains were six hundred miles away.

Horton brooded on the problem until the memorable day when his belief in the value of intelligence proved itself once more. Always seeking information, he learned that the SR-71 people at Kadena also kept a treasure under glass—the preserved carcass of an Okinawan snake, the Habu, which had been adopted as the symbol of their squadron.

When Horton learned that a cargo plane would be making a flight to Okinawa and returning the next morning, he chose three of his most reliable troops, including Hopper, and advised them that such opportunities were extremely rare. "It's the weekend coming up, and we'll invite ourselves to stop by for a reunion. We will accept the invitation of the sled drivers with the grace and dignity it deserves and spend the night in good fellowship. We will admire their luxurious accommodations and foster an atmosphere of sweet understanding. Those of you who feel themselves incapable of such emotion, those who might be prejudiced about our national assets, may withdraw now." There were no rejections.

The gathering at Kadena propelled itself into a roaring success, and everyone agreed that Japanese beer was superior to Korean beer. The U-2 contingent were all on their very best behavior and lavished praise on the SR-71 base, the food, the beverage supply.

At midnight, when the bar at the Officers' Club was closing, there was a touching scene as U-2 people and SR-71 people swore their admiration of each other and their devotion to a common cause. No one wanted to bring such a mellow evening to an end.

The cargo plane was scheduled to return to Osan at seven in the morning. At six, long before his hosts were awake, Horton led his team to the office of the SR-71's commander. There, in agreement with Horton's recently acquired intelligence, they found Oscar's jewels prominently displayed. They carefully packed the glass jar in a duffle bag, and as added booty took the jar containing the Habu.

Yet Horton was not quite satisfied. He eyed the commander's desk with increasing interest. It was of Oriental manufacture, a great, heavy accumulation of carved mahogany that Horton estimated might weigh three hundred or four hundred pounds.

It was while Horton was speculating what his squad might do with such an awkward prize that four of the base MP's arrived. They were interested in why the lights were on at such an hour on a Sunday morning. It was just not standard routine.

Horton rose instantly to the occasion. He made certain the

sergeant of the MP's saw the silver oak leaf on his flight cap, then spoke with the tone of authority the badge represented. "I'm sure glad y'all came, sergeant. We have to move this desk out of here, and we just can't handle it without help. How about lending a hand?"

The MP's glanced uncertainly at each other. This was highly unusual, but a lieutenant colonel was a lieutenant colonel. "Why do you have to move it, sir?"

"Because it's Sunday, and since this office is closed today, we're going to paint the ceiling. The last thing we want is any marks on the commander's desk."

It was thus that the desk belonging to the commanding officer of the swiftest airplanes in the world was transported down a long hallway and, along with a full symphony of gruntings, maneuvered through the only doorway wide enough to accept its bulk—the officer's latrine.

Horton considered taking the desk back to Osan, but realized reluctantly that it would be impossible to hide.

The final parting took place just outside the cargo plane. There was much shoulder-slapping and overfirm hand-squeezing as the formal farewells were declared. And to a man they vowed to remain steadfast friends in the future. When at last the huge doors of the cargo plane were closed, Horton was reasonably content with all that had transpired. He saw a ring of smiling faces standing on the ramp until the very last salute.

Horton was still smiling when the cargo plane lifted off from Kadena Air Base. He saw the sun come up over the Pacific, and he thought that Driskill and Hinkle and, yes, even Pinsky, would approve of his actions. This mission would, of course, remain classified as most secret, but the true high fliers of the air force would know of it before one more revolution of the earth.

· · ·

It was a subdued Oscar who bade Cecil Hopper farewell on his first operational mission. Now, some ten days after his arrival in Osan, Hopper had seen what there was to see in the town; he had taken his share of beers in the Honeymoon Club, where he had been initiated by the notorious "Miss Penny"; he had been to the Tick-Tock Club, the Fifth Avenue Club, and even Papa Joe's. As if confirming his residence in Korea, he had ordered a sport jacket and a pair of slacks from Mr. Oh's, a shop that catered entirely to the military and kept prices so low few Americans could resist.

It was not Driskill's parting words that kept Hopper from establishing closer relationships with the club girls of "beautiful downtown Osan"; it was the prospect of his upcoming flight. Nothing must go wrong. No one must be able to say that this rookie failed his first mission—no matter what happened.

Ten anxious days had passed before Hopper saw his name scheduled for a flight, and at last there it was on the operational blackboard—a nine-hour sortie with take off scheduled for the second hour of the new day. If all went well, he should be over the targets soon after sunrise. After a few minutes orbiting in the vicinity of each target, he could turn for home. Home? He found it difficult to believe that only four months back he had never heard of Osan.

Rain drummed on the roof of the Physiological Support Unit (PSU) at Osan, which was housed in a large trailer parked alongside Operations and Horton's office. Within the trailer the staff maintained, dried, and cleaned the pressure suits, helmets, and all the gear necessary for high flight. There were also the same leather reclining chairs, test stands, pressure-suit wall consoles as at Beale, Hopper noted, and the same concern for his personal well-being.

The sergeant, a short, hyperactive man, greeted him warmly. "Never mind the nitrogen in your blood, Captain, how's your libido on this moist morning?"

"Outstanding."

"That's a nice way to put it." The sergeant held out a yellow pressure suit. There was a cloth plaque on the chest with CECIL HOPPER, CAPT. embroidered in white on a blue background. "Just came in last night," the sergeant said, as if he had made it himself. "Cut to measure, but if it doesn't fit, we'll give you your money back."

Hopper stared at the suit. It seemed incredible that he was looking at his own name so fixed in position. The sense of impermanence, which had plagued him ever since his arrival, suddenly evaporated.

"You don't like the style, sir? We sell a lot of these . . . very popular . . . very chic."

"I'm just pleased they spelled my name right."

The sergeant held out a fishbowl helmet. "They played it safe here, sir."

HOPPER was spelled in bold letters across the back of the helmet.

"Welcome to Det Two." The sergeant smiled and glanced at the ceiling. A sudden shower caused such a commotion on the roof that the sergeant's voice was barely audible. "Believe me, sir, it's not always such a nice night for flying around here. We do have worse, but I have trouble remembering when."

Just before Hopper lay back to absorb his quota of pure oxygen before flight, Oscar appeared in the trailer and stood staring at him quizzically. He cocked his head and licked one paw, all the while keeping his harvest-moon eyes on Hopper.

"That's a good sign," the sergeant said, "it's not everybody Oscar bothers to see off, especially at this hour of the morning."

While he assisted Hopper into his space suit, the sergeant launched into a solemn commentary on Oscar. "He ain't the same man he was by a damn sight, which, of course, is understandable. Like, how would we feel if the same thing was done to us? I mean, you know, it would slow a guy down. It might even change his personality and he might become a murderer even, or beat up on people, you know. I notice the change in Oscar. Of course, he never does say much, so it's hard to tell if his voice . . ."

Hopper was relieved when the sergeant slipped the goldfish bowl over his head and he heard the security locks click into place. This midnight he wanted to concentrate on one subject: his flight. He had rehearsed over and over again in his mind the obvious things that could go wrong, but there were always surprises. As he lay back and knew the now-familiar sensation of actually separating himself from the rest of humanity, it occurred to him that slipping into eternity might be a very similar experience. He shook his head inside the goldfish bowl and looked at Oscar, whose stare remained uncompromising. Was there a hex in those amber eyes? Was Oscar expressing vengeance on every detachment member he encountered?

"Suspicion dies hard," Hopper whispered as he lay back to dispense with the nitrogen in his blood.

Now, lying almost prone in the second hour of a new day, when a man should be in his deepest sleep, it was easy to pretend he was looking back at what had turned out to be a fatal mistake. There was Oscar barely to be seen along the lower rim of the goldfish bowl. He was still at his vigil—waiting for what? Why, when given a possible choice, do the quick cats survive and the dullards perish?

It was strange how a man could ring all the wrong bells right in the midst of his personal doom. Here in this U-2 business a man was properly trained for everything but the unknown. Even so, even if he had his wits about him, he could easily make the wrong decision . . . turn right instead of left, and so bring about a calamity.

Was he dreaming? He saw a beautiful girl descending a flight of stairs. She tripped and fell. The balustrade speared her cranium. He saw it clearly. If she had turned her body one-half inch as she tripped, her head would have missed the balustrade. The balustrade had no choice—the girl died, and she made the wrong one. Did bullfighters feel this way, think such nonsense before they entered the arena . . . or afterward?

Pinsky had obviously made all the right choices when the need was there. He was still alive and healthy. Likewise Driskill. And that old-timer known as "Snake" Pierce, who had been through the worst of wars and managed to keep his body intact. They all looked so different in dress uniform. It was as if they were leading one life and pretending to be in another. They were full of good humor, some of it silly. They posed such questions as why God invented women when airplanes were so much fun, and they praised the joys of sleeping with a flying machine. Yet they had all made the right decisions—many times.

Hopper thought about the rain. This was the third day of it, and there was no explaining why it had not turned to snow.

It would be an instrument takeoff, of course. The base of the clouds was at five hundred feet, and the visibility was one mile. So if for some reason he would have to return to Osan immediately—say, the gear failed to retract—then he would have his hands full with an instrument approach. No strain there unless something else went wrong. Think ahead of your airplane, Hopper. Hours ahead.

Why was it, he thought, as he watched Oscar make himself comfortable on the other reclining chair, that he always had these bouts of gloom and doom just before an important flight? Then it all went away the instant he entered the cockpit. Euphoria replaced melancholy, and all was as it should be.

"All right, sir, up and away with you."

Strange. The sergeant's gruff benediction was beginning to sound familiar. And then suddenly there was Horton standing at the door of the trailer. His flight jacket was dripping with rain, and his face was studded with droplets. It was said through the detachment that Horton had never missed seeing off a sortie no matter the time of day, but it was reassuring to see him now.

It was even better when Horton walked beside him to the U-2. There was something inspiring about the way he ignored a puddle of water and sloshed right through it, the way he walked with his head up in spite of the rain.

"Good!" Horton shouted as soon as he saw the U-2's cockpit was protected by a howdah. "They got things repaired. At least you won't get your ass wet. We had some problems with this airplane, but I understand it's all cured now."

There was a pat on the back as Hopper mounted the howdah. Some commanders, he thought, were naturals.

At the top of the stairs the airplane crew was waiting for him. "Good morning, sir!" someone yelled above the sound of the turbine generator. Hopper stepped on the parachute that formed the bottom of the cockpit seat and lowered himself awkwardly into position. He plugged into the communications system, and soon there were many voices. "Wherever you're going, sir, it's got to be better weather than here. . . ."

"You might have some trouble with that new view sight, sir, but I think it's fixed now."

"I hope." How was that for casual?

"The tacan was replaced this morning, and the number-two transmitter checked out okay. Those were all the squawks."

Somewhere from beyond the protection of the howdah a voice penetrated the communication system. There was a laugh, then: "There must be some mistake. I joined the air force, not the goddamned navy. I'm either a frogman or in a submarine."

"Getting wet, Jackson?"

"No, no. I'm taking a sunbath down here."

Down where? Hopper supposed they were still working on one of the equipment bays that had developed a leak. There had even been talk of scratching the mission unless it could be fixed.

It was cozy enough in the cockpit. All the personal trinkets a guy found comforting were at hand—his favorite soup (bean); just open the packet. Applesauce and Gatorade and chocolate pudding—each in its own packet. Then a small, much-worn copy of *The Prophet* from the library.

Ah, the library! He must not even think about it now, because Willie Horton was standing out there in the rain and he expected 100 percent concentration on the mission. A few minutes ago Horton had been standing on the howdah making sure of a personal sendoff. According to his custom.

His soft, licorice voice had drawled through the intercom, "You sure got a nice mornin' to fly, Cecil. Hark to the angels for me."

Now how could any guy ever let a man like that down? Three o'clock in the morning, raining a Niagara, a new guy on this mission, and Horton easy as always.

Of course, there was more to this library than just books. There was, thank God, the librarian. She had pressed a copy of *The Prophet* in his hand and said he should carry it for good luck on his first operational sortie. It was a very small book, so no strain. And it was sort of nice to have it along.

No more thinking about her now. The crew chief was standing down there in the rain rotating his electric wands, and he was already pissed off because the auxiliary power unit had almost caused a delay. Something he would have to explain in writing, and he did not care for writing anything about anything. His men were moving away into the gloom like stagehands caught after the curtain rose, Hopper thought. And now, the fat lady must sing. Cecil Hopper was the star. Trumpets, please! This was what he was born for and paid for. It seemed incredible that both were true. Was it only yesterday that he had been in Hinkle's school? Always with nursemaid Napolitano close at hand.

He flexed his arms and stretched his gloved hands. No need to consult the approach plates for Osan at this time. He had them all memorized down to the last digit. He remembered something the librarian said to him. She was small and feisty and she had warned him of the three "C's"—never criticize, complain, or compare. A little rain with probably some icing in the clouds just made things interesting. Anybody could fly with a full moon.

The howdah vanished into the night, and the crew with it. As the engine spooled up, Hopper ran his gloved finger down the last of the checklist. Circuit breakers? . . . Pitot heat ON . . . INS mode switch? . . . suit cool lever UP . . . flaps UP . . . throttle friction set . . . spoiler ARM . . . IFF . . . set . . . Defog handle IN . . . very necessary tonight . . . canopy closed and locked.

He saw the mobile car pull up beside Horton and watched him run for the door. Just as he entered the car, he turned for a quick look at the U-2 and made an okay sign with his fingers. Plus a smile. No wonder Willie Horton was treasured as a commander. He was so in love with his work. And that makes two of us, Hopper decided.

His face swam from side to side in the goldfish bowl, his eyes alert to anything in the dark perimeters that might present a collision factor to the U-2's long wings. A stray mobile unit, a parked jeep, a forgotten auxiliary unit; he deliberately reminded himself that he was surrounded by several hundred chances to make a mistake. Now, and for the balance of his mortal days.

This foul night was illuminated only by his taxiing lights and the magenta cockpit lights. They both had a way of fostering illusions. It might even be accepted that this flight was not really happening, since there would be no official record of it. He was bound to gather priceless information in which he could never share. If he failed, the mission coded "Sacrament Five" would fail, and the consequence of that he would never know. Only Horton and a handful of people in Washington would know that Cecil Hopper had fucked up.

Hopper was astonished at the electric speed of his thoughts. If he had a bride, he might say to her that he would return in the late afternoon and surround himself with what passed for real life. But he had no wife, which was a good thing, because there was always some chance he would not return at all. It was possible that he would be marooned forever in the limbo for which he was bound.

Of course, nothing could go wrong with something that didn't happen.

He reached the threshold of the runway and paused. So, inexplicably, did his attention. It was as if he must gather himself and suddenly his brain had rejected the preparatory signals. Now, in a nanosecond of time, he left the cockpit. Frivolous thoughts took command in the very heart of complexity. Greetings to the world's most enchanting librarian! Would she understand that even in this space suit a man could commit the folly of remaining human? Go away, woman! You are not invited to this collection of instants when concentration has got to stay at the peak, when distraction could possibly bring the failure of Sacrament Five, when blooming roses are not on the program.

He had bought the roses from a farmer's stand, barely budding, fresh and vigorous, as are so many things in Korea. And he had taken the roses back to his quarters and brought with him a can of spray paint—black. Then, delicately, as if he were a master origami artist, he sprayed the outside of the roses black. Next, he saw to it the roses would be delivered to her when he had already been some time aloft. Up in the high country where few men flew as a regular thing.

Now, he was hoping that after sunrise, when all the world lay far below him, in a region where his blood would boil instantly were it not for his manufactured skin, the scent of his roses would mark her thoughts.

"What a surprise!" his mind heard her exclaim, golden-voiced. "How like him . . . how precious!"

When he returned, he could say modestly, "It seemed right. Our squadron colors, you see?"

Even as he descended, if his timing was right, the roses would open, revealing themselves in a pattern of dead blacks surrounding little islands of crimson.

"You are so thoughtful," she might say.

"It's how I feel." Or, better . . ., "It's nothing."

There, he thought, were soft things.

His mind once more became obedient. *Here* were only hard things.

Pitch trim set zero point—five degrees nose up.

Continuous ignition on.

IFF mode and code set as briefed.

Pitot head on.

Engine and flight instruments, check, check, check.

Nearby in the darkness were the flashing red lights of the mobile car. Behind the wheel Horton picked up a microphone. "On your way, pal . . . pogo sticks?"

Men from the truck were moving beneath the wingtips, unlatching the long sticks with wheels on the bottom end. They would fall away as the U-2 accelerated. The men in the truck would retrieve them when the U-2 was airborne. In thirty seconds he knew he would be climbing into the Korean night and he would no longer be the new boy.

"All clear?"

"You're a go."

A moment's hesitation. Hopper swiveled his head right to left and back again. He blew out his checks as he had done as a little boy just before attempting the difficult. Then determination locked his jaw. Here was his true passion. The love of challenge did not need red roses.

His left hand was already on the throttle. He eased it full

forward and was satisfied with the pressure of himself against the back of his seat.

Power percentage—check.

Exhaust-gas temperature—check.

A soft rumbling now throughout the U-2.

Runway lights flashed past, swirling along the limits of his peripheral vision. Next the familiar sense of levitation. The U-2 became airborne.

Airspeed 160 knots. Hopper was tunneling into a black abyss at a sixty-degree angle. At fourteen thousand feet there was still runway below. Sacrament Five was in business.

It was quiet inside Hopper's helmet. He could hear himself breathing.

There were many things Hopper did not know when he left Osan behind, punched through the overcast, and disappeared almost instantly. The weather reports of his target area were sketchy and based on what little information was available. The North Koreans and the Russians, with whom much of the Asiatic weather reports originated, were not given to supplying a detailed description of the climatic situation for foreigners. He had been briefed that the local weather at Osan was supposed to improve as the day progressed, and there were several clear alternates in Japan if the prophecy was wrong. He was satisfied that at least a back door would be open to him. The winds at his operating altitude were "best guesses."

There was still considerable mystery about the winds at or above seventy thousand feet; no meteorologist would venture a positive prediction, because experience had proven that there was no reliability about the region. So high, where the fences of space began, the winds were normally calm or very light, and yet full gales had been encountered many times. The same fickle behavior applied to upper-air turbulence; mostly it was smooth sailing, but there were periods when it could be so rough it tried the integrity of both machine and man.

Limited visibility in the haze. As yet, no stars this morning.

A voice rattled in the goldfish bowl, unmistakably Horton's. "Have a good day."

"Thanks. See ya."

The U-2 climbed steeply upward through the black overcast; then, suddenly, the cloud cover became translucent and the morning exploded—first an amber line across the eastern horizon, then a bomb of outrageous scarlet to match the roses.

Now, passing through sixty thousand feet, Hopper noticed something sneaking along like a minnow in the depths below. An airliner of unknown nationality and origin. He watched it a moment. If the roses did their work, if by some wild chance he married the librarian, would he leave this and settle down? Become a businessman? A ground-bound citizen worrying about taxes and promotions? He dismissed the fancy almost instantly. Even the thought was far below the salt of his current realm.

He was monitoring many things now, for the U-2 was subservient to the automatic pilot, and at these altitudes it gradually took on a new character. He liked to think of it as a gnat perched very precariously on the tip of a needle. Sensitive. Fickle when flown by hand.

Today the task is to monitor the activities of certain people who had been saying for two generations that their way of life was best for mankind and that sooner or later they would conquer the world. Maybe? Lately, they had changed their song and added sweet lyrics. It was a fair guess that Sacrament Five was looking for proof that the music was genuine.

Let the Soviet submarine flotilla play in the Sea of Okhotsk this glorious morning. Their activities were otherwise well covered.

And then there were the North Koreans. Morning to you!

What is the purpose of those new roadworks leading toward your still-bitter enemy the South Koreans?

The ore pocket just east of Chongjin? How many tons mined to make the steel that will build the rails to connect four new depots . . . in the middle of nowhere?

Why has the North Korean 6th Brigade changed from permanent quarters to a temporary bivouac near Tsau Manjang—at least that is the way the intelligence spooks pronounce it. Is their change of station a feint of some kind? The truck tracks, or better yet the tank tracks, if there are any to be photographed, will reveal the truth. If the sun casts a good shadow. Two hours and forty-two minutes from now.

Someday, Hopper resolved, he was going to spend more time with the spooks. He would very much like to see down there what he was supposed to see from up here. This was like trolling for a fish, catching it, and never seeing it again.

He leveled off in the brilliant sunlight. Seventy thousand feet. Chongjin down there. The weather was clearing, even in the depths below. Somewhere ahead, beyond the curvature of the planet Earth, would be Vladivostok, which would not exactly hang out a welcome mat if he strayed that way. No peeking.

He yawned and reached to scratch his nose. His glove slammed into his faceplate. Jesus, would he ever learn? U-2 pilots could not have itchy noses. You could blow up the clown suit with compressed air, which would raise the rim of the helmet high enough to scratch your chin, but noses were out—specifically if you had one that turned up at the end instead of down.

Aside from Sacrament Five, this day was going to be made up of such trivialities. It was written, as the old-timers always said. And you did not argue with the word. You wiggled your nose around as much as you could and waited for the itch to go away.

. . .

Sacrament Five was far to the north of Osan when Detachment Commander Horton bade an official farewell to the man his new pilot had replaced. He was Major Maxwell Peabody, a New Englander who expected the rest of the world to keep their place. Peabody was flying home via one of the Flying Tiger contract planes, and Horton escorted him directly to the boarding ramp. He knew instinctively that this was a moment of hidden joy, the last jewel in the crown of a grand performance.

For Peabody was unique to the 99th Squadron, and was an even rarer bird to the Second Detachment. Assignment to Korea was considered an honor, yet somehow, to Horton's near despair, one of Hinkle's more notorious assholes had somehow slipped through the screen. He had been at Osan for nearly six months, and anyone who understood Horton would not have taken his farewell with quite the conviction he put into it. "We're sure going to miss you around here," was rendered profoundly. Anyone but Peabody would have realized that if Horton had said, "We'll be glad to get rid of you," then he would truly be missed. "You've done a lot for the detachment." Indeed he had, for Peabody's personality was scribed forever among his peers. He proved there was one of his kind in every outfit. He gave them something to loathe.

Peabody was such a miser he was often suspected of delving into alchemy, and his record as a goldbrick tended to confirm the rumor. He was known to reuse mail envelopes, if he could not steal the government-issue variety, and he had never been known to buy anyone a drink. Even so, he was quick to accept when other members of the Black Cat Detachment paid for his beer in the vain hope that he might reciprocate. His quarters were always immaculate, the more so since the morning of his departure, when he packed everything that could be considered as government property, including towels and drinking glasses, which he added to his own gear.

Peabody's parsimony knew no limits. To save on barber fees, which in Korea were possibly the cheapest in the world, he cut his own hair. As his time remaining in Korea waned, he heard of a remarkable bargain available in a Japanese car. Once he found a way to ship it home at government expense, he haggled for several days before he finally bought it. It was then that his talent for boring recitations ran away with him, and the patience of Horton and his otherwise merry men.

Peabody had never married. He declared that marriage was like a weeping willow, a tree that drooped with age and demanded upkeep forevermore. It was, Horton had long ago decided, the only interesting thing Peabody had ever said.

Peabody was a gaunt man with ears resembling radar dishes, and a nose that led him into everything that was none of his business. He had an overlarge mouth, which one of the detachment said reminded him of a toilet seat, even though Peabody had never been known to use profanity. There had been times when Oscar the cat chose to weave a pattern between Peabody's ankles, a sort of sinuous dance to keep his coat sleek. Peabody's reaction was always the same. If Horton was within sight range, he would move Oscar away gently, using the toe of his boot. If Horton was absent, he applied the same boot with considerable force, and seemed pleased when Oscar screeched with anger.

As soon as he became the owner of the car, Peabody began to brag about the mileage-per-gallon it attained. He launched into the consumption virtues of his vehicle every time he could find an audience, and since normally the officers of the detachment ate together, this was at least three times a day. Any conversation had to compete with Peabody's idolatrous lectures on automotive fuel consumption.

A week passed before outright objections were made to Peabody's interminable monologues. Then, at last, Horton resolved that something must be done. His solution was typically Hortonian. First he began pretending to hear what Peabody was saying, and even expressed interest in his miles-per-gallon marvel. "Maybe you would like to sell me your car and make a slight profit?"

When Peabody was convinced he had a brother enthusiast, Horton roused himself in the middle of the night and put an extra gallon of gas in the car's tank. He waited a few days, then repeated the process. He continued for the better part of a month and was gratified when Peabody's mileage reports approached ecstasy. Never in the history of the world had there been such an economical automobile!

Then, one night, Horton decided he had lost enough sleep. Peabody's magic fuel supply ceased forever, and Horton had only a few days to wait before his gravely concerned nemesis confessed, "I can't understand . . . my mileage has dropped from forty-five-point-two down to thirty. I think there must be something wrong with the carburetor."

Horton was quick with suggestions, as were all the other officers who had suffered Peabody's interminable droning on a single subject. "It must be your fuel line . . . Your plugs need cleaning . . . The fuel pump, they were no good in that year . . . Maybe a leak in the tank. . . ."

The benefits to the detachment were immediate and satisfying. Peabody the bore, Peabody the skinflint, the malingerer, and the complainer, became a whirlwind of energy. He tore at the fuel system of his almost-new car apart, and on the frequent advice of Horton and his comrades made several expensive trips to Seoul to buy new parts—to replace the nearly new. And yet all to no avail, for despite his Herculean efforts and the tender care he took with his numbers, he was never able to regain what he had come to regard as his personal mileage standard.

As Peabody disappeared into the airliner, Horton employed his most sincere wave of farewell, but he had trouble keeping the enthusiasm out of his smile. Maybe, he hoped, the air force would get lucky and Peabody would next find himself sentenced to the Pentagon. Maybe a fine detachment like the Second of the good old 99th Squadron would be safe from the likes of him.

❖

Three hours into the flight now. Chongjin already a hundred miles behind. Hopper sighed in contentment. Number-one job completed according to schedule. En route to the next way-point. Outside temperature dropping. Fractured cumulonimbus below. Sky still deep indigo to the west. Bad-guy territory, but everything sailing along just fine.

For a moment Hopper thought about the U-2's long nose. He had never been invited to examine all the equipment up there. Or beneath the wings in special pods. All that was none of his business, in spite of his top-secret clearance. He had been told that some of the cameras were so smart the spooks could identify a football held horizontally or vertically—from seventy thousand feet. Or above. And from miles away on either side.

The targets for Sacrament Five were like all others—classified. He was not supposed to be here. Every country in the world had reserved the airspace above them. By whose authority? God's? Their territory extended to how high? No one cared to be specific. As far as the Milky Way? Further yet, or not so far?

The melody of the left hand, Hopper thought, was not necessarily in the same key as the right hand. The upper atmosphere was for the taking. If you could get away with discovering what the other guy was up to without killing your informant, just how you went about it was none of his affair.

Lunchtime. Hopper inserted a plastic straw through the valve in his helmet and sucked on a packet of applesauce. He followed it with a meat stew and decided they both tasted about the same. The bean soup would come later.

Now, his limbs were stiffening. He tried a few isometrics, and some of the tension left him. Embalmed. The Egyptian mummies never had it so good. They must have the world's most tired asses.

He stretched as far as he could, then turned a valve in the side of his clown suit, blowing himself up until he resembled an orange potato. The squeezing sensation was a pleasant relief for a time—until he let the air out again. He checked and rechecked his oxygen gauge. Was it because he was suffering from hypoxia that he felt better than he had in his entire life? His capacity for admiration was exhausted. There was just no way, he thought, to absorb all that met his eyes.

He remembered breaking out of the overcast above Osan as he passed through thirty thousand feet. It was like escaping from a dungeon. Suddenly, where there had been swirling darkness, there was the black sky studded with glittering stars, and on the western horizon a chunk of old moon. There stood Sirius, blue and bold, and then Capella near the zenith. Castor and Pollux, of course, then low in the sky Arcturus, creamy and sparkling like a toy balloon gone a great distance. Soon after there was that bonfire in the east. As the U-2 climbed, he was hoisting his own sun.

All was distance here. There was nothing within reach—even of the mind. This world aloft was a civilized wilderness with all things controlled for eternity, but the brain could not accept the concept of eternity. It was impossible to conceive of anything without termination.

Very well, he thought. We might be puny microbugs, but somehow, while still alive, we have invented a machine that can soar toward infinity. And come home.

Seventy-one thousand. A lighter U-2 now, with almost three hours into the mission and that much fuel burned. There was almost no sound—only the most gentle purring of the engine. The air was smooth. Below, nothing. This area of earth was still blanketed by an overcast. Still, he had a long way to go.

He kept looking toward the north, hoping to catch a break in the overcast. If the weather guys were to be believed, there should be a change in ground cover about here, but then perhaps they had miscalculated.

Seventy-one thousand, two hundred. That seemed almost as high as the old bird intended to go.

Hopper suddenly remembered something a very old pelican of an aviator had told him. "It's when things are going just right that you'd better be suspicious. There you are, fat as can be. The whole world is yours and you're the answer to the Wright brothers' prayers. You say to yourself, nothing can go wrong . . . all my trespasses are forgiven. Best you not believe it."

The old pelican had then gone on to talk of his friend Tallman, an extraordinarily versatile aviator. He had flown all manner of aircraft in all kinds of situations, and yet had, inexplicably, crashed into a low hill in terrain he knew like his own yard. No one was ever sure why.

Tallman's partner, Mantz, was an equally talented airman. "A natural," as the flying ancients used to say. At least his end was explainable. He was flying an experimental airplane for a movie—a job he never completed.

Then, as if to relieve his mournful intoning of lost friends, the old pelican told again of Hoover, who was recognized by the world's most skillful aviators as in a class by himself. Just recently, his Mustang had caught fire during an airshow. Thanks to Hoover's exceptional ability, he executed an immediate all-or-nothing landing and made a hasty exit while the flames still roared. He performed that flight wearing his trademark—an ordinary business suit.

"Now, he has compromised." The pelican smiled. "Now, he wears a neoprene flameproof flight suit. So just remember, Cecil, nobody who gets too damned relaxed builds up much flying time.

The emergencies you train for almost never happen. It's the one you can't train for that kills you."

At last there was a bar of dung-colored ground beneath. True overcast. And a patch of sunlight was stabbing at it. Appropriate cheers. Business was picking up.

Hopper twisted in his harness. Five hours yet to go, and his muscles were already stiffening. The little numbers blinking so reliably on his navigational computer were a constant reminder that he was not up here just to view the scenery. In terms of degrees and minutes, they were reporting his exact position relative to the equator and to Greenwich, a suburb of London that had been famous for generations simply because cartographers had to start somewhere. It was magic unless the computer went ape, and then it was back to basics with as little confusion as possible. It was quite pleasant to realize the computer could link itself directly to the future of Cecil Hopper. It would keep him from wandering from his preplanned flight. Usually.

Hours before he had rolled out of his bunk, showered and shaved, and put away his high-altitude breakfast, the flight planners had extracted a series of numbers from their charts, placed them on a card that would be mated with the on-board computer. The numbers represented chosen "way-points" along the route, which Hopper carefully monitored. And his computer was joined to the automatic pilot, which took over the physical effort of keeping the U-2 flying level and straight. The more he thought about it, the more the whole process seemed rather humiliating.

Maybe it was the fault of the almost faultless genii who designed all this apparatus. Those electronic wonder boys believed they had attained perfection; and except for one factor, they nearly had. In their absorption with mastering the energies of tiny silicon chips, they had overlooked the frailties of humans— who sometimes slept the numbers away.

At last the sun was high enough to start heating the planet's atmosphere, and Hopper saw that there were large breaks in the overcast some fourteen miles straight down. He saw segments of the Sea of Japan, black and forbidding between wreaths of gray cloud. The changing shape of the segments from round to oval gave him his only visual sense of progress. Otherwise, he thought, he might as well have been suspended from a string.

He glanced at the outside temperature gauge. Minus fifty centigrade. Cold. Yet in his yellow clown suit he was comfortable, except that his nose itched. Why did this perversity come to be only when he was unable to reach his nose?

Now, the day came quickly. He was hungry, so he chose a packet of "Sloppy Joe," removed the guard cap, and stuck the plastic straw through the valve in his helmet. He sucked in about half of the packet's contents, then returned it to the supply box. Not exactly a breakfast of champions, he thought, but it did carry a sterile guarantee.

There were more important things ahead, it seemed, for the horizon was becoming indefinite, and there was a haze developing over all of the target area. The Wild-Heerburg camera in the nose would be photographing in infrared, and its twelve-inch lens would reach far beyond anything he could see with his own blue twenty-fifteens. All as advertised. Press trigger switch and start the ragtime band. The Soviets were reported as being restless again, and there was supposed to be considerable submarine activity near Petropavlovsk. Their private lake, the Sea of Okhotsk. Or so they behaved.

Questions. Would the information he was gathering wind up at Wakanai, the once-secret U.S. intelligence station on the northern tip of Japan? Or would it go all the way back to the National Security Agency at Fort Meade in Maryland?

It suddenly occurred to Hopper that there might not be anything at all operating in the nose of this beast—that maybe all the machinery had been deliberately turned off and his sortie was just a practice chore set up for the new boy in town; or could he be acting as a decoy while some other device did the serious business? Or how about the bad guys down in the far below? Were "they," as "they" had done in the past, laying out some nice displays cleverly designed to be photographed by you and assessed by the spooks back in Washington—also decoys?

Mine is to ask, Hopper thought, and never be told. Next dragon?

Hopper yawned at the dark blue sky above the U-2's canopy. Indigo. Yes, that was the color.

Now was temptation hour. A nap would do nicely, thank you, but this was not sleepy-time land. Electronics were rascals, and they lay awake nights trying to find some way to screw you during the day. You could not reason with them. They had a brain and intestines, but no heart. They would never understand painting red roses black on the outside, just as it was better if a recce guy did not always understand the details of his mission. No one could guarantee that a man might just have an extra beer some night and tell his chick something she should not know, or if caught on his job, he might have to tell somebody else. After all, the brass knew he was human. Any man could be made to talk.

Damn! He was so anxious that everything be perfect on this first operational mission. Driskill deserved a confirmation of his faith. So did Hinkle and Horton and, of course, Napolitano. They must not feel they had made an error in appointing Cecil Hopper to such a high and fancy-pants office. Not even a billionaire could arrange a view like this. Now, the sun had matured and the haze was melting away.

Never mind. The airspeed needle was sitting right between the barber poles. He was "in the throat" and sailing free. According to a tacan reading he had taken from a transmitter in Japan, he would be over the last target area in seven minutes. Way-point six.

He made several entries on his green card—oxygen supply, engine readings, fuel remaining—then he checked the numbers against a graph on the back side of the card, which had been calculated as part of his flight plan.

Okay, here was way-point number six. Earth plainly visible, but weak shadows. Check through view sight. Not reality—more like inspecting brain plasma through a microscope. Wiggle the sight around a bit with the toggle switch on the right lower panel. Presto! Buildings along a harbor. Railroad tracks leading to largest complex . . .

The sun had crossed the zenith. Everything as advertised. A shallow turn back for Osan in two minutes. If the haze did not negate the final product, his job was well done. He began to whistle softly, "Home on the Range." Then he eased the U-2 around in a gentle left turn. Back to the stable, old cowboy. Sacrament Five was in the bag.

Once he was on the reverse course, the reflected light was so brilliant Hopper pulled down the sunshade over his faceplate. Now there were only scattered cumuli below, marching in sheep-like little bands across the grizzled sea. And the further south he flew, the better the visibility. He sat as far back as he could and urinated. A guy just couldn't go on forever, even if he wanted to.

It was time to start a descent for Osan. He checked his fuel. Ample. He checked the oxygen supply. The same.

New way-points coming up now. A straight course for the old corral. Howya doing' there, honcho?

Mind the rate of descent. It's important. Not only keep the airspeed under control, but have a care for timing and so avoid embarrassment. It would never do to arrive over Osan with twenty-odd thousand feet to spare, as some guys on their first mission had done. Or worse, fly the last hundred miles too low and waste fuel.

He disengaged the automatic pilot and pushed gently forward

on the control yoke. Nothing happened. Surprise? He pushed harder. The yoke refused to move.

Autopilot still engaged? Negative on the switch. He reached down and pulled the circuit breaker. A hard push this time. No movement.

Hopper frowned at the sun. What the hell was going on here?

He tried a gentle bank to the left, and the U-2 responded normally. He tried another to the right. No problem. He shoved on the right rudder pedal. The plane slewed to the right. He tried the left pedal. The plane slewed to the left. He pushed again on the yoke. No movement of any kind.

He tried pulling gently. Then harder. He could not move the yoke. It was locked in position.

He placed his hands on his thighs and reviewed all he knew of the U-2's control system. This was impossible. But it was also a reality. Something was jammed.

He pressed the trim-tab switch. The nose of the U-2 descended immediately. Hey!

The trim was activated by a thumb trigger. It moved the whole elevon on the tail and gave the U-2 very small and precise degrees of changes in up-and-down attitude.

The artificial horizon was indicating a descent, and the altimeter was slowly unwinding . . . very slowly. So slowly that if this were the best rate of descent possible, fuel would be very short before he touched earth again.

He was beginning to sweat. Shape up, man. A U-2 could not be landed with just a trim tab, but maybe something would break loose before it was too late.

He tried hauling back on the control yoke again. No amount of heaving would move it a millimeter. What was it that Driskill said, ". . . shit happens"?

Somehow the control yoke had to be unblocked. All right, Cecil Hopper. Just don't hyperventilate. And don't be too dumb-proud to ask for advice. Either that, or ask God to pass a miracle.

He switched the autopilot on and off several times. He was a lone castaway on an invisible sea, and there seemed to be no safe escape. Zero result as far as the yoke was concerned.

He considered ejecting. It would be easy just pulling the yellow handle, and poof—there he would go. Usually. But here the situation was different. During a normal ejection the yoke would be automatically shoved forward as the rocket exploded and the seat went up. But now the yoke could not be moved, and with the column still in place between his legs, the force of the rocket would obviously remove something—his legs, at about mid-thigh.

Later, when he'd descended to a decent altitude, he could consider bailing out the old-fashioned way. When the T-handle on his left was pulled, the two little cartridges at eye level on the canopy would blow it away. He could then crawl out and jump, or roll the U-2 on its back and fall out. And if all went as planned with separation of man and machine, he might be lucky and land somewhere near Osan. There were other possibilities, such as the Sea of Japan, a mountaintop, or a drift into the hospitality of the North Koreans.

Maybe the U-2 could be landed using only the pitch trim and engine power?

There was a gnawing in his stomach. Was he going to fuck up his very first mission? Crawling out from beneath the yoke was going to be extremely awkward, and at the last moment, when the canopy was gone, he might find it impossible.

He looked around his deteriorating world. He noticed the "whiskey" compass was reading 170 degrees. That compass, an ancient relic of former times, was hanging just above the big round view sight. It was a primitive backup in case his gyrocompass lost its mind, and he had rarely bothered to look at one for a long time.

At least the descent was holding steady and his altitude was now a mere sixty thousand feet.

"Hello, Osan? Sacrament Five is with you and I have a problem. . . ."

"Stand by. . . ."

Now, he thought, he had done it for sure. He could visualize one of the detachment airmen slipping into Horton's office with an urgent look on his face. He would hand him a slip of paper, and Horton would wish that one of the older hands were up here sailing beneath the sun and fucking things up. One of the more experienced guys would recognize what was wrong and know how to fix it. This strange combination was just as ridiculous as it was frustrating. How could any pilot lose the most basic control in the entire airplane? Directional control was important, but up-and-down was just plain absolute necessity.

Everything on the instrument panel spoke of the U-2's well-being. The engine RPM was right on the book for descent, and the exhaust gas temperature was right where it should be. The tacan was reading ninety miles from Osan, and there was not a warning light on the panel. He should be singing.

There was Horton's voice on the horn. Here came the Confederate cavalry. Why did he resent Horton now that he had to share his trouble?

"What is the nature of your problem, Sacrament Five?"

"I can't move the control yoke."

"You sure it's not locked into the autopilot?"

Was there a hint in Horton's voice that he thought the basis for this problem could only be pilot stupidity?

"Absolutely, sir. I even pulled the circuit breakers."

"And still no movement?"

"Negative, sir." The Soviet listening posts as well as the North Koreans must be enjoying this, he thought. "I've tried everything I can think of, sir. The ailerons work fine. Rudder the same."

A long pause, then: "Cecil? Will the yoke move at all? Just a bit, maybe?" Horton was certainly not one to excite. It was more as though he had just asked for a mint julep.

"No way, sir."

Another pause. Even longer this time. Hopper noted that he was down to forty thousand feet. Soon he would put the gear down and the spoilers to increase his rate of descent. But then what?

Horton's voice became calm and reassuring. "Cecil . . . maybe you'd better think about taking some vectors from us, and after we find a good place . . . you shut down, blow the canopy, and climb out." Horton sounded as if he were ordering a plate of hominy grits.

"I'm not very enthusiastic about that, sir. I think with the control column so solid, I might have a rough time getting out of here."

A note of solemnity in Horton's tone now. "Cecil, we've been discussing the problem here, and the Lockheed rep is with us. We seem to think the same on this . . . that your yoke is frozen. The temperature here was okay, but when you reached your altitude . . ."

What the hell was Horton trying to say? That this mission was about to be written off? And along with it the career of one Cecil Hopper?

"How can that be, sir? We fly in a lot colder weather than this and never have any trouble."

"What do you want to do, Cecil?"

Hopper exhaled heavily. What did he want to do? Of course. When it came right down to the nitty-gritty, there was only one individual up here . . . and he had a bad case of the frights. It was no good just wishing the yoke would suddenly become functional. The people on the ground were presumably thinking more clearly, if only because they were not sitting up here with the herald angels singing hark.

Silence. What were they doing down there?

Horton again. At last!

"Cecil? I find out now that during the early part of last evening, they were working on your airplane and failed to put the howdah in place. The canopy was open, and the rain must have collected in the belly of the fuselage. The yoke fore and aft connection is down there, and we believe that when you reached your altitude the water froze. That's why you can't move your elevators."

Hopper found that he was suddenly relieved. At least this was not his fault.

"We think you should consider your options. We have radar contact with you now, and when you decide to leave your aircraft, we'll come get you."

"Understand." Understand that the mission, your very first, was beginning to look like a $20 million calamity—not to mention the cost of your training if . . .

What was it that old pelican said? If an airplane is still in one piece, don't cheat on it. Ride the bastard down.

Hopper glanced at the depths below. A chopped-up land of corrugated bronze. Not a soft spot anywhere.

"Osan . . . Sacrament Five."

"Go ahead."

"I'm going to carry on to Osan and land."

"Understand you intend landing here?" There was neither approval nor disapproval in Horton's voice.

"Affirmative. I'll make one pass, and if that doesn't work . . ."

"You're sure?" Dismay. At least he had their attention. What could they say? No one, not even Willie Horton, wanted to be responsible for a decision that might result in a fatality.

"How's your fuel situation?"

"Enough. I don't think that will be a problem unless it takes too long to descend. I think I can trim just enough with the stabilizer to get away with it."

A pause. He could see Horton's face twisting with uncertainty. And Oscar? Maybe Oscar would know of a Plan B.

"We'll clear all traffic for you, Cecil. The wind is calm. You're sixty miles out and cleared to land."

Hopper made his first pass over Osan at three thousand feet. He could see an assembly of emergency equipment standing by near the end of the long runway. The mobile car with lights flashing was just off the runway threshold. Horton's now-familiar voice in the goldfish bowl. "Have you in sight, Cecil. Relax. Oscar is with me, and he says it's a piece of cake."

"Roger. I'm going to come in very flat, nose high and plenty of speed."

It occurred to Hopper that his commanding officer could order him to bail out, which would be the safest policy. That would cover him if things went wrong. It would be hard to prove later that under the circumstances leaving the airplane was close to an impossibility. So Horton was gambling right along with him. Nice to have company, boss.

There was the runway, a long, beautiful stretch. How could concrete be so beautiful?

He had slowed the U-2 to 120 knots with everything hanging out. He could feel the warning burble of a stall in the seat of his pants, which was just what he wanted. The nose rose slowly as he ran the trim back more and more. Now, the task was to keep the speed just there . . . just shy of a stall . . . not one knot slower or faster.

He forced himself to believe this was a perfectly normal landing—the kind Napolitano would have approved. Instinctively he tried to pull back on the control yoke as the concrete rose. It was still immovable. As he retarded the engine power, there was Horton's voice.

"Twenty feet, Cecil . . . easy down some more . . . fifteen feet . . . looking good . . . five feet!"

One hundred and twenty knots! He was going too damn fast!

He eased back on the throttle very gently, lest the nose drop and what could be a fatal porpoising might follow.

"Easy Cecil . . . five feet . . . still plenty of runway left . . ."

Now was the time, if there was going to be one.

"Three feet, Cecil!"

Hopper pulled all the way back on the throttle, and the U-2 sank to the concrete. It bounced once gently and then again. He concentrated on keeping the wings level and the U-2 on the runway. It was not quite a perfect landing, but it would do. As he taxied toward the ramp, he realized he was soaked with sweat and his hands were trembling.

When at last he cut the engine, he saw Horton jump out of the mobile car and stand where he could easily be seen. He was clapping his hands together and smiling.

Hopper had to delay a moment before he could reach for the canopy-release lever. There was a mist inside his goldfish bowl he could not explain.

❖

At 1730 Beale time Colonel David Pinsky, commander of the Ninth Wing, which included the 99th Squadron, closed his weary eyes for a moment and rested his head on his hands. Now what to do? News had just come from a friend on the selection board that he had not made general. There were several hundred applicants who had also been passed over and it was certainly no disgrace, but it was hard to take, even so. Very hard, after a man had given so much for so long.

Well, hell, the record was still a proud one, as anyone could see. Not very many guys wound up with stars on their shoulders. So? Hang in there at some obscure job at the Pentagon, awaiting the day of mandatory retirement? Not Dave Pinsky. No way. He would resign with colors flying. There would be a band and a parade of some sort, and speeches. Then a retirement party in the evening, which would be ego-building according to form—and difficult to endure.

The future was outside—somewhere in the civilian world. A job with an aircraft company? An airline? After more than twenty-five years, what kind of world was outside? It had been so long since he had even paused to look at the outside.

Too old to fly? Wither away on some golf course? Not Pinsky.

❖

While Pinsky was contemplating his future, the recce business continued. Now transferred from instructing, Napolitano was skirting an area called Kurdistan at seventy thousand feet. He watched in deep appreciation as the terminator slipped behind him and appeared to pause as he paralleled the Syrian border. It dissolved rapidly as he slipped past Urfa, Mardin, and then on to look down on a vague blob that was supposed to be Hakkari. Now the eastern light was blinding. It magnified every scratch in the U-2's cockpit windows so there wasn't too much a man could see. But not to worry. The little old computer was churning out the navigational numbers, and it said, loud and clear, that he was right on course.

Back at Fantasy Island by, say, ten hundred hours?
Mission accomplished.

❖

Chairman of the Joint Chiefs of Staff, Admiral Crowe, left the "tank" in the Pentagon with Air Force General Welsh. Twenty-thirty hours, Washington time. They slipped into a White House limousine, moving quickly lest a drop of rain spot the crispness of their uniforms. They had been briefed in the "tank" by a lieutenant colonel in the air force, a young man whose rapid-fire command of language and grasp of several "situations" around the world left his superiors with a vague sense of being patronized. Astonishing how intelligent the younger officers were these days. And somewhat dismaying. Yet Intelligence had come through handsomely this time. Tonight the two chiefs knew they had much to offer a president who often complained that no one ever told him what the hell was going on in the world.

Fifteen-thirty hours, Anchorage time. Orville Tosch was sitting far back in a taxi that was transporting him from the airport to the Captain Cook Hotel. He viewed the urban growth passing his window with disapproval. Too goddamned many people had moved to Alaska. Eskimos drunk. Indians drunk. But! Going out to Wien's house for supper. There would be a bunch of old bushwhackers gathered. Talk about Nome when it was Nome, and Naknek and Point Barrow just before the ice let go. Bud Rude would be there. He would remember a lot of things. One of the best damn flyers ever. Jesus, it was a pain getting old. Sitting around telling old flying stories. It was like the elephants going far away to die.

❖

General John Chain, Commander in Chief Strategic Air Command, was seated in his upholstered chair, a bit irritable now because it was 2230 hours, Omaha time, and he had yet to find time for a meal since his 0500 hours breakfast. He was in the large underground Operations Post at SAC headquarters waiting for reports on an SR-71*now speeding over Honduras and a U-2 in the same area. Mission "Samson," another U-2 assignment, was

*Three months before publication an SR-71 was lost on take-off from Kadena. Although the loss of one aircraft would ordinarily not indicate the end of a series, it is now even more likely that the "sleds" will not long continue to be operational.

out of Florida, and the large projection screen before him simulated the U-2's position in real time. All the data was projected in a small luminescent box on the left side of the screen. The pilot was a Captain Laidlaw.

General Chain prided himself on his vast acquaintance throughout his command, but he could not recall ever having met a Captain Laidlaw.

❖

Twenty-thirty hours, Washington, D.C. Undersecretary Griswold, project chief on operation "Sacrament Five," waits impatiently for a report from Japan. It will come from the director of Reconnaissance, Fifth Air Force, a Lieutenant Colonel Steve Brown. Warm regards. But it is messy doing things this way. Hell, it is 1030 hours in Japan, and "Sacrament Five" could not possibly have landed, with the film developed and the negative deciphered in time for explanations to the president and chiefs of staff at 2100 hours, Washington time, tonight. They would need at least another two hours over there, but the scoop was that the president became mighty testy about missing his early bedtime. And then the report could still be a dabble of *maskirovka*. The Soviets had developed some new on-surface tactics for units of six submarines—the old wolf-pack stuff with modern twists. The DOD said it was their baby, but it wasn't. Hell, the basic information originated right here in State. The president would be pleased, if not the chiefs. One-upmanship maybe, but who requested the U-2 flight in the first place? If the Soviets were going to play games in the Sea of Japan, then State had a right to know about it. And never mind the out-of-joint noses in the CIA. Not to mention the navy, which sometimes went to sleep. "Sacrament Five" would show them who was on top of things.

· ❖ ·

Nor had it been too bad a day for Lieutenant Colonel Driskill, some eight thousand miles to the east of Horton territory. Driskill had thoroughly enjoyed a T-38 flight for an hour at 1600 hours and then a meeting with Butch Hinkle about switching around some administrative duties. Two lieutenant colonels involved, three majors, and one captain. His "in" box was emptied, and since it was now 1730, Beale time, it seemed mandatory to drop by the Heritage Room for a beer before striking out for home. Hay-ell, it was time for a man to unravel hisself. . . .

Also at Beale, Debra Van Heeswyk tried valiantly to keep her thoughts calm and in order, the way she liked things to be. It was difficult because her special flier, whom she had not seen for three months, was scheduled to arrive on one of the tankers at five-thirty . . . seventeen-thirty by his military time. But then, of course, he would be on some other time, some secret time of a place no one cared to mention, which was at least somewhere in the real world—or so they claimed. Avoiding goose bumps before reunions was becoming ever more difficult. . . .

❖

Eight-thirty, Washington, D.C., time. Senator Drexel was usually well away from his office by this hour, but his day had been full of frustrations and he was far behind schedule. Now, his staff had long gone home and he was alone with a special report on the military budget. He found it more than usually discouraging. The goddamned military was breaking the treasury of the United States! Hadn't anyone in this history-blind town ever read about the Roman Empire? Or the British? Or the Spanish, for Christ's sake?

The senator tossed the report into his briefcase and went to the window. He stood looking down at the rain bubbling on the street, but he could not drive the essence of the report from his thoughts. Hell, the reconnaissance business alone was costing so much it made a man choke on the numbers. And it didn't even go bang! The future cost projections were even more stunning—particularly in this new atmosphere of mutual understanding with the Soviets. Tomorrow or the next day at the latest he would be summoned to vote "aye" or "nay" on those sums. With some cuts here and there, to be sure, but then the military always asked for more than they really needed. Or was that always true?

What price to let your guard down? Two dollars? Twenty million? Fifty million and twenty cents?

He was going to walk the few blocks to his house at 312 C Street in a few minutes, and he did not expect to be mugged en route. Why? Supposedly because there was a police force standing by that at least discouraged violence. And supposedly they knew the habits and styles of most muggers because their reconnaissance was good. Would it be reasonable to assume that if they did not have that information, it would be extremely risky to walk home in the rain? Even at this hour?

❖

Oscar stretched languorously, extending his legs full length and then flexing his toes. He expanded his nostrils when he caught the eye of Lieutenant Colonel Willie Horton, who was sitting behind his desk and staring thoughtfully into Oscar's tiger eyes.

"Greetings," Horton said to him. "May you live for a hundred years." And he added as he had countless times before, "The birds of care may fly over your head and mine, but there's nothing we can do about it. Just don't let them build nests in our hair."

Horton glanced at the glass bottle behind him, then slowly began to massage his bald scalp. It was noon, Osan time. Time, he thought, for Oscar to discontinue his morning slumbers and take command of his detachment.

About the Author

Adventurer, filmmaker, and author of many best-selling novels and films (*The High and the Mighty, Fate Is the Hunter, Band of Brothers,* and others), ERNEST GANN's first love is flying. He has piloted all types of planes, all over the world, in peace and war. He lives with his wife, Dodie, on a cattle ranch in Washington state.